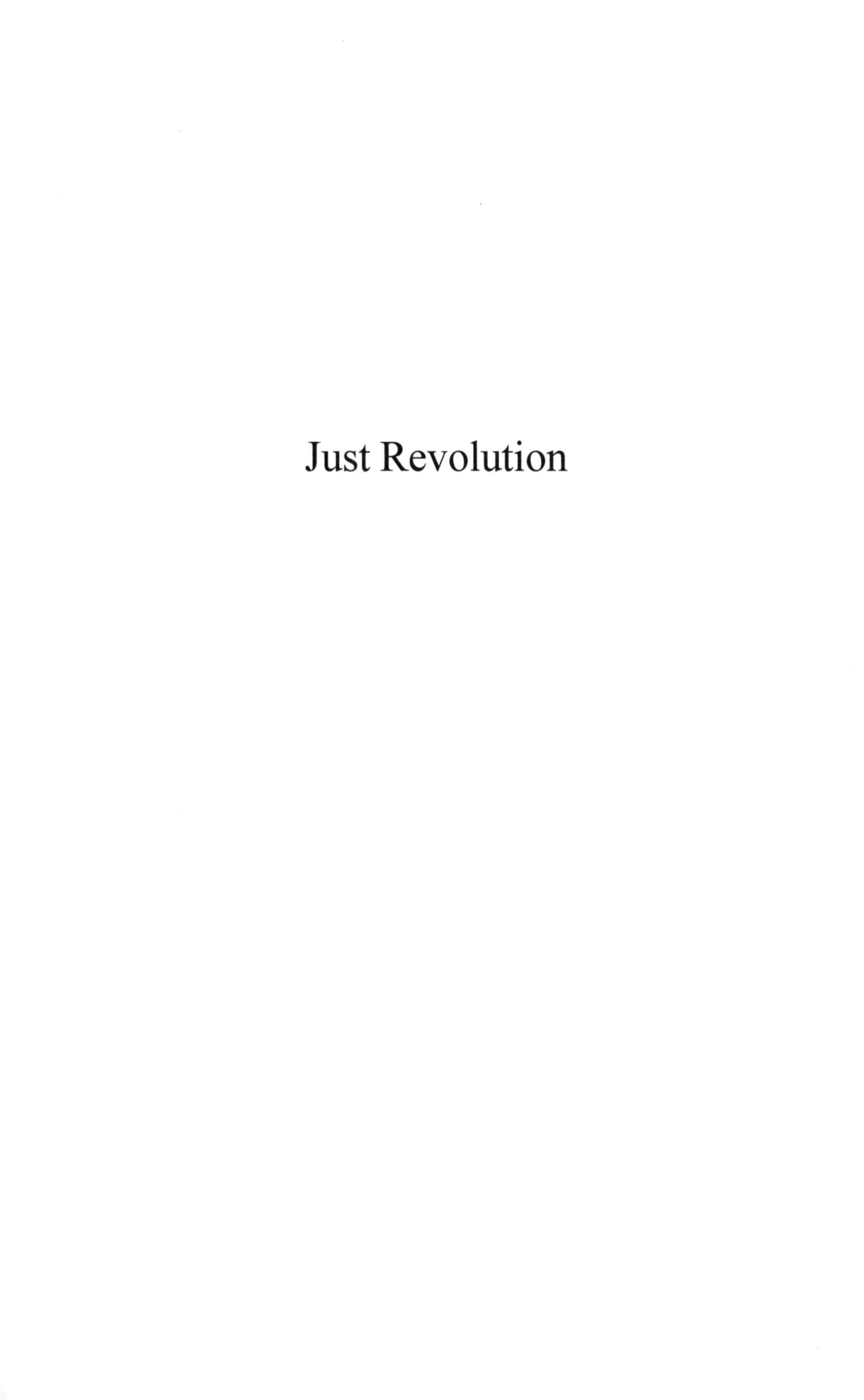

Just Revolution

Just Revolution

A Christian Ethic of Political Resistance and Social Transformation

Anna Floerke Scheid

LEXINGTON BOOKS
Lanham • Boulder • New York • London

Published by Lexington Books
An imprint of The Rowman & Littlefield Publishing Group, Inc.
4501 Forbes Boulevard, Suite 200, Lanham, Maryland 20706
www.rowman.com

Unit A, Whitacre Mews, 26-34 Stannary Street, London SE11 4AB

Copyright © 2015 by Lexington Books

Cover image "To the Sky," © 2009 Nathan Ackman. www.nathanackman.com

Excerpts from *Interpersonal and Social Reconciliation: Finding Congruence in African Theological Anthropology*, by Anna Floerke Scheid, *Horizons*, Volume 39, Issue 01 (Spring 2012), pp. 27–49, copyright © 2012 The College Theology Society. Reprinted with the permission of Cambridge University Press.

"Waging a Just Revolution: Just War Criteria in the Context of Oppression," by Anna Floerke Scheid, was previously published in *Journal of the Society of Christian Ethics*, 32.2 (Fall/Winter 2012): 153–172. Reprinted with permission of The Society of Christian Ethics.

"Under the Palaver Tree: Community Ethics for Truth-Telling and Reconciliation," by Anna Floerke Scheid, was previously published in *Journal of the Society of Christian Ethics*, 31.1 (Spring 2011): 17–36. Reprinted with permission of The Society of Christian Ethics.

All rights reserved. No part of this book may be reproduced in any form or by any electronic or mechanical means, including information storage and retrieval systems, without written permission from the publisher, except by a reviewer who may quote passages in a review.

British Library Cataloguing in Publication Information Available

Library of Congress Cataloging-in-Publication Data

Scheid, Anna Floerke, 1977-
  Just revolution : a Christian ethic of political resistance and social transformation / Anna Floerke Scheid.
   pages cm
  Includes bibliographical references and index.
  ISBN 978-0-7391-9094-4 (cloth : alk. paper) -- ISBN 978-0-7391-9095-1 (electronic) 1. Revolutions--Religious aspects--Christianity 2. Government, Resistance to--Religious aspects--Christianity. 3. Peace--Religious aspects--Christianity. 4. Just war doctrine. 5. Christianity and politics. 6. Apartheid--South Africa. I. Title.
  BT738.3.S3175 2015
  241'.621--dc23
                            2015013902

∞ ™ The paper used in this publication meets the minimum requirements of American National Standard for Information Sciences Permanence of Paper for Printed Library Materials, ANSI/NISO Z39.48-1992.

Printed in the United States of America

Contents

Acknowledgments		vii
Introduction		ix
1	Historical Context for a Case Study: Oppression in South Africa	1
2	Theological Roots of the Just War Tradition and Just Peacemaking Theory	11
3	Just Peacemaking Practices for Resisting Oppression	39
4	The Just War Tradition and Revolution	71
5	Restorative Justice for the Common Good	109
6	Just Revolution and the "Arab Spring"	135
Bibliography		157
Index		163
About the Author		171

Acknowledgments

I am filled to brimming with gratitude to so many who inspired, supported, and assisted me throughout the process of writing this book. Chief among these are my extended network of family, friends, and colleagues who provided motivation and encouragement in the form of conversations, questions, and oftentimes active and compassionate listening.

I am monumentally indebted to my mentors in theology and ethics, many of whom read iterations of this text and all of whom have influenced the development of my thinking and writing. In particular I thank David Hollenbach, S.J., Lisa Sowle Cahill, Stephen J. Pope, Thomas Nairn, O.F.M., and Robert Schreiter, C.PP.S.

Several institutions and organizations have afforded me the opportunity to present this material at both U.S. and international conferences where colleagues encouraged me to develop my thought across cultures, to pursue new resources, and to sharpen lines of argumentation. I am grateful to the Society of Christian Ethics, the Catholic Theological Society of America, the College Theology Society, the Hekima Institute of Peace Studies and International Relations, and Catholic Theological Ethics in the World Church. Likewise, I am grateful to my home institution, Duquesne University, most especially for their generous support of my work via the Presidential Scholarship Award.

Moreover, I express my gratitude to all of my colleagues in the theology department at Duquesne for their gracious support and to my research assistants Jeffrey Schooley and Arlene Montevecchio for their hard work and diligence.

In addition, several of my colleagues including Mark Allman, James P. Bailey, Meghan Clark, Beth Haile, Marinus Iwuchukwu, Matthew Shadle, Elochukwu Uzukwu, Elsabeth T. Vasko, and Tobias Winright read drafts of chapters and offered invaluable constructive criticism that has greatly strengthened this book. Their friendship and colleagueship is indispensable to my life as a scholar.

I am truly fortunate that my cousin, Nathan Ackman, is both a talented and generous artist. I am extraordinarily thankful for the stunning and evocative cover image, "To the Sky," that he created for this book.

Finally I thank those closest to me, who bore the brunt of my anxiety as I wrote this text, but also share most deeply in my delight at seeing it come to fruition. Thank you to my children Henry Daniel, Clare Susanna, and Eamon Patrick, and to my husband and partner Daniel P. Scheid. Dan and I have the somewhat rare blessing of being not only spouses and friends, but also colleagues. We are both theological ethicists, with offices just two doors apart. When discovering this, people often remark that it must be difficult to work with one's spouse. Not so. Dan is the first sounding board for all of my ideas, the kindest but most honest (and thus most valuable) critic, a deeply intelligent and vastly compassionate person, to whom I am ever grateful. Working closely with my spouse is indeed a blessing, and one that I cherish.

This book is dually dedicated: first, to Dan, whose love and support enabled me to write it; and second, to oppressed people—this book's agents and subjects—who endeavor to forge a more just and peaceful world.

Introduction

In their 1983 pastoral letter, *The Challenge of Peace: God's Promise and Our Response,* the U.S. Catholic bishops note that "insufficient analytical attention has been given to the moral issues of revolutionary warfare."[1] Over twenty-five years later, there remains little systematic analysis of what constitutes a just or justifiable revolution within theological scholarship on war and peacemaking. The need for ethical reflection on revolution has been heightened over the last several years, given the ongoing events across North Africa and the Middle East.[2] Beginning in 2011, popular revolutionary movements have forced regime change in Tunisia, Yemen, and Egypt, though the long-term consequences remain uncertain. In Libya, armed revolutionaries drew the international community to their cause and ousted Muammar Gaddafi, who had held power for over four decades. As I write, government forces continue to clash brutally with armed revolutionaries in Syria. Meanwhile, the international community, including the United States, continues to debate what role it ought to play.

To be sure, revolutionary efforts do not always succeed, and even when they do effect change, the full implications and consequences may not be able to be evaluated for decades. In Iran, for example, Green Movement activists led peaceful protests in 2009 against what they understood to be a rigged presidential election. Yet the protests were crushed by the Iranian government, which has retained political control.[3] On the other hand, in Burma (Myanmar) in 2007, nonviolent protesters, led by Buddhist monks, instigated what came to be called the Saffron Revolution.[4] The military regime carried out harsh repression against these protests, but it also promised reforms, beginning with a constitutional referendum held in 2008 and elections in 2010. Whether or not these elections were free of fraud remains a matter of dispute. Finally, in 2011 popular uprisings across Egypt led to the end of the three decades-long regime of Hosni Mubarak and a subsequent round of elections. However, by June 2013 thousands of protesters were again demanding change. Seemingly in response to these protests, the Egyptian Armed Forces carried out what many observers have called a coup d'etat, declaring an end to the rule of democratically-elected president Mohammed Morsi. Although the armed forces initially promised quick new elections, Egypt's future remains precarious and many consider the revolution unfinished.

While assessing revolutions from a political standpoint admittedly remains complex and murky, it seems appropriate that these geopolitical events receive a more rigorous response from Christian theological ethicists. Christian theologians have been engaged with the moral questions that arise in situations of war and violence for centuries. At its best, Christian theological ethics insists that the dignity of the human person, created in the image of God, be respected with as much care as possible, even in the midst of situations of social and political conflict, including warfare. Considering the observation of the U.S. bishops about the lack of attention to revolution, and the ongoing reality of geopolitical revolutionary activity, Christian theological ethicists ought to attend more closely to the ethics of revolution. This book is an attempt to begin to address this lacuna. I do not pretend to answer the questions surrounding the ethics of revolution in full. Instead, by construing a possible model of just revolution rooted in Christian theology, but attentive to the discipline of political science, I hope to begin and to contribute to conversations regarding revolution and theological ethics.

Revolutionary activity is as diverse as the cultures and contexts in which it arises. Lisa Anderson, president of the American University of Cairo, reminds us that while perhaps the uprisings across the Middle East are related, it would be naïve to view them as one "cohesive Arab revolt."[5] Given the different kinds of experiences, dynamics, and circumstances surrounding revolutionary activity in the examples of the countries above, it is reasonable to ask the question, what exactly is a revolution? What distinguishes revolution from diverse kinds of conflict ranging from coups, to insurrections, civil wars, and wars of aggression or defense? My working definition of revolution throughout this book is influenced by one of the premiere philosophers of revolution, Hannah Arendt. Drawing from her work, I understand revolutions to be intrastate "overthrows and upheavals" which aim to engender "a complete change in society."[6] For Arendt, who was thinking primarily in terms of the American and French revolutionary contexts, revolutions are necessarily violent, but they are distinct from insurrections, civil wars, or coups. Each of these, Arendt contends, shares the feature of violence, "but violence is no more adequate to describe the phenomenon of revolution than change; only where change occurs in the sense of a new beginning, where violence is used to constitute an altogether different form of government, to bring about the formation of a new body politic, where the liberation from oppression aims at least at the constitution of freedom can we speak of revolution."[7] Thus, as I use the term here, revolution refers to the attempt by the citizens or subjects of a tyrannical state to overthrow a government that oppresses them with the goal of liberating themselves from that regime and instituting a new government and social order that recognizes the inherent freedom and rights of its citizens.

While I affirm Arendt's argument that revolutions seek a specific kind of social change that establishes greater freedom, I disagree with Arendt that revolutions are necessarily violent. Again, Arendt's thesis was influenced by the case studies she chose—the French and American revolutions. My own case study, that of the South African struggle against apartheid, affirms a robust role for nonviolent revolutionary activity. Indeed, the aims of revolution that Arendt identifies—an "altogether different form of government," or "a new body politic," or "the constitution of freedom"—can also sometimes be achieved through nonviolent means.[8] Sociologist Sharon Erickson Nepstad has, for example, argued for the efficacy of nonviolence in overthrowing various dictatorial regimes, looking particularly at the end of the East German state, the ouster of General Augusto Pinochet from Chile, and the "Bloodless Revolution" in the Philippines.[9]

My understanding of the ethics of revolution, then, combines the insights of Nepstad and Arendt. Following Nepstad, I will argue that nonviolent resistance ought to form the initial response to government oppression, and that a revolution that can achieve its goals through the use of nonviolent resistance alone ought to endeavor to do so. However, as a theological ethicist committed to the just war tradition, I also argue that under certain circumstances revolutionaries may legitimately take up arms against an oppressive regime. Indeed, if the just war theory is a valid, useful tool for thinking about the ethics of warfare and how a nation defends itself against assault or aggression, then we can and should employ the tools of the just war tradition to consider how a people might defend themselves against assault or aggression perpetrated against them by their own government. In other words, we should assess how the just war theory might be viewed in situations of oppression or how it might be transformed into a theory of just revolution. Specifically, I argue for a new understanding of the traditional just war criteria to evaluate when the use of armed resistance is ethically licit in revolutionary contexts.

Method

The manner by which I develop an ethics for just revolution might be called a hybrid of deductive and inductive ethical methodology. The principles which I suggest for just revolution are drawn deductively from established practices of nonviolent resistance and the criteria of the just war tradition. I also work inductively by describing these principles as they emerged in the actual experience of a relatively recent revolution, which employed both nonviolent and armed strategies: South Africa's struggle against apartheid. This hybrid method is not unlike the approach taken in one of the classic texts of political philosophy, Michael Walzer's *Just and Unjust Wars,* which placed the traditional just war criteria in conversation with historical examples meant to sharpen and help redefine the just war tradition.[10] I place the established practices of nonviolence and the principles of the just war tradition in conversation with an actual contemporary revolution widely considered to have been just in order to illuminate the most ethical and effective strategies for oppressed peoples seeking revolutionary change.

As a case study for Christian ethics for gleaning principles to guide a just revolution, South Africa is particularly felicitous for at least three reasons. First, it is broadly recognized as a revolution that had a just cause and a right intention. The movement against apartheid clearly qualifies as revolutionary struggle. It endeavored to engender, in Arendt's words already noted above, "change . . . in the sense of a new beginning . . . to constitute an altogether different form of government, to bring about the formation of a new body politic, where the liberation from oppression aims at least at the constitution of freedom."[11] Moreover, few would deny the justice of its cause or the rightness of its intention: to overthrow a racist and repressive regime which routinely disenfranchised and violated the human rights of its own citizens, in order to establish a non-racial, democratic government dedicated to justice, the preservation of human rights, and post-conflict reconciliation.[12] Given the relatively uncontroversial nature of the cause and intention propelling the South African revolution, and the fact that it employed both nonviolent and armed means of resistance toward social transformation, it provides a relatively clear case study for generating and analyzing principles and practices to guide a just revolution. Note that it is not my purpose to argue that every aspect of the South African struggle against apartheid was just. Indeed, atrocities were committed in the South African revolution by those fighting for liberation that shock the conscience of any person dedicated to human rights. However, it is because South Africa employed both nonviolent and armed resistance in carrying out a revolution that accords uncontroversially with the criteria of just cause and right intention that it becomes an invaluable case study for illustrating both what should and what should not happen in revolutions which seek to be both effective and ethical.

Second, discussion of the South African revolution has been deeply theological, with hundreds of books and articles devoted to theological analyses of its various facets, especially most recently its post-conflict efforts at reconciliation through the famous Truth and Reconciliation Commission. Theologians and theological ethicists from around the world have formed interdisciplinary partnerships and engaged in research with sociologists, political scientists, practitioners of conflict resolution, and scholars of international law to tease out the legal, political, philosophical, and theological implications of apartheid, the struggle for liberation from it, and the reconciliation of former enemies in its aftermath. This book fits into the range of that discussion, while offering a unique contribution to it—the South African struggle as a touchstone for understanding the ethics of revolution more broadly.

Finally, history suggests that the African National Congress (ANC) was among the most effective liberation movements insofar as it brokered a transition to democracy in South Africa that was remarkably and unexpectedly peaceful, and that left open the possibility of the pursuit of post-conflict reconciliation amongst long-standing enemies. Indeed, the South African revolution against apartheid—while not without considerable bloodshed, and though it did make use of armed resistance—nevertheless struck the world as being astonishingly more peaceful than anyone had imagined possible. Despite the common expectation that the conflict would end in full scale civil war, in the simple words of South African Archbishop Desmond Tutu, "It did not happen." Instead, South Africa "confounded all the prophets of doom by making a remarkably peaceful transition from repression and injustice to democracy and freedom."[13] Thus, for anyone concerned with how to protect human dignity and establish human rights, with how to work toward peace, justice, and reconciliation in the face of dictatorial regimes, the South African revolution begs for further analysis. What happened in this highly volatile context that allowed for so peaceful a transition with such auspicious prospects for building a just peace marked by sincere efforts at post-conflict reconciliation? The successful struggle against apartheid emerges as a critical site for exploring the possibilities of a Christian ethic of political resistance and social transformation.

Overview of Chapters

Following this introduction, this book is comprised of six chapters, each of which presses the argument of the book forward in different ways. Chapters 1 and 2 are largely explanatory and descriptive. They lay the groundwork necessary to understand the various components of the model of just revolution I propose in chapters 3, 4, and 5. In chapter 6, I make some tentative observations about how the ethics of just revolution interact with what we currently know about the Arab Spring.

Specifically, chapter 1 provides a brief introduction to the context of the South African revolution. Mindful again that I do not intend here to write a history of South Africa, but rather to use the context as a touchstone for ethical reasoning, I outline the origins of apartheid in the contentious relationships amongst native South Africans, British colonists, and Dutch colonists, who call themselves *Afrikaners*. I discuss the ideology of racism and the political dynamics that led to the rise of the National Party, the party of apartheid, in South Africa. The National Party would wield power in South Africa for roughly four decades, systematically disenfranchising and dehumanizing the vast majority of South Africa's inhabitants.

Chapter 2 introduces the two conceptual interlocutors—the just war tradition and just peacemaking theory—that will converse with the South African case study in chapters 3 and 4. The development of the just war tradition spans most of Christian history. Just peacemaking theory, by contrast, is a relatively recent endeavor by Christian ethicists to systematize a pragmatic nonviolent approach to global conflict. These two ethical systems are the foundations from which I work deductively to suggest principles to govern nonviolent and armed resistance in a just revolution. Besides simply describing the just war tradition and just peacemaking theory, this chapter considers the theological roots of each system. Readers who already have a good grasp of the just war tradition and just peacemaking theory may choose to move directly to chapter 3.

The remainder of the book follows a trajectory that will be familiar to students and scholars of the just war tradition. It proposes a model of just revolution that spans four potential stages: *jus ante* armed revolution, *jus ad* armed revolution, *jus in* armed revolution, and *jus post* revolution. In chapters 3 and 4, the hybrid method I described above is most apparent—I am using the practices and criteria of the just peacemaking theory and just war tradition, deductively, in conversation with an analysis of the South African struggle against apartheid, inductively, to formulate a model for just revolution.

Chapter 3 explores *jus ante* armed revolution, or justice before any call to take up arms. The chapter looks at the period of exclusively nonviolent confrontation against the apartheid regime, in the light of several practices of just peacemaking theory. First, I point to the need for nonviolent direct action against oppressive regimes, showing how ordinary South Africans rebelled against apartheid using strikes, marches, boycotts, and other forms of protest. Second, I emphasize the importance of advancing democracy and human rights by attending to the South African revolution's emphasis on broad participation. Third, I show how the South African context demonstrates the importance of developing grassroots organizations to continue nonviolent resistance even in the midst of repression. Finally, I turn to how South Africa's revolution illustrates the importance of strengthening the United Nations and international efforts for cooperation and human rights for achieving revolutionary goals. Each of these nonviolent practices can be understood as components of a just revolution when viewed in the context of the struggle against apartheid. I will argue that these and other forms of nonviolent resistance should be major components of any revolution which seeks to be just.

Chapter 4 examines *jus ad* and *jus in* armed revolution, or justice as we begin to consider armed resistance, and justice in the midst of armed resistance. It suggests that the just war tradition's criteria for *jus ad bellum* (legitimate authority, just cause, right intention, last resort, reasonable hope of success) and *jus in bello* (proportionate means, noncombatant immunity) must undergo certain revisions to address adequately a revolutionary context. For each criterion, I begin by stating the manner in which it must be revised to apply to just revolution, and then I demonstrate how the South African context illustrates that particular revision. While the main thrust of chapter 4 is the ethics of armed resistance, it also marks the emergence of what I call the "tandem approach" to just revolution: revolution that engages in both nonviolent resistance practices and armed resistance simultaneously.

Chapter 5 explores *jus post* revolution, or justice in the aftermath of regime change. Relevant for this chapter is just peacemaking theory's argument that peace-building includes an effort to "acknowledge responsibility for conflict and injustice and seek repentance and forgiveness."[14] I argue that some form of transitional justice must be pursued following revolution. Transitional justice will seek to stave off cycles of retaliation and revenge by developing a shared history of past abuses, validating the experiences of victims, and finding ways to hold perpetrators accountable. Following revolutionary upheaval, restorative justice—the type of justice pursued by South Africa's Truth and Reconciliation Commission—may best meet these goals, and promote social reconciliation for the common good.

Finally, in chapter 6 I examine how the principles and practices of just revolution that I have described interact with the revolutionary activity across North Africa and the Middle East. My observations here are tentative given the ongoing nature of these conflicts.

The criteria of the just war tradition coupled with the nonviolent practices of the just peacemaking theory, and viewed in the context of the South African struggle against apartheid yield a rich and theologically grounded ethics of just revolution. The model of just revolution that I propose endeavors to limit violence to do the least possible harm while overcoming political oppression, working toward a just peace, and promoting long-term reconciliation. This dual approach of just peacemaking and just war principles maintains the Christian ideal of nonviolence but supports the right to armed resistance in accordance with revised just war criteria. It comprises a dynamic and ethical model for political resistance, and it represents a unique approach to promoting social transformation.

NOTES

1. U.S. Bishops, *The Challenge of Peace: God's Promise and Our Response,* 89. Available at http://old.usccb.org/sdwp/international/TheChallengeofPeace.pdf.

2. For a comprehensive resource on these events see Council on Foreign Relations/Foreign Affairs, *The New Arab Revolt: What Happened, What It Means, and What Comes Next* (New York: Council on Foreign Relations, Inc., 2011).

3. See Charles Kurzman, "The Arab Spring: Ideals of the Iranian Green Movement, Methods of the Iranian Revolution," *International Journal of Middle East Studies,* 44.1 (2012).

4. The Burmese Buddhist monks wear saffron-colored robes. For more information see Benedict Rodgers, "The Saffron Revolution: The Role of Religion in Burma's Movement for Peace and Democracy," *Totalitarian Movements and Political Religions,* 9.1 (2008) and Natalie Keefer, "The Struggle for Human Rights in Myanmar," *Social Education,* 76.5 (2012).

5. Lisa Anderson, "Demystifying the Arab Spring," *Foreign Affairs,* 90.3 (2011), 2.

6. Hannah Arendt, *On Revolution* (New York: Penguin Books, 1990), 22–23.

7. Arendt, *On Revolution,* 35.

8. There is solid grounding for the notion of nonviolent revolutions. Martin Luther King, Jr. spoke of a "revolution of conscience." See Greg Moses, *Revolution of Conscience: Martin Luther King and the Philosophy of Nonviolence,* New York: The Guilford Press, 1998. Others who speak of nonviolent revolutions include: André Trocmé, *Jesus and the Nonviolent Revolution,* Charles E. Moore, ed. (Farmington, PA: Plough Publishing House, 2007); Barbara Epstein, *Political Protest and Cultural Revolution: Nonviolent Direct Action in the 1970s and 1980s* (Berkley and Los Angeles, CA: University of California Press, 1991); and Michael J. Nojeim, *Gandhi and King: The Power of Nonviolent Resistance* (Westport, CT: Praeger Publishers, 2004).

9. Sharon Erickson Nepstad, *Nonviolent Revolutions: Civil Resistance in the Late Twentieth Century* (New York: Oxford University Press, 2011).

10. See Michael Walzer, *Just and Unjust Wars: A Moral Argument with Historical Illustrations* (New York: Basic Books, 1977).

11. Arendt, 35.

12. Consider that James Childress includes protection of the innocent from unjust attacks, restoring rights wrongly denied, and establishing a just order as just causes for war. James Childress, "Just War Criteria," in *War or Peace,* T.A. Shannon, ed. (Maryknoll, NY: Orbis Press, 1980), 40.

13. Desmond Tutu, *No Future Without Forgiveness* (New York: Doubleday, 1999), 8–9.

14. See Glen Stassen ed., *Just Peacemaking: The New Paradigm for the Ethics of Peace and War* (Cleveland, OH: The Pilgrim Press, 2008), chapter 4.

Chapter One

Historical Context for a Case Study

Oppression in South Africa

One of the first lessons regarding the ethics of revolution that we can draw from the South African struggle against apartheid is that severely oppressive contexts radicalize citizens and inculcate a spirit of revolution. The context of South African apartheid, as both a political philosophy and a set of social structures, was one of severe oppression and repression. It placed undue and unjust burdens on the majority of South Africa's inhabitants and denied them legal, meaningful participation in the systems which affected their lives. This brief chapter introduces the context of apartheid. It provides the necessary backdrop for understanding how the South African struggle against apartheid functions as a case study in the proceeding chapters.

In the introduction, I described several reasons why the context of the South African struggle against apartheid provides an especially valuable case study for examining the ethics of revolution. The first reason I note is that the struggle against apartheid is widely regarded as a revolution which had a just cause and a right intention—to overthrow a racist and repressive regime that violated the human rights of its own citizens, in order to establish a non-racial, democratic government dedicated to justice and human rights. Here, I provide a brief illustration of the historical context that led to apartheid, and thus to the just cause for revolutionary activity. To this end, I organize my approach to the South African context using three broad socio-historical subjects that taken together paint a picture of the terrain of oppression on which the South African revolution was conducted: (1) Colonialism and concomitant racism, (2) Afrikaner nationalism, and (3) The codification and legalization of discrimination.

COLONIALISM AND RACISM

While South Africa's National Party did not begin to codify apartheid into law until they won power in 1948, South Africa's colonial history is laced with a racist white supremacist ideology. The colonial occupation of South Africa originated with Dutch settlers in the mid-seventeenth century. During this early colonial period Africans were traded as slaves, and white settlers confiscated broad swaths of land on which slaves were forced to work.[1] While slaves were officially emancipated in 1838,[2] the late nineteenth century nevertheless saw new waves of exploitation of black workers as prodigious amounts of diamonds and gold were discovered in 1867 and 1886, respectively.[3] Colonizers recognized the opportunity for enormous wealth and profits. The growing mining industry would, however, require a vast, steady supply of cheap labor. Thus the exploitation of native Africans, who had already endured two centuries of oppression and enslavement, continued.[4] Prior, then, to the official codification of apartheid, the South African landscape was already stained by a deliberate system of colonial oppression based both on the economic interests inherent in European colonial projects and a relatively easily recognizable criterion of identity—skin pigmentation.

The policies of apartheid were made possible by the ideology of white supremacy and the structures of institutional racism that had already been entrenched in South Africa. Indeed, racism imbued all of South African society prior to the codification of apartheid. For example, forms of the infamous pass books—identity papers that black Africans were required to carry when traveling in white areas during apartheid—had been used since the sixteenth century to control the movement and migration of native South Africans and slaves. Moreover, the Native's Land Act which reserved ownership of 87–93 percent of South African land to whites was passed in 1913, some forty-five years prior to the political platform of apartheid. Indeed, racism so imbued pre-apartheid South Africa that most anti-apartheid scholarship and activism throughout the era of apartheid largely presumes this backdrop of racism and white supremacy. Nevertheless, in an attempt to understand how apartheid came to be, and why so many felt compelled to revolt against it, it is helpful to briefly remind ourselves of what racism is and how it functions.

Racism is a product of prejudiced or biased thinking which categorizes and values people in accordance with their skin color. Sociologist Allan G. Johnson describes "racial prejudice" as including "values that elevate whiteness above color and the belief that whites are smarter. It also includes negative feelings about people of color—contempt, hostility, fear, disgust, and the like—along with positive (or at least neutral) feelings toward whites. Thus prejudice is a powerful force that provides fuel for discriminatory behavior and a rationale for justifying it."[5] Anti-racist scholars and activists also distinguish between individual racist attitudes and behaviors on the one hand, and institutionalized racism on the other. To make this distinction theological ethicist Bryan N. Massingale distinguishes between the "common sense understanding of racism" and "culturally entrenched racism." The common sense understanding of racism views racism as primarily intentional and conscious attitudes and behaviors, "usually, but not always" on the part of whites toward a person of color, "because of the color of his/her skin."[6] On the other hand, "culturally entrenched racism" is "a set of shared beliefs and assumptions that undergirds the economic, social, and political disparities experienced by different racial groups. . . . This set of meanings and values not only answers questions about the significance of social patterns, customs, and policies. As a culture, it is also formative: racism is a communal and learned frame of reference that shapes identity, consciousness, and behavior."[7] The cultural entrenchment of racism leads to institutional or structural racism. These distinctions are important since anti-racist scholars and activists tend to agree that racism is not simply prejudice or bias, but rather the combination of prejudice and power. Prejudice disposes people and groups with power to use their power to discriminate against those they are biased against. Since racial prejudice had influenced the attitudes, thoughts, and behavior of South Africa's white inhabitants throughout the colonial period, and had been institutionalized via the social, economic, and political structures of South Africa, the country's white minority was primed for an extreme experiment in racial segregation: apartheid.

AFRIKANER NATIONALISM

The ideology of racism was exacerbated in South Africa due to its particular colonial history marked by the profound nationalism of the Afrikaner *Volk* (People). South Africa was initially colonized by the Dutch, who created a settlement in Cape Town in 1652. The British conducted an additional wave of colonialism in the late eighteenth and early nineteenth centuries clashing repeatedly with the descendants of the original Dutch colonizers, known as the Boers and later Afrikaners. In response to British imperialism, including the unilateral abolition of slavery, a group of Afrikaners conducted a "Great Trek" further into the South African mainland. This event looms large in the historical imagination of the Afrikaner *Volk,* who view it as an act of both resistance against and freedom from British hegemony. They conquered natives and set up two republics independent of British rule: the Transvaal and the Orange Free State. The republics were subsequently crushed and annexed into the emerging South African state during the Anglo-Boer War by the British who felt threatened by the new wealth generated by the Transvaal's lucrative mining industry.[8] The long-term impact of the Anglo-Boer War on the inhabitants of South Africa as well as the British colonial state should not be underestimated. Historian William Beinart suggests that the Anglo-Boer War was Britain's "greatest colonial war" and that had it not been overshadowed just a decade later by the onset of World War I it would be considered a far more momentous event in the course of world history.[9] The war wreaked havoc and humiliation on Afrikaners in part because the British Empire refused to "negotiate with lesser states controlled by Boers."[10] Instead, the British implemented a "scorched-earth policy, burning farmhouses and collecting women and children into concentration camps where death rates from disease were very high."[11] Approximately 28,000 Afrikaner civilians died as a result of the war.[12] Following this humiliation and loss, Afrikaners understandably harbored a sense of injustice. Their outrage found its outlet in an intense spirit of nationalism.

Sharply distinguishing themselves from both native Africans and South Africans of British descent, who they viewed as favoring native Africans, Afrikaners identified themselves as the *Volk* whose "history became a search, sanctioned by God" for "independence and identity"[13] over and against other ethnic groups in South Africa. Indeed, the preservation and promotion of the *Volk* was imbued with religious significance. The *Volk* saw themselves as a chosen race, destined to inhabit and rule South Africa as a kind of Promised Land.[14]

Afrikaner nationalism followed a common historical pattern of loss and humiliation, leading to political oppression and violence—even against a group that was not the original perpetrator of injustice. Joseph V. Montville, a former U.S. diplomat and expert in political psychology, describes extreme nationalism as

> a state of collective mind that is filled with rage alternating with despair, and it can create an environment that can lead to political violence and war. Extreme nationalism is a result of painful, traumatic experiences in history or recent times, or both, with each reinforcing the sense of loss which has not been mourned. Extreme nationalism is usually nourished by a powerful sense of injustice on the part of the victimized nation or identity group, and a feeling that the outside world does not care about the injustice it has suffered. The historic wounds are felt as assaults on the self-concept and therefore ultimate safety and security of the victim group. Its very existence could be threatened. Such assaults generate an automatic instinct toward counteraggression or revenge.[15]

In the case of Afrikaners, the instinct toward counteraggression manifested itself in the segregationist policies of apartheid. By separating themselves as whites and Afrikaners from other ethnic groups in South Africa, the *Volk* sought to establish for themselves a sense of security in a land in which they felt threatened, and historically had actually been threatened. However, what is, of course, crucial to keep in mind is that Afrikaners, not powerful enough to vent their aggression on the British who were responsible for their historical pain and humiliation, instead directed their animosity toward black South Africans, a group who had been politically disenfranchised throughout colonial history and was thus easier to dominate and humiliate. The extreme nationalism of the Afrikaner *Volk,* combined with white supremacy and racism, constitutes the ideological bedrock and the scaffolding on which apartheid was built.

This analysis of the Anglo-Boer War and the relationship between the British and Afrikaner provides a context for the National Party's initiation and implementation of apartheid. "There is nothing so dangerous as people who feel they have been deeply wronged, and are blinded by their own sense of injustice."[16] In the 1960s and 1970s, when other African countries were winning their independence, the Afrikaner-dominated National Party maintained a despotic stranglehold over South African political life. The particular colonial history of South Africa, in which Afrikaners experienced a measure of the brutality of British colonialism normally reserved for Africans, offers some explanation, but no justification, for this historical reality.

THE CODIFICATION AND LEGISLATION OF DISCRIMINATION

The Afrikaner-dominated National Party came to power in 1948 with the intent to "meet new challenges with a tighter set of racial policies."[17] Throughout the 1950s the Nationalists would implement their program of apartheid. The word *apartheid* literally means "apart" or "apartness" and segregation of the races is its hallmark. At its inception South African Prime Minister Hendrik Verwoerd remarked that it "could much better be described as a policy of good neighborliness,"[18] but this euphemism masks apartheid's intrinsic injustices. Despite apartheid's having been shrouded, as we shall see, in the seemingly innocuous language of "separate development," the National Party's "statements and documents over many years agreed on the irreducible aims of the 'maintenance and protection' of Afrikanerdom, white power, and the white race."[19] In their quest for security and independence, the Afrikaner *Volk*, represented by the National Party, molded an elaborate system of racial segregation and subjugated the majority of South Africans. The system was characterized by oppressive laws and brutal repression of anyone who resisted those laws. Three major pieces of legislation—some codependent with additional smaller pieces of legislation—formed the foundation of political oppression under South African apartheid: the Population Registration Act, the Group Areas Act, and the Bantu Education Act.

Population Registration

The Population Registration Act (1950) required that all South Africans submit to national registration according to race.[20] This legislation arose partly as a practical way of enforcing the Mixed Marriage Act (1949) and Immorality Act (1950), both of which prohibited sexual contact between persons of different races.[21] The Population Registration Act was thus intended to protect the "purity" of the white race from "miscegenation." The purity of races was considered so crucial that one Afrikaner politician remarked "that he was better able to raise money for the [National] party by mentioning the fact that white women were dancing with black men in Cape Town" than by stressing independence from the British.[22]

According to the Population Registration Act, all persons were issued papers affirming their inclusion in a particular racial group:[23] White; Coloured—used to describe those with a "mixed origin" believed to be descendants of the indigenous Khoisan, white settlers, and non-indigenous slaves brought from the East; Black (those of African descent); and Indian.[24] A "Race Classification Board" was developed to decide unclear cases.[25] The Coloured population was especially burdened by the National Party's insistence on racial classification and separation. Because persons of racially mixed backgrounds did not fit easily or obviously into the dominant categories of white and black, apartheid officials resorted to crude methods to determine their racial classification. These included the now infamous so-called "pencil test" in which race was determined by whether or not a pencil inserted into a person's hair stuck, and another practice in which race was determined by the color of "the patch of skin on the inside of a person's arm."[26] Such methods of "testing" resulted in arbitrary pronouncements on a person's race, so that members of the same family could be classified differently and forced to separate in to distinct "homelands" described below.[27]

Group Areas and Separate Development

The second piece of legislation that formed the backbone of apartheid was the Group Areas Act (1950) which coupled with the Prevention of Illegal Squatting Act (1951) to define racial zones and to restrict movement between them.[28] This legislation was designed to enact apartheid's promise of "separate development." The schematic of separate development proposed that each of South Africa's nine native tribal groups should have its own "homeland." The rationale was that separate homelands would "reduce [racial and ethnic] 'friction' to the benefit of all."[29] Apartheid officials suggested that these "homelands" would eventually operate as independent nations, even instituting a separate law—the Bantu Authorities Act (1951)—which created local and regional governing structures modeled on the old tribal structures. Thus African "chiefs" were appointed by the government and named as rulers of various homelands.[30]

While the architects of apartheid claimed that separate development would secure the rights and wellbeing of all in South Africa, it proved to be a contrivance for solidifying white political and economic power. Rather than promoting independence and self-sufficiency for various tribal groups, the Group Areas Act functioned to protect "white workers from competition, [to control] African movements to town," and thereby to curtail their access to labor markets and reserve certain jobs for whites.[31] The land of South Africa was reordered and redistributed according to these goals. "Cape Town, Durban, and other cities were pulled apart and reassembled to conform to the new pattern."[32] Thousands of people were uprooted from their homes, many of which were expropriated by the Group Areas Board and then sold cheaply to white real estate developers. Developers then "improve[ed] them and [sold] them off as whitewashed cottages to whites" or cleared the land for new office and housing development projects.[33] For example, the dismantling of District Six in Cape Town resulted in the forced removal of some 60,000 people, mostly classified as Indians and Coloureds.[34] Many of its buildings, particularly those created in the British Victorian style—recall the Afrikaner's historical claims against British injustices—were destroyed.[35] What remained was an urban wasteland with few businesses or occupants to speak of. Beinart reports that "reoccupation" of District Six "remains a politically charged issue."[36] Sophiatown in Johannesburg endured a similar fate. It had been a bastion of black urban culture, from prominent black politicians and writers to great jazz musicians. Sophiatown "epitomized the urban African culture anathema to apartheid."[37] The residents were removed and the neighborhoods were dismantled and replaced with houses reserved for whites.[38] Sophiatown was renamed "Triomf." The displacement of Sophiatown with Triomf is the stuff of lament and tragic poetry: black Wisdom destroyed by white Triumph.

The Group Areas Act was coupled with the Urban Areas Act (1952) to further restrict the lives of black South Africans, especially in South African cities.[39] In order to qualify for residence in urban areas, black South Africans had to prove that they had been born in that particular city, or that they had worked there under the same employer for at least ten years, or that they had lived in the city for at least fifteen years.[40] Any person who did not qualify under these conditions had seventy-two hours upon arriving in the city within which to register as a "work-seeker." This enabled the apartheid government to create a class of migrant workers—people who could not qualify for residence in the cities, but who could come for temporary employment. In this way, the Urban Areas Act separated thousands of people from their families, as migrants struggled to find work in cities, while their families remained in the economically depressed homelands.

Education

Finally, the third pillar in the edifice of apartheid was the Bantu Education Act (1953). Education was a critical component of the apartheid government. During apartheid, twenty percent of the national budget was spent on education but "the trouble was that about eighty-five percent of the total went on educating whites."[41] In an effort to emphasize ethnic differences and condition black South Africans for subjugated roles in apartheid society, the government passed sweeping education legislation.[42] This set of regulations removed control of education from local authorities and placed it under a centralized Bantu Administration. The legislation's provisions changed the languages in which school was taught: native languages would be used in the early years of education, and in later years Afrikaans would be used alongside English.[43] Teaching strictly in native languages in the first years of schooling was meant to emphasis ethnic identity and difference among African children in concert with apartheid's philosophy of separate development. It was also likely intended to discourage Africans of different ethnicities from uniting in a common revolutionary cause against the minority white regime. Moreover, the National Party was concerned that missionary schools were providing "an academic training with too much emphasis on English and 'dangerous liberal ideas.' It was seen as the foundation of an African elite which claimed recognition in a common society."[44] Instead, a new model of education was promoted by then education minister Hendrik Verwoerd who, in speeches to the South African parliament, remarked: "There is no place for . . . [Africans] in the European community, above the level of certain forms of labor." Thus the school system should not confuse a black child "by showing him the green pastures of European society in which he is not allowed to graze."[45] Thus emphasis in the African schools was placed on technical skills only, a clear attempt to prepare Africans for and keep them in low-level, low-wage jobs.

CONCLUSION

Apartheid emerged from a context of colonialism and racism in which whites were viewed as superior to all other races, especially blacks. The racist worldview and structures already present in South Africa were harnessed by those Afrikaners whose experiences of violence and humiliation at the hands of the British left them feeling harassed and insecure. When the National Party won the elections of 1948, they used their power elaborately to codify and legislate their racist ideology. The early legislation of the apartheid regime thus illustrates the extent of the oppression that South African revolutionaries sought to resist and overcome. Apartheid was designed to solidify white economic and political power. Under the veneer of separate development the regime segregated South Africans by race, restricted their freedom of movement and employment, eviscerated the education system, and guaranteed that there would be a permanently impoverished Black South African underclass. For nearly four decades following the implementation of the National Party's policies of apartheid, thousands of South Africans would participate in revolutionary activity to overcome injustice and oppression. They would reject the ideology of racism and white supremacy that gave birth to apartheid, as well as the ethnicized and racialized nationalism of the *Volk*. They would refuse to follow unjust laws, and endure severe consequences for their rebellion. When the National government met their nonviolent resistance with violent repression, some revolutionaries would even take up arms against the regime. Throughout chapters 3, 4, and 5, South African freedom fighters' successful struggle against apartheid acts as a touchstone for constructing an ethic of just revolution.

NOTES

1. For more on slavery in early South African colonial history see Wayne Dooling, *Slavery, Emancipation, and Colonial Rule in South Africa* (Scottsville, South Africa: University of KwaZulu-Natal Press, 2007).

2. Dooling, 113.

3. For more on the early South African mining industry, see William Beinart, *Twentieth Century South Africa*, 2nd edition (New York: Oxford University Press, 2001), 27–35.

4. The legacy of injustice in the mines reaches even into post-apartheid South Africa where the mining industry remains a source of serious tension and a locus of social justice and human rights activity. Miners' unions organize strikes and advocate for better pay. In August 2012, South African police forces killed several protesting miners. This event, dubbed the Marikana Massacre, shocked South Africans and evoked memories of illicit police activity in repressing protest against apartheid.

5. Allan G. Johnson, *Privilege, Power, and Difference* (New York: McGraw-Hill, 2006), 55.

6. Bryan Massingale, *Racial Justice and the Catholic Church* (Maryknoll, NY: Orbis Books, 2010), 13.

7. Massingale, 25.

8. Beinart, 64.

9. Beinart, 2.

10. Beinart, 65.

11. Beinart, 65.

12. Beinart, 65.

13. Beinart, 65.

14. For more on the religious component of Afrikaner nationalism see J. Alton Templin, "The Ideology of a Chosen People: Afrikaner Nationalism and the Ossewa Trek, 1938," *Nations and Nationalism*, 5.3 (1999), 397–417. See also Sandra Joireman, *Nationalism and Political Identity* (London: Continuum, 2004), 60.

15. Joseph V. Montville, "Religion and Peacemaking" in *Forgiveness and Reconciliation: Religion, Public Policy, and Conflict Transformation,* Raymond G. Helmick, S.J. and Rodney L. Petersen, eds. (Radnor, PA: Templeton Foundation Press, 2001), 101.
16. Beinart, 65.
17. Beinart, 143.
18. Transcript, *Mandela: An Audio History* [Joe Richman, Radio Diaries and Sue Johnson, Radio Diaries, 2004], "All Things Considered" (NPR: Broadcast, April 26–30, 2004). This sentiment was repeated by P.W. Botha in 1998, after he had been ousted from power by his own cabinet who subsequently dismantled the regime. Speaking to reporters at his trial on charges of contempt of court for ignoring a subpoena from South Africa's Truth and Reconciliation Commission, Botha said, "Apartheid is an Afrikaans word and can easily be replaced by a positive term—good neighborliness" (Andrew Maykuth, "Botha Gives No Apologies for Actions on Apartheid," *The Philadelphia Inquirer*, January 24, 1998).
19. Beinart, 147.
20. Beinart, 148.
21. Beinart, 147.
22. Beinart, 147.
23. Beinart, 148.
24. For a brief explanation of these racial classifications see Desmond Tutu, *The Rainbow People of God: The Making of a Peaceful Revolution* (New York: Image, Doubleday, 1994), xix.
25. Beinart, 148.
26. Deborah Posel, "What's in a Name? Racial Categorisations Under Apartheid and Their Afterlife," in *Transformations: Critical Perspectives on Southern Africa,* 47 (2001), 58–59.
27. Beinart, 143. The treatment of Coloured persons and families in South Africa bears witness to the idea that race is a social construct. If biologically related families were assigned different racial categories and forced to separate, then race is clearly a social construct rather than a biological reality.
28. Beinart, 147.
29. Beinart, 148.
30. Beinart, 154.
31. Beinart, 155.
32. Beinart, 153.
33. Beinart, 153.
34. Beinart, 153.
35. Beinart, 153.
36. Beinart, 153.
37. Beinart, 154.
38. Beinart, 154.
39. Beinart, 158.
40. Beinart, 158.
41. John Grimond, "A Survey of South Africa: Africa's Great Black Hope," *The Economist* (February 24–March 2, 2001), 6.
42. Beinart, 159.
43. Beinart, 160.
44. Beinart, 160.
45. Quoted in Tutu, *The Rainbow People of God,* 5.

Chapter Two

Theological Roots of the Just War Tradition and Just Peacemaking Theory

Providing a conceptual framework for the ethics of revolution that includes both just war and just peacemaking demonstrates the possibility of a harmonious and even cooperative relationship between these two systems. It affirms that both the just war tradition and just peacemaking theory can contribute to peaceful outcomes in conflict situations; and that both can contribute to an outcome characterized by justice. I will stress that when possible in situations of revolution the nonviolent practices of just peacemaking theory should continue to be employed even when armed resistance has been initiated as a last resort. In this way, the just peacemaking theory acts as a reminder of the best ideals of the just war tradition to those engaged in armed resistance: peace is the goal of armed force. Thus, rejecting any notion that the just war and just peacemaking theories are opposed to one another, my approach to the ethics of revolution couples the possibility of the last resort of armed force with the continued use of nonviolent confrontational strategies as a practical way to curb and contain violence, to overcome oppression, and to work toward a just peace with the goal of reconciliation.

Accordingly, this chapter serves as an introduction to the two conceptual frameworks that will undergird the ethics of a just revolution. It discusses both the just war tradition and the just peacemaking theory, paying special attention to the roots of both in Christian theology. Laying these foundations here will allow for a more fluid conversation amongst the just war tradition, just peacemaking theory, and the ethics of revolution in chapters 3, 4, and 5.

THE JUST WAR TRADITION

The just war tradition has been embraced in the secular spheres of political science and international law; however, it is important to remember that the just war theory was initially promulgated and discussed in a Christian theological context. Indeed, "the western theory of just war originated . . . from the interior of the ethics of Christian love."[1] The theological roots of the tradition are key to understanding how best to interpret and apply its principles, both for war in general and, for our purposes, the ethics of revolution.[2] My task here will be to illustrate the convergence of the just war tradition with Christian theology, especially through Augustine and Aquinas, whose thinking on war and peace continues to influence theo-political discussions of global conflict today.

In concert with the historical development of the just war tradition, contemporary Christian just war theorists typically hold that the telos of a just war is a just peace. While there are numerous thinkers across the centuries who have contributed to this understanding of the proper end of a just war, two theologians stand out as particularly important and influential for understanding the just war tradition, and especially the theology from which it flows: Saint Augustine and Saint Thomas Aquinas.

Augustine and the Tranquility of Order

Early adherents to Christianity debated whether or not participation in the Roman military was morally licit. Allegiance to Jesus Christ, some thought, was incompatible with military service that required allegiance to the emperor.[3] "Studies of early Christian attitudes toward military service have found no evidence that Christians served in the military up until approximately the year 170 or 180 AD."[4] The early church fathers "were generally adamant that discipleship requires close adherence to the nonviolent and countercultural example of Jesus's own life."[5] The conversion of the Roman Emperor Constantine, with the concomitant implementation of Christianity as the religion of the Roman Empire, is widely considered a defining moment in Christian history;[6] one that generated innumerable questions and discussions as to the relationship of Christianity to society and politics, and the role of individual Christians in social and political life. At the same time, questions surrounding the morality of military service became somewhat less pronounced and "Christian participation in the military became much more general."[7] Instead of asking whether or not military participation was morally justified, questions surfaced inquiring as to the legitimacy of warfare itself. Was it possible for a state characterized by faith in Jesus Christ to wage war, and if so, under what circumstances and in what manner?

Augustine addressed questions related to the use of military force in several places, most notably his dialogue with Faustus, the Manichean Bishop *Contra Faustum*[8]; his letters to the general, Boniface[9] and to the politician, Marcellinus[10]; and in his major treatise against paganism, *The City of God*. Given the dispersed nature of Augustine's writings, his discourse on the morality of war is not nearly as systematic as some contemporary scholars might wish. Indeed, he writes more about peace than war per se, and it is only in the context of his theology of peace that his contributions to Christian thinking about war can be properly understood. To illustrate the foundation of Augustine's thinking regarding the morality of warfare, I set out here to do three things. First, I will describe Augustine's understanding of Manichean dualism and his ultimate rejection of it. Augustine's related conceptions of sin and evil emerge from his spiritual and intellectual struggles with Manichaeism. How he understands sin and evil is arguably crucial to comprehending his entire worldview[11]—including his thoughts regarding peace and war. Second, I will draw out the connections between Augustine's conception of evil and his understanding of peace as its opposite. Evil is the result of a perversion of order, while peace is the result of harmonious order. Finally, I examine how Augustine's affirmation of peace as "the tranquility of order" leads to his articulation of what eventually become the first three criteria of the just war theory.

Key to Augustine's understandings of war and peace is the battle he waged—both interiorly in his intellectual and spiritual life, and publically in his writings—with the Manichean religious sect. Augustine reports having spent nine years in what he comes to call the "delusion" of Manichaeism[12] as part of his epic struggle with questions of theodicy, specifically how evil and suffering come to exist in a universe that Christians believe is created by a good God. The Manicheans proposed a solution to this dilemma that was, for a time, rather attractive to Augustine. Augustine suggests that the Manicheans espoused a form of dualism which allowed them to deny the notion that the universe was created by a good God. Rejecting traditional Judeo-Christian monotheism, the Manicheans instead believed in two deities: the Christian god, the Father of Jesus Christ depicted in the New Testament, and the "Creator" god depicted in parts of the Hebrew Scriptures. For the Manicheans, the Father of Jesus Christ is benevolent and seeks to redeem humankind. The good and benevolent Father is opposed to the Creator who is neither good nor benevolent.[13] In describing his understanding of these two deities and their relationship Augustine writes: "I imagined that there were two antagonistic masses, both of which were infinite, yet the evil in a lesser and the good in a greater degree."[14]

As part of their understanding of the nature of these two deities, and the concomitant dualistic structure of reality, the Manicheans posited that only spiritual realities were good, while matter—from figs and the trees they grow on, to the human body—is permeated with the substance of evil. The soul, as a spiritual substance, was deemed good, and the body evil. This allowed Manicheans to reject the idea of free will and to view "sin" as more a force of nature, than a result of human choice. Thus Augustine, under the thrall of Manichaeism, remarks, "I still thought that it is not we who sin, but some other nature that sins within us."[15] Augustine portrays the Manicheans as holding that the physical world is a prison that spiritual realities seek to escape. Manichean religious rituals were in part designed to free these spiritual energies from their physical prisons.[16] This dualistic worldview allowed the Manicheans to deal with the question of theodicy by asserting that the material world had not been created by a good God, therefore the question that theodicy seeks to answer about the origins of evil simply does not apply.

Augustine ultimately rejected Manicheism and instead proposed a different response to the question of theodicy. We can imagine Augustine asking, if God is good, and God generates and contains all creation, which is also therefore good, can it be that evil does not exist as a substance at all? In what Augustine describes as a kind of mystical moment of "light pouring over [his] soul" he begins to understand that "even those things which are subject to decay are good."[17] Indeed, Augustine chooses faith in God's goodness as a point of departure and reasons that since God is good and the Creator of all, "whatever is, is good."[18] Corruptibility, for Augustine, is in fact a testament to the goodness of created things, which are only corruptible because they are good to begin with.[19] In creation however, there are good things that we think of as imbued with evil because they are at odds with other good things.[20] This then, is Augustine's concept of conflict, which occurs when we perceive good things to be at odds with one another; and when we freely choose to esteem a lesser good over a greater one, we sin. Thus evil, Augustine argues, does not exist as a positive substance at all, but only as an absence of goodness.[21] It occurs, so to speak, via a "perversion of the will when it turns aside from . . . God . . . and veers toward things of the lowest order."[22] The origin of evil and suffering in this world is the human choice to sin: to misprioritize the good things of creation, loving them more than their Creator, and in ways that are disordered. Sin and evil are intimately related.

Augustine's explanations for the origins of sin and evil directly inform his theology of peace. If evil comes from the human capacity to sin by disordering our love for God and the goods of creation, then peace is the harmonious ordering of our love for God and the good things of creation, generated by divine grace. We experience peace insofar as we prioritize love for God, and then love created goods in ordered ways, and with reference to the Creator. Hence Augustine names peace "the tranquility of order."[23] But this tidy image of serenity ought not tempt us to adopt too rosy a vision of Augustine's theology of peace. Augustine develops his vision in the context of two "comingled"[24] polities—the earthly and the heavenly cities—in his major work *The City of God*. It is in his description of the earthly city in particular that Augustine earns his reputation for pessimism.

In contrasting how philosophers understand the pursuit of happiness, versus how Christians understand it, Augustine leaves no doubt that life on earth can be and often is brimming with conflict and misery. Augustine argues that "the philosophers" seek happiness in themselves, particularly their practice of virtue. Augustine, however, understands virtue as a battle with vice, which connotes less the pursuit of happiness and more the constant struggle that Christians must wage against sin. Virtue does not inculcate peace, but rather a restlessness as we marshal virtue as a bulwark against the temptation to sin. For example, "fortitude," argues Augustine "is the plainest proof of the ills of life, for it is these ills which it is compelled to bear patiently."[25] Though he notes that "the Stoic philosophers" simultaneously argue that infirmity and misfortune do not affect a happiness born of virtue "at the same time they allow the wise man to commit suicide and pass out of this life if [these ills] become so grievous that he cannot or ought not to endure them."[26] This contradiction prompts the mordant exclamation, "O happy life, which seeks the aid of death to end it!"[27] In an effort to illustrate that life in the earthly city is vile when compared to that of the heavenly city, Augustine calls virtue an "intestine war" that seeks to reign in the vices and pull them toward moderation.[28] Thus, the citizen of heaven understands that even to exercise virtue in the earthly city is to subject one's self to the mal-ordered folly of social and political life on earth.

Augustine's understanding of this folly is made most apparent in his famous example of the wise judge.[29] The judge is ignorant as to the guilt or innocence of a given suspect, and so he orders the subject to be tortured to elicit a confession. Suppose, suggests Augustine, that the suspect *is* innocent and chooses "in obedience to the philosophical instructions to the wise man, to quit this life rather than endure any longer such tortures?"[30] The suspect would then confess to a crime of which he is innocent in order to compel the judge to cease the torture and simply put him to death. The judge is then in the position of having tortured an innocent man to discover his guilt, and, still ignorant of his innocence, condemns the accused to death. Since he truly is wise, the judge will recognize that under the circumstances he remains ignorant of the subject's guilt or innocence, even after the torture-induced confession, but he is nevertheless compelled to order the execution. For Augustine this pandemonium points to the perversion of goods in the earthly city—to the disorder and chaos that prevent true peace. The situation Augustine describes defaces even the most orderly functions of social and political life in the earthly city. We ought not detest the judge, who is in fact laudable for doing his duty, but rather we must "condemn human life as miserable."[31] For Augustine all human activity is tangled in these perversions of what is good, in sin that is inescapable without the grace of God. Nevertheless Christians are duty-bound, like the wise judge, to use their positions to mitigate evil as much as possible. Thus Jean Bethke Elshtain notes, "Pilgrims on this earth understand that life around them was created by human beings to achieve some good, to avoid greater evil."[32]

In the midst of this misery we can attain only a shadow of the peace that is promised in the heavenly city. There we will exercise the virtues with ease rather than as a struggle against vice. The limited peace of earth mirrors that of heaven in that it comes from attention to order, including obedience to hierarchical authorities: God in heaven, and those God ordains to rule on earth. Indeed, ordered relationships are key to both earthly and heavenly peace. On earth, "peace is realized provisionally, albeit defectively, whenever order or harmony prevails in earthly relationships, whether they be among members of the body, between body and soul, among members of a family, among citizens and rulers, or between humanity and God."[33] Moreover, peace in one sphere contributes to peace in the others.[34] What is defective on earth is perfected in heaven, where God reigns, sin is conquered, and death is no more. "The peace of the celestial city is the perfectly ordered and harmonious enjoyment of God, and of one another in God. The peace of all things is the tranquility of order."[35]

Peace in the earthly city is provisional, but that does not, for Augustine, depreciate its value as earthly peace. It is "mere misery compared to that final felicity,"[36] but it is misery much to be sought, and is certainly preferable to war—indeed, as we shall see, it is the only thing worth warring for. "The earthly city, which does not live by faith, seeks an earthly peace, and the end it proposes in the well-ordered concord of civic obedience and rule is the combination of men's wills to attain the things which are helpful to this life."[37] Peace on earth facilitates the positive—if tainted with sin—functioning of earthly relationships. Indeed, Christians are called to contribute to earthly peace and recognize its instrumental value: peaceful and harmonious relationships free Christians to focus on God.[38] Conflict and chaos detracts from this focus. Peace, even the derivative peace of the earthly city, is to be consciously pursued; so much so that Augustine contends that the only valid reason for waging war is to reestablish peace when it is threatened by sin and disorder.

Among the texts that likely earn Augustine the title "Father of the Just War Tradition"[39] is his response to the theological ideas of the Manichean bishop, Faustus. The response is not a systematic attempt to generate a "just war theory" and Augustine likely had little sense that his statements on war in this text would become the foundation of a major ethical approach to conflict that would stand for centuries. Nevertheless the first three criteria of the just war theory are drawn initially from this interaction with Faustus.[40] As in many of his writings, Augustine composes *Contra Faustum* as a dialogue, in this case between Faustus and himself. Of primary concern to Augustine is Faustus's rejection of the divine authority of the Old Testament, or Hebrew Scriptures,[41] partially on the grounds that the deity it describes approves of and orders evil actions.

A good God, for Faustus, could neither participate in nor sanction the evil acts of war and violence described in the Hebrew Scriptures. Echoing his approval of the wise judge who does his duty even though it may involve participation in the misery of the earthly city, Augustine suggests that the circumstances of our activities and the intentions with which we carry them out matter. "Some actions have an indifferent character, so that men are blamed for presumption if they do them without being called upon, while they are deservedly praised for doing them when required."[42] War is "indifferent" in this way for Augustine: when it is done in the wrong way, at the wrong time, and for the wrong reasons, it is wrong, but under the right conditions it is a duty. Augustine embraces the divine authority of the Hebrew Scriptures, and retains his monotheism, in part by rejecting the notion that evil entirely permeates all war. Moreover, Augustine is deeply concerned about limiting God's will according to imperfect human standards of good and evil. In responding to Faustus's disgust at the plight of the Egyptian soldiers drowned in the Red Sea,[43] Augustine warns, "Your feeling of disapproval for the mere human action should be restrained by a regard for the divine sanction."[44] Whereas Faustus charges that the good God cannot will such an evil as war (and thus the deity described in the Hebrew Scriptures is not good), Augustine, intent on God's unity and sovereignty, counters that God can and is free to will anything. Nevertheless, God does not will anything that is evil, since evil is the result of a perversion of the human will when it chooses lesser goods over greater ones. Thus it must be possible, Augustine reasons, for God to will a just war. Augustine appeals to the example of Moses to support his view: "Now, if this explanation suffices to satisfy human obstinacy and perverse misinterpretation of right actions of the vast difference between the indulgence of passion and presumption on the part of men, and obedience to the command of God, who knows what to permit or to order . . . the wars of Moses will not excite surprise or abhorrence, for in wars carried on by divine command, he showed not ferocity but obedience; and God in giving the command, acted not in cruelty, but in righteous retribution, giving to all what they deserved, and warning those who needed warning."[45] Thus for Augustine certain wars—those waged for a just cause, by a legitimate authority, and with a right intention—may be sanctioned by the good and sovereign God for their contribution to the maintenance of a proper social order and earthly peace.

Augustine understands just causes for war to be activity that disrupts or compromises earthly peace and social order, and such wars should be fought only as necessities.[46] A good grasp of Augustine's theology of peace, detailed above, is essential to understanding his willingness to justify war as an ethical possibility. Civic order is fostered by rightly ordered love of God and the goods of creation, and this rightly ordered love advances the establishment of peace. Earthly peace is the end result of rightly ordered relationships in civic and political life. When these relationships are deeply disturbed by grave wrongs or injustices, war may be necessary to reestablish civic order, or peace.

The criterion of legitimate authority also finds its basis in Augustine's theology of peace. God has ordered all things in creation toward the end of peace.[47] When Augustine declares that only a legitimate authority can justly wage war he points to this divinely inspired order because he generally understood the legitimate authority to be the emperor or monarch whose position of power, he believed to be divinely ordained.[48] In waging war, the authority acts as part of the "natural order" established by God, "which seeks the peace of mankind."[49] Thus it is the responsibility of the divinely ordained civil authority to maintain civic order, and peace, even when necessary through recourse to the sword.[50]

The final of the original three just war criteria, right intention, also emerges from Augustine's conception of peace. Those who consider waging war must examine their intentions, or the interior dispositions of their hearts. Thus Augustine reasons that a just war is waged only "for the natural order which seeks peace,"[51] and to establish a "well-ordered concord" amongst the civic community.[52] The result of rightly ordered loves is peace, and so the just war, in intending to reestablish order, pursues peace. Indeed, contrary to Faustus's claim that war is intrinsically evil, Augustine is adamant in his theo-ethical belief that evil is a perversion of goods. Thus he remarks, "The real evils in war are love of violence, revengeful cruelty, fierce and implacable enmity, wild resistance, and the lust of power."[53] Note that these evils manifest as "loves" or desires that are disordered. One *ought not* love violence, engage in cruelty, hold grudges, and lust after power as these detract from civic peace. These loves are perversions of the will that was originally created by God to love in an ordered way. The recognition of these disordered loves prompts Augustine to suggest that "good men undertake wars" to "inflict punishment" for exactly such perversions of order. "Right conduct requires them to act, or to make others act in this way"[54] and in acting they seek to reestablish order, and thus peace. Again, Augustine rejects any motivation for war that arises from a perversion of goods. Across several of his writings Augustine warns against the glorification of violence for pleasure, revenge, or personal gain.[55] Instead, the ruler's intention in war must correspond in obedience to God's intentions for creation: to maintain peaceful order.[56] Augustine advocates for the Roman military to be an army of peacemakers, telling the general, Boniface that "Peace should be the object of your desire; war should be waged only as a necessity, and waged only that God may by it deliver men from the necessity and preserve them in peace."[57]

Rooted in an Augustinian conception of rightly ordered loves, "social order as a form of peace is also a form of love."[58] Love properly orders the goods of creation, and always prioritizes obedience to the will of God. Thus an interior disposition of love seeks peace, guiding right intention in warfare. Augustine contends: "When war is undertaken in obedience to God, who would rebuke, or humble, or crush the pride of men, it must be allowed to be a righteous war."[59] It should be noted that connecting a right intention to love is not a point devoid of controversy as Augustine's understanding of just war also includes killing one's enemies as an expression of love.[60]

For Augustine war is sometimes an unhappy necessity to secure earthly peace. Elshtain writes, "The just ruler waging a justifiable war of necessity to rescue innocents from destruction, for example, doesn't look down the road and see parades and banners and kudos all round, but he sees mangled bodies and destroyed villages and torn and shredded human lives."[61] War, even when it seeks to correct severe injustices, is never to be sought or celebrated, but only undertaken as a duty to participate in and promote the well-ordered harmony of civic and political life. This harmony is also called peace, and Christians make use of it to focus their attention on God. The more a political community is able to cultivate peace, the nearer it will be to the happiness that is ultimately fulfilled only in the heavenly city. War represents a deeper descent into the misery and folly of earthly life, but it is a descent that is sometimes required for the purpose of peace-building. It should thus, for Augustine, be regulated by a legitimate authority, whose power comes from God, and who is motivated, even in the midst of war, by peace as a form of a rightly ordered love.

Aquinas and the Common Good

Aquinas's contributions to the just war tradition build on Augustine's and evidence his strong concern for the common good, understood as the product of justice. It is from the tradition of Thomistic theology and ethics that we draw the widely accepted idea that justice is a prerequisite for true peace.[62] Indeed, Lisa Sowle Cahill notes that "for Aquinas, peace in the political community is accomplished by justice and the rule of law much more emphatically than for Augustine."[63]

For Aquinas, the primary function of government is to care for the common good. Care for the common good will necessarily involve justice since justice is, for Aquinas, "definitive of the common good."[64] This conception of good government emerges from Aquinas's understanding of God—especially God's goodness and authority as the eternal law which encodes all creation with a natural law. To illustrate these relationships I first describe Aquinas's understanding of God as the ultimate good. Second, I show how Aquinas's understanding of God affects his conception of good government, in particular government's role of inculcating virtue and more specifically, justice in the commonweal. Finally, I return to the original three criteria of the just war theory illustrating how Aquinas's focus on justice colors the principles of just cause, legitimate authority, and right intention.

In his Treatise on God,[65] Aquinas reasons that God is the ultimate good which all creation seeks as its end. Thus good government and just rulers will seek to mirror God's goodness. Aquinas equates "the good" with God's being, via themes that resonate with how God is depicted in the Hebrew Scriptures. As the uncaused cause of all creation, God is pure being.[66] Aquinas's insight here harkens back to the Hebraic name of God—*YHWH*, I AM—and he reminds us that "a proposition effected by the mind [joins] a predicate to a subject . . . this proposition which we form about God when we say 'God is,' is true."[67] As pure being God is also one, an undivided unity since "the being of anything consists in indivision."[68] Thus, Aquinas argues: "God comprehends in himself the whole perfection of Being . . . all things that exist are seen to be ordered to each other . . . but things that are diverse do not agree in one order unless they are ordered thereto by someone being . . . what is first is most perfect and is so *per se* and not accidentally, it must be that the first which reduces all into one order should be only one. And this one is God."[69] For Aquinas, God's goodness flows from God's unity of being. Aquinas remarks, "Good and being are really the same, and differ only according to reason . . . a thing is desirable only in so far as it is perfect . . . everything is perfect so far as it is in act. Therefore it is clear that a thing is good so far as it is being."[70] Since God is pure being, God is the perfect and absolute good. All other goods are only good insofar as they participate in the goodness of God. In perhaps his most complete description of God, Aquinas remarks, "There is then something which is the truest, something best, something noblest . . . to all beings the cause of their being, goodness, and every other perfection."[71] Since goodness connotes desirability, and God is wholly good, God is the final and ultimate desire of all creatures.[72] Thus, for Aquinas, we strive to model our existence—including our socio-political life—after God, who is our most ardent desire.[73]

Modeling our socio-political life after God involves recognizing God as the first cause or prime-mover of all things, and thus as a sovereign eternal law over all creation.[74] We strive for order and authority in the temporal world in part due to our having been created in the likeness of God and invested by God with the capacity to attain our natural ends, one of which is life in society.[75] Thus, deviating in tone from Augustine for whom misery abounds in this earthly city where human beings can never hope to attain the peace they will participate in in the heavenly city, Aquinas more optimistically views our natural ends as within our grasp given the proper use of reason. More so than Augustine, Aquinas trusts human beings to use reason effectively to pursue our natural ends. To aid people in achieving their natural ends, all earthly government ought to be a participation in God's wise and just governance of creation. Just as God, by virtue of God's ultimate unity and absolute goodness, orders creation, all legitimate governmental authority encourages and maintains order toward peace and the common good. Moreover, good government arranges and adjusts socio-political life so as to eliminate discord and injustice and to ensure that peace, social unity, and the common good can be enjoyed by society as a whole. For Aquinas, the maintenance of peace and the common good is facilitated in at least two ways. First, the government ought to encourage the development of virtue in its citizenry; and second, a government's legitimacy is tethered to its exercise of justice.

Aquinas emphasizes the role of structures and law in training people in the virtues. Good government promotes and encourages virtue in individuals and society. While some people more easily obey their natural inclinations toward the good most manifest in God, others need to be "restrained from evil by force and fear, in order that at least they might cease from evil-doing and leave others in peace."[76] Such people must be persuaded toward virtue by fear of punishment. "Men who are well disposed are led willingly to virtue . . . but men who are evilly disposed are not led to virtue unless they are compelled."[77] The "discipline of laws" restrains vice, and it can lead people to do good and thereby acquire virtue.[78] Aquinas reasons that the duty of rulers is to inculcate virtue in the citizenry, ensuring that those subject to their rule "live well."[79] Following Aristotle, for whom happiness depended mostly on virtue but also on having sufficient physical resources to meet one's own needs,[80] living well for Aquinas included not only virtue but also "a sufficiency of bodily goods, the use of which is necessary to virtuous conduct."[81] Here Aquinas seems to argue for a relationship between virtue and vice on the one hand and justice and injustice on the other. For people to grow in virtue they must first be able to meet their basic needs. While social justice assists the development of virtue, injustice breeds greater vice. Hence, for Aquinas a just and virtuous ruler will be a key component of good governance, and will inculcate virtue and an appreciation of justice in the people.

Second, Aquinas links law and governance to justice, rooted in the natural law. He avers that the human (or positive) law should not contradict the natural law because the natural law promotes justice through the exercise of reason. Since, "the force of a law depends on the extent of its justice," and justice is established according to the rule of reason, which is the province of natural law, "every human law . . . is derived from the law of nature. But if in any point it differs from the law of nature, it is no longer a law but a corruption of the law."[82] For Aquinas then, natural law places moral limits on human law and urges human law toward justice.[83] Governments that attend to justice in adherence to the natural law are legitimate. Those which corrupt the natural law through injustice can become illegitimate.

In his political thought, Aquinas, echoing Aristotle, generally details five forms of government.[84] First, he describes monarchy, "that is, when the state is governed by one,"[85] who rules as a virtuous King.[86] This is Aquinas' preferred form of government for his understanding of how it mirrors the one God's benevolent and just governance of creation. A second form of government, aristocracy, is characterized by a ruling elite of "the best men or men of highest rank."[87] Here a relatively small group of elite and virtuous men guide the larger community. Third is oligarchy, a lesser form of aristocracy in which a few wealthy and powerful individuals control all governance. Oligarchies are essentially group tyranny. While no single ruler seeks to wield all power and wealth for himself, the ruling elite seek to benefit at the expense of the common good. Fourth, Aquinas describes democracy, or rule by the majority of the people. Although this is generally viewed as the most just form of government in contemporary, Western culture, Aquinas, operating out of his medieval context, counts it among the disordered forms of government for at least two reasons. First, under Aquinas' requirement that rulers be virtuous, democracy presents peculiar problems. To keep from becoming simple mob-rule in which the majority tyrannizes the minority, democracy demands a higher level of virtue from its citizens (higher, perhaps, than Aquinas is willing to expect) than any other type of government. "The democratic principle of equal participation, without morally responsible citizens, risks anarchy."[88] Nevertheless, as we will see when we discuss the criterion of legitimate authority in revolutionary contexts, Aquinas does seem to suggest that, at least to some extent, the will of the people must guide a legitimate authority. Second, he worries that democracy encourages dissention and therefore acts against unity.[89] Unity here is intricately related to peace. For Aquinas, peace includes concord, but adds something to it.[90] This "something" is essentially a lack of needs. One cannot be at peace if one has unfulfilled needs. These unfulfilled needs represent a lack of unity between the appetitive and rational powers. Peace, then, is related to the overarching desire within all of our desires and needs—that is, a desire not to have wants, a desire to be completely fulfilled. Thus in addition to being difficult for Aquinas in a democracy because of its lack of unity and probability of dissention, peace is also impossible in Aquinas' fifth form of government: tyranny. As a product of the love of God and neighbor, peace is a result of charity, or love. No peace can exist in a tyrannical regime because the tyrant loves neither God nor neighbor. Peace, being unity, absence of needs, and ultimately, fulfillment of desires, is categorically impossible under a tyrannical dictatorship. Tyranny constitutes the rule of one who elevates his personal desires above the common good. Tyrants are "utterly corrupt" and thus tyrannies lack any "corresponding law."[91] Under such a regime, reason, justice and virtue are abandoned, and disorder and chaos abound. All "law" in a despotic regime bends to the caprices of the ruler, so that its value is significantly diminished. "Law" in such a political system can hardly be called law at all as it is at odds with natural order, justice, or virtue.

With this backdrop on the role of government in promoting justice and the common good, we turn now to Aquinas's thoughts on warfare. Aquinas adopts Augustine's three criteria for when a war may be justified—just cause, legitimate authority, and right intention. Nevertheless, Aquinas's focus on justice for the common good engenders both subtle and overt shifts from Augustine's understanding of these criteria.

Aquinas concurs with Augustine that just causes for waging war include serious wrongs and injustices that threaten peace. "Those who are attacked," Aquinas reasons, "should be attacked because they deserve it on account of some fault."[92] In citing Augustine, Thomas Aquinas contends that just causes involve avenging and punishing wrongdoing or restoring "what has been seized unjustly."[93]

Thomas Aquinas likewise concurs with Augustine that only a legitimate authority can rightly wage war. Where Augustine stresses the duty of political authorities to keep order for peace, Aquinas articulates the ruler's responsibility in terms of the common good. The task of the political authority is to care for the common good,[94] and "just as it is lawful for [rulers] to have recourse to the material sword in defending that common weal against internal disturbances when they punish evil-doers . . . so too it is their business to have recourse to the sword for war in defending the common weal against external enemies."[95] Only rulers have a right to wage war, and implicit here is that it is a right limited to the defense of the common good. Private individuals, Aquinas contends, have no need to conduct wars to punish wrong-doers since they have recourse to civil authorities for resolving personal disagreements and maintaining security.[96]

Augustine and Aquinas's conceptions of legitimate authority raise several questions, and because the criterion of legitimate authority is one of the most difficult to reform for a revolutionary context, it is helpful to discuss some of those questions here. Specifically there are three claims these theologians have made that ought to be considered.

First, Aquinas's suggestion that individuals are not fit to wage war because they have recourse to just civil authorities is a presumption that must be questioned given that despots routinely violate the human rights of their own people. Lack of recourse to a just and impartial civil authority is one of the legitimate grievances that may lead to revolutionary activity. Aquinas's own socio-political thought acknowledges as much in his suggestion that a tyrannical regime is not a legitimate form of government since it is directed not toward the common good but to the private good of the ruler.[97] Accordingly, Aquinas claims that it is not sedition to overthrow a tyrant, but that it is "the tyrant rather that is guilty of sedition, since he encourages discord and sedition among his subjects."[98] Nevertheless, Aquinas does not give a clear account of who would be the legitimate authority to carry out a rebellion against the unjust ruler. This will be discussed further in chapter 4 when I revise the criterion of legitimate authority for the ethics of revolution.

Second, Augustine's claim that God uses rulers—including even tyrants—as conduits for divine punishment does not adequately account for Augustine's own theology of sin, in which we are utterly mired, unable to do anything good without the grace of God.[99] All human beings, whether peasants or kings, are lost in this abyss of sin; all are subject to error and vulnerable to temptation. Rulers are no exception. It is thus important to acknowledge the capacity of a ruler to do genuine wrong in waging an unjust war instead of suggesting that even an unjust war is somehow divinely providential as a form of "punishing" or "humbling the vanquished."[100] John Langan's critique of Augustine is salient here: "Augustine's insistence on the power and mystery of God's providence leads to a kind of agnosticism about the value of what human beings do and suffer in the course of war."[101] Indeed, as we have come to understand more deeply the attraction of power and its corrupting qualities, the notion of the *de facto* ruler as a divinely ordained legitimate authority who providentially administers reward and sanction has come to be seen as morally bankrupt. Instead under certain political circumstances civic authority may be more of an occasion for sin than for doing good. Of particular relevance here is the critique that Rosemary Radford Reuther makes concerning the proximity of sin to power.[102] The more power one has, the more one finds opportunities to sin, and the more one ought to guard against the corrupting capacities of power. Indeed, it is likely that Augustine developed a nuanced understanding of the relationship between sin and power. Speaking of the relationships between power and authority for promoting order in the family, the Church, and the state, Elshtain suggests that Augustine understood that "the temptations of arbitrary power and excess grow greater the more power there is to be had."[103]

Aquinas's understanding of the task of the legitimate authority as promoting the common good may mitigate this concern for the corruptive possibilities of power somewhat. Nevertheless, the focus on the common good when considering whether to wage war also raises a third concern. Especially in an era in which more destructive wars are fought more and more often "for reasons based in local rivalries, typically inflamed by historical animosities, ethnic disparity, or religious difference,"[104] in arguing that just wars are fought by legitimate authorities who care for and defend the common good, we ought to ask ourselves certain questions about the common good in order to avoid clannish exclusivity. Who exactly is included in the "common" good? Who and, given the ecological crisis we face, what is encompassed in our notion of "common" when we profess to defend the common good? Can the degree of havoc wrought by modern wars rightly be attributed to the common good? If so, then how do we define the common good and how do we justify excluding some and sacrificing others to attain it? Again, the implications of these questions for an ethics of revolution are clear: revolutions are generally the result of, at least, competing notions of how the common good ought to be defined, and/or who ought to be included in the common good, and what a just distribution of social benefits and burdens in the community entails.

The final of the original three just war criteria is right intention and nowhere is Aquinas's emphasis on justice more apparent than in his discussion of this criterion. Aquinas argues that war is not inherently contrary to peace, but rather that peace is the goal of just war: "Those who wage war justly aim at peace, and so they are not opposed to peace, except to the evil peace, which Our Lord 'came not to send upon earth.'"[105] The reference to "evil peace" points to Jesus's declaration that he came not to bring peace but the sword.[106] Coupled with Aquinas's stress that wars should be waged only against those who "deserve it on account of some fault,"[107] and his vehement arguments against tyranny[108] this suggests that for Aquinas a superficial peace devoid of justice is not a "good" peace. War is opposed only to the "evil peace" that comes at the price of justice.

Later Developments and Additional Just War Criteria

The original three just war criteria developed by Augustine and Aquinas—just cause, legitimate authority, and right intention—form the bedrock of what is known as *jus ad bellum,* or the consideration of what is just as we approach the possibility of warfare. The remaining four just war principles emerged in the tradition as distinct criteria following Augustine and Aquinas. Last resort and reasonable hope of success join the original criteria as *jus ad bellum* restraints when considering the initiation of war. Also considered here is macro-proportionality. Proportionate means (also called "micro-proportionality") and noncombatant immunity (also called discrimination) are *jus in bello* criteria, or restraints that seek to maintain justice during the actual fighting of a war.

The criterion of last resort requires that all other possible means for establishing the desired outcome of a just peace be attempted prior to the use of force. Mark J. Allman and Tobias L. Winright trace the roots of this criterion to Cicero's *De Officiis*. Cicero argues that human reason demands that we settle differences peacefully, through discussion rather than physical force. Force is justified only "in case we may not avail ourselves of discussion."[109] The presence of this criterion in the just war tradition, though, is typically credited to the sixteenth century Spanish theologian and philosopher Francisco de Vitoria who, in his criticism of Spanish colonial violence declared war to be "the *ultima ratio,* the last resort."[110] Today, last resort demands that "all peaceful alternatives" to war be "exhausted."[111] As Allman and Winright point out however, the criterion of last resort "does not preclude the immediate use of force for defensive purposes"[112] if a nation is actively under violent attack.

The criterion of reasonable hope of success must also be considered prior to engaging in armed conflict. It is generally attributed to another Spanish theologian, Francisco Suárez, who studied with de Vitoria as part of the School of Salamanca, a group of philosophers and theologians devoted to the study of the natural law and Thomistic thought as it relates to war, politics, and economics. Suárez's concern for the successful outcome of war applied in his mind primarily to punitive wars. Since rulers were responsible to protect the common good, they have no choice but to engage in wars of defense. Wars of defense protect the common good from unjust aggressors. But in wars undertaken as punishment rulers should consider whether their own people will suffer more in punishing another than in letting a punishable offense go unanswered.[113] A retrieval of Suárez's insistence that wars of defense are compelled, not chosen, will be helpful as we revise this criterion's meaning for the context of revolution. In the contemporary understanding of the just war theory, just wars are only waged for defense, and punishment, if it is ever valid, is subsumed under defense. Thus in the just war theory today reasonable hope of success (sometimes called "probability of success") involves a calculation of whether or not the goal of a just peace is likely to be achieved by the resort to war. The United States Bishops concede that "this is a difficult criterion to apply,"[114] and Suárez himself noted that he meant for this criterion to consider the probability, and not the certainty, of success.[115] Still "its purpose is to prevent irrational resort to force or hopeless resistance when the outcome of either will clearly be disproportionate or futile."[116] One important effect of the criterion is that it encourages the civilian and military leaders of armed forces to include clear missions and goals in all war plans since it is impossible to predict success without understanding what the goals are for a given course of military action, or what the mission is in a given conflict situation. Success must be defined and there must be a plan for achieving it.

The final *ad bellum* criterion of macro-proportionality requires that the good outcome sought by war is proportionate to the evil that will be suffered in war. As Augustine understood, war inevitably engenders chaos. Moreover, all war involves the loss of human life through killing.[117] Likewise, Aquinas conveyed at least an implicit concern for macro-proportionality in his caution that it may be better to suffer the rule of tyranny than to attempt to overthrow it if either failure or success in toppling the despotic regime will lead to something worse than the present conditions.[118] *Ad bellum,* then, proportionality judges whether or not "the overall good achieved by the use of force [is] greater than the harm done."[119]

Proportionality also functions *in bello* on a "micro" level to restrict the means of warfare so that unnecessary, or disproportionate, harm is avoided during the fighting of wars. Micro-proportionality is at least in part derived from Thomas Aquinas's treatment of killing in self-defense.[120] Aquinas argues that, "Though proceeding from a good intention, an act may be rendered unlawful, if it be out of proportion to the end. Wherefore if a man, in self-defense, uses more than necessary violence, it will be unlawful: whereas if he repel force with moderation his defense will be lawful."[121] This reasoning is also the source of the traditional principle of double-effect, which scholars of the just war tradition use to adjudicate ambiguous moral issues such as whether or not deadly forced can be used against military targets in situations that will also likely result in the deaths of civilians.[122] Aquinas is adamant that good intentions alone do not suffice to make good acts, and ends do not in themselves justify means. Political philosopher, Michael Walzer succinctly sums up the need for a criterion of micro-proportionality to restrain the means of war: "Proportionality is a matter of adjusting means to ends."[123] It is crucial since "there is an overwhelming tendency in wartime to adjust ends to means instead."[124] Aquinas's declaration that the means must be proportionate to the end holds true not only for acts of personal self-defense, but also for acts of war.

The final *in bello* criterion for a just war is noncombatant immunity, or discrimination. This criterion, which precludes belligerents from directly and intentionally harming civilians, has become increasingly important in contemporary warfare with the rise of civilian deaths in conflict situations and the intentional targeting of noncombatants as a means of waging war.[125] Noncombatant immunity demands that innocent human life be respected even in the midst of violent conflict.[126] Put positively, the criterion of noncombatant immunity requires that civilians be protected as much as possible against the damaging effects of war, including not only death but also severe damage to civilian infrastructure and quality of life. James Turner Johnson rightly sees this criterion as tied to proportionality in that the two seek to "make sure that war does not destroy everything that is worth living for in peacetime."[127]

Rooted in Christian theological commitments to peace and justice, exemplified by the work of Augustine and Thomas Aquinas, the just war tradition seeks to limit and restrain force when its use is determined to be absolutely necessary to secure a just peace. Untethered from its theological foundations, the just war theory can seem like a checklist of procedures for justifying warfare. It is not. In the spirit of promoting order and advancing the common good, its purpose is to reign in the human propensity toward sin and excess and direct us instead toward peace and justice. This same purpose can apply to the use of armed resistance. The criteria I have introduced here will be revised in chapter 4 to apply specifically to situations of revolution. Remembering that the telos of a just war is a just peace will be particularly crucial to understanding how the just war theory might function in a revolutionary context since revolution seeks to liberate people from unjust oppression.

JUST PEACEMAKING THEORY

From Gandhi's movement for Indian independence, to the U.S. Civil Rights Movement, to numerous revolutionary movements across the globe, nonviolent practices have been intentionally used in pursuit of peace and justice for decades. Recently, however, a broad array of these practices has been compiled by a group of theologians and activists into what they call "just peacemaking theory." In 1993 at a meeting of the Society of Christian Ethics, Glen Stassen, a Christian ethicist from Fuller Theological Seminary, led a group of twenty-three scholars who began to identify practical strategies for building peace and justice and for deterring war. Their work generated several articles introducing just peacemaking theory and later Stassen compiled and edited a comprehensive text now entitled, *Just Peacemaking: The New Paradigm for the Ethics of Peace and War*.[128] Just peacemaking theory has emerged as a powerful rubric for thinking about war, peace, and justice, as well as a practical route to addressing situations of conflict and promoting peacebuilding. In developing a theory of just revolution, I have turned to the notion of just peacemaking to provide the bedrock for *jus ante* armed resistance; just peacemaking theory acts as a conceptual framework for thinking about how justly to employ nonviolent tactics against oppression. It also constitutes one wheel of what I call the "tandem approach" to revolution in which nonviolent strategies are used alongside armed resistance. Now, I aim to introduce the just peacemaking theory, and describe its relationship to the just war tradition and pacifism, as well as its theological underpinnings.

The aim of just peacemaking is not to provide an answer to the question of whether or not war is ever justifiable. The just peacemaking scholars offer a practical theory which they hope will "take its place along with, but not . . . replace the established paradigms of pacifism and just war theory."[129] These scholars "disagree on the important question, 'When, if ever, are war and military force justified?'"[130] Rather the theory seeks to provide crucial content to both just war theorists and pacifists, acting as a corrective and supplying something that is lacking in each approach. Using only, or primarily, the just war theory as our lens for conflict resolution, just peacemaking theorists contend, can cause "tunnel vision,"[131] in which we focus too heavily on military solutions to conflict. Likewise, espousing only a pacifist orientation to conflict resolution lacks clear guidance on what kinds of practices can best promote a just peace.[132] For pacifists, just peacemaking theory offers a positive agenda for the pursuit of a just peace, including concrete actions that can be taken to build peace and avoid war. For just war advocates, just peacemaking theory offers strategies crucial to implement in order to fill out the criterion of last resort. Just war theorists who advocate just peacemaking theory "are not renouncing military force as a last resort, but they are committed to just peacemaking practices to try to divert events from leading to the horror of another war."[133] Thus, "the just peacemaking paradigm fills out the original intention of the other two paradigms. It encourages pacifists to fulfill what their name means, 'peacemakers.' And it calls just war theorists to fill in the contents of their underdeveloped principles of last resort and just intention—to spell out what resorts must be tried before trying the last resort of war, and what intention there is to restore a just and enduring peace."[134] In a world where 90 percent of the casualties of conflict are civilians, Stassen argues that governments, citizens, and all people of faith—whether they espouse pacifist or just war principles—have a moral duty to promote and bolster these practices of peacemaking so as to lessen the humanitarian crises of war.[135]

The theological foundations of just peacemaking theory are in some ways more self-conscious and explicit than those of the contemporary just war theory. Just peacemaking theory divides its ten practices into three thematic sections which highlight their Christian theological underpinnings: peacemaking initiatives, justice, and love and community. First, promoting "peacemaking initiatives" is part of the call to Christian discipleship. Second, "justice" is acknowledged as a precondition for peace, necessary for building up the Reign of God. Third, a broad commitment to "love and community" begins in the Christian understanding of Church as a community of witness to values like peace, liberation, and compassion.

The category of "peacemaking initiatives" is based on an incarnational or embodied Christology. This Christology places emphasis on Jesus's teachings, which present an "authoritative model for our ethical practice."[136] As Christian disciples, our ethical practice must be based on Jesus's own commitments to "nonviolent love, community-restoring justice, and peacemaking initiatives."[137] Stassen et al. argue that the Christian requirement that we take concrete initiatives to build peace is most evident in the Sermon on the Mount, in which Jesus offers a vision of peacemaking that precludes "either passive withdrawal [from society] or violent confrontation."[138] This vision is supported by a triadic interpretation of the sermon in which Jesus suggests initiatives we can take for restoring relationships. In each triad, Jesus first makes an appeal to "traditional piety"[139] —for instance, reminding his followers "You have heard of old, you shall not kill." Second, Jesus illustrates a "mechanism of bondage"—for example, "nursing anger, or saying 'you fool.'"[140] Last, Jesus presents us with a "transforming initiative"—"go therefore, be reconciled."[141] The Sermon on the Mount

> consists of fourteen such triads. In each of them the second member of the triad (the mechanism of bondage) does not use imperatives but continuing-action verbs, realistically diagnosing the vicious cycles that we get ourselves into when we serve some other lord than God . . . The third element is always an initiative, not merely a prohibition. It is always a practical participation in deliverance from a vicious cycle of bondage, hostility, idolatry, and judgment.[142]

Through these triads, especially the initiatives suggested in the third part of each triad, Jesus teaches us how to restore right relationships that have been damaged within society. From this exegesis of the Sermon on the Mount, just peacemaking theorists glean the necessity of peacemaking initiatives—proactive steps to confront social evils, avoid violence, and create and sustain peace. The practices which the just peacemaking theorists name as peacemaking initiatives are: (1) *Support Nonviolent Direct Action*, (2) *Take Independent Initiatives to Reduce Threat*, (3) *Use Cooperative Conflict Resolution*, and (4) *Acknowledge Responsibility for Conflict and Injustice, and Seek Repentance and Forgiveness*.

The second theological theme under which just peacemaking practices are categorized is "justice." This theme is based primarily on the foundational idea that "injustice is a major cause of war. To make peace, we must make justice."[143] In other words, just peacemaking theorists support the notion that justice and peace are intimately linked and indicative of one another. This notion is expressed throughout the Bible beginning with the Hebrew Scriptures, which present a vision of *shalom* as deep peace, characterized by justice. Shalom peace is a "gift from God, inclusive of all creation, grounded in salvation and covenant fidelity, inextricably bound up with justice."[144] In the New Testament, the relationship between justice and peace is evident in Jesus's praxis of preaching and promoting the Reign of God. The Reign of God will be infused with justice, and as such is "good news . . . that is hopeful and encouraging to the poor."[145] Christians who would be peacemakers are called "to transform the world"[146] and "to participate in the liberating power of God's reign"[147] by promoting justice. Promoting justice is key to establishing true peace because "the goods of peace and justice are interdependent, but justice is regarded as the precondition of peace in the concrete political order."[148] This idea is further echoed in Catholic Social Teaching. Throughout his encyclical *Pacem in Terris*, Pope John XXIII links peace to the protection of human rights. The Second Vatican Council reinforces this concern, declaring "peace is not merely the absence of war," but instead it is also "an enterprise of justice."[149] The U.S. Bishops further confirm that "justice is always the foundation of peace."[150] Two just peacemaking practices are included in the category of justice: (1) *Advance Democracy, Human Rights, and Interdependence,* and (2) *Foster Just and Sustainable Economic Development.*

The peacemaking practices included in the theme of "love and community" are rooted in an ecclesiological vision of church as a covenant community built up in radical love that "includes enemies, outcasts, and the neglected."[151] In this way, peacemaking is contiguous with building relationships across boundaries and with addressing the structural inequalities and injustices that lead to conflict.[152] Just peacemaking theorists argue that community efforts to build peace are a sign of love "understood realistically, rather than sentimentally."[153] The Christian understanding of love is a force for building community that includes enemies and marginalized persons. This radical love has been modeled by Jesus through his care and compassion for those typically considered outsiders or enemies in relation to his own Jewish people—Samaritans, tax collectors, lepers, and prostitutes.

The task of the church community toward building a just peace is twofold. First, the Church acts as a "community of memory and hope to nurture the paradigmatic story that orients the community in time and sustains a vision of God's reign."[154] In this way, the Church commits itself to remember and share narratives, such as the Exodus story, and the Good Samaritan, that speak to alternative values like liberation and compassion.[155] Second, "the church structures a process of practical moral reasoning where members of the community can listen to one another as they discern together what discipleship means."[156] Membership in a Church community involves commitment to "conversation" and "active participation" in the life of that community.[157] This provides a model for conflict resolution in the world, where active listening, negotiation, and participation are crucial to building peace. This theological focus on community thus begins in the Church, but then broadens to include the global community. In its broader context, it warns against the dangers of both individualism in interpersonal relationships, and excessive individualism's group-equivalent, nationalism. In a community committed to values like peace, liberation, and compassion, individualism and nationalism as forces for exclusion have no place. Just peacemaking practices included under the theme of "love and community" are (1) *Work with Emerging Cooperative Forces in the International System,* (2) *Strengthen the United Nations and International Efforts for Cooperation and Human Rights,* (3) *Reduce Offensive Weapons and Weapons Trade,* and (4) *Encourage Grassroots Peacekeeping Groups and Voluntary Associations.*

The ten practices of just peacemaking theory offer practical guidelines for staving off the last resort of war. In the context of a just revolution, their consistent use even during armed resistance can also help limit and restrain the use of force by putting continual economic and political pressure on the oppressive regime, and by acting as a reminder that a just peace marked by reconciliation is the revolution's final goal.

CONCLUSION

Both just peacemaking theory and the just war tradition can contribute to securing a just peace in situations of conflict and oppression. Just peacemaking theory offers practical strategies for conducting a just revolution that is entirely nonviolent. Nonviolent revolutions have been successful in a variety of historical situations, and some have even argued that they are more effective than revolutionary movements that take up arms.[158] However, under certain circumstances, these nonviolent practices alone may not be enough to secure the aim of a just peace. A truly just revolution that has come upon the last resort, and deems force necessary to establishing a just peace, will continue to use the practices of just peacemaking theory alongside armed strategies guided by the just war tradition. In the next several chapters, I aim to show how this model—just peacemaking and just war strategies working together to secure the common aim of a just peace, marked by reconciliation—enacted in the context of South Africa, generates principles to guide how it may be enacted elsewhere.

NOTES

1. Paul Ramsey, *The Just War: Force and Political Responsibility* (Lanham, MD: Rowman and Littlefield Publishers, 1983), 142.

2. Note what Lisa Sowle Cahill has written regarding the theological framework for the just war tradition: "Loss of the essentially theological horizon of Augustine's political theory will result in a distortion of his perspective on justified political action." Cahill, *Love Your Enemies: Discipleship, Pacifism, and Just War Theory* (Minneapolis, MN: Fortress Press, 1994), 66.

3. For more on the early Christian debate regarding military service see Cahill, 39–54.

4. David Hollenbach, S.J., *Nuclear Ethics: A Christian Moral Argument* (Mahwah, NJ: Paulist Press, 1983), 8.

5. Cahill, 41.

6. Cahill quotes Louis J. Swift on this point: "It is a truism that the reign of Constantine (AD 306–337) represents a watershed in the development of Christian attitudes concerning war and military service" (55).

7. Hollenbach, 9.

8. Available at http://www.newadvent.org/fathers/1406.htm.

9. Letter 189. Available at http://www.newadvent.org/fathers/1102189.htm.

10. Letter 138. See especially chapter 2. Available at http://www.newadvent.org/fathers/1102138.htm.

11. On this point see Jean Bethke Elshtain, *Augustine and the Limits of Politics* (South Bend, IN: University of Notre Dame Press, 1998).

12. Augustine, *Confessions*, R.S. Pine-Coffin, trans, (London: Penguin Books, 1961), 71.

13. For a succinct description of these Manichean propositions see John Langan, S.J., "Elements of St. Augustine's Just War Theory," *Journal of Religious Ethics*, 12.1 (1984), 20.

14. *Confessions*, 104.
15. *Confessions*, 103.
16. Augustine describes such a ritual with no small amount of sarcasm in his *Confessions:* "I was gradually led to believe such nonsense as that a fig wept when it was plucked, and that the tree which bore it shed tears of mother's milk. But if some sanctified member of the sect [Manicheans] were to eat the fig—someone else, of course, would have committed the sin of plucking it—he would digest it and breathe it out again in the form of angels or even as particles of God, retching them up as he groaned in prayer. These particles of the true and supreme God were supposed to be imprisoned in the fruit and could only be released by means of the stomach and teeth of one of the elect" (67).
17. Augustine, *Confessions*, 146, 148.
18. Augustine, *Confessions*, 148.
19. Augustine, *Confessions*, 148.
20. Augustine, *Confessions*, 148.
21. "Evil, the origin of which I was trying to find, is not a substance, because if it were a substance, it would be good" (*Confessions,* 148). See also Augustine, *City of God,* Marcus Dods, trans. (New York: The Modern Library, Random House Publishing Group, 1950) "Evil has no positive nature; but the loss of good has received the name 'evil'" (354).
22. Augustine, *Confessions*, 150.
23. Augustine, *City of God,* 690.
24. Augustine, *City of God*, 346.
25. Augustine, *City of God*, 678.
26. Augustine, *City of God*, 678.
27. Augustine, *City of God*, 678.
28. Augustine, *City of God*, 677.
29. Augustine, *City of God*, 682.
30. Augustine, *City of God*, 682.
31. Augustine, *City of God*, 682.
32. Elshtain, 42.
33. Cahill, 63.
34. Elshtain, 34.
35. Augustine, *City of God*, 690.
36. Augustine, *City of God*, 686.
37. Augustine, *City of God,* 695.
38. Augustine *City of God,* 695.
39. Or, for Elshtain, "the great-great-grandfather of the just war tradition" (107). Though some also see this title as a misnomer since, as James Turner Johnson has shown, the just war theory in its modern formulation is derived not only from "Augustine through Thomas Aquinas and the canon law" but also from "Roman law, the chivalric code, and common practice among men." See Johnson, *Ideology, Reason, and the Limitation of War* (Princeton, NJ: Princeton University Press, 1975), 150.
40. See especially *Contra Faustum,* XXII 74–75. These passages are also referenced by Thomas Aquinas in his question on war (*Summa Theologiae* II.II.40) where the criteria are named explicitly.
41. While for many centuries Christian theologians made reference to the Old Testament, it is common in scholarly theology today to refer to the Biblical books of Genesis through Malachi as the "Hebrew Scriptures." This is done to avoid understanding these texts merely as preludes to a superseding "New Testament" and to recognize their worth as sacred texts in their own right.
42. *Contra Faustum*, XXII.73. Augustine expresses a similar thought in Letter 138 to Marcellinus: "For just as in the cases of different persons it may happen that, at the same moment, one man may do with impunity what another man may not, because of a difference not in the thing done but in the person who does it, so in the case of one and the same person at different times, that which was duty formerly is not duty now, not because the person is different from his former self, but because the time at which he does it is different" (I.4).
43. Exodus 13.

44. *Contra Faustum*, XXII.73.
45. Augustine, *Contra Faustum*, XXII.74.
46. Augustine, *Contra Faustum*, XXII.75 and Letter 189 to Boniface, 6.
47. Augustine, *City of God*, 692.
48. Augustine, *Contra Faustum*, XXII.75.
49. Augustine, *Contra Faustum*, XXII.75.
50. Augustine, *Contra Faustum*, XXII.75.
51. Augustine, *Contra Faustum*, XXII.75.
52. *City of God*, 690.
53. *Contra Faustum,* XXII.74.
54. *Contra Faustum,* XXII.74.
55. For an excellent analysis of this theme in Augustine's writings see, J. Joyce Schuld, *Foucault and Augustine: Reconsidering Power and Love* (Notre Dame, IN: University of Notre Dame Press, 2003), 160–180.
56. *Contra Faustum,* XXII.74.
57. Augustine, Letter 189 to Boniface, 6.
58. Cahill, 62.
59. Augustine, *Contra Faustum,* XXII.75.
60. Cahill attributes Augustine's notion of right intent as love partially to a tendency in Christian thinkers of Augustine's time to seek to accommodate the "hard sayings" of Jesus (e.g., "love your enemies") by distinguishing between "sayings that define a 'higher' Christian life . . . but need not be taken literally on the 'lower' plane" (56). Such commandments, "apply to the inner realm of loving intention, but not to the outer realm of just action" (56). Thus Augustine can urge soldiers in war to keep love for their enemies "in readiness of mind" even as they kill them, so long as the cause of war is just.
61. Elshtain, 108.
62. The notion that justice is a prerequisite for true peace is ubiquitous in Christian social ethics. A few examples pertinent to the subject matter of war and peace-building include the United States Conference of Catholic Bishops (USCCB), *The Challenge of Peace: God's Promise and Our Response,* 60, available at http://www.usccb.org/issues-and-action/human-life-and-dignity/war-and-peace/nuclear-weapons/upload/statement-the-challenge-of-peace-1983-05-03.pdf; and Martin Luther King, Jr., "Letter from a Birmingham Jail," available at http://www.africa.upenn.edu/Articles_Gen/Letter_Birmingham.html; and *The Kairos Document*, especially chapters 3 and 4, available at http://www.sahistory.org.za/archive/challenge-church-theological-comment-political-crisis-south-africa-kairos-document-1985.
63. Cahill, 92.
64. Cahill, 87.
65. Thomas Aquinas, *Summa Theologiae,* trans., English Dominican Fathers, I.1–26. Available at http://www.newadvent.org/summa/. Hereafter ST.
66. Aquinas, ST I.3.3 and 4.
67. Aquinas, ST I.3.4 ad 2.
68. Aquinas, ST I.11.1.
69. Aquinas, ST I.11.3.
70. Aquinas, ST I.5.1.
71. Aquinas, ST I.2.3.
72. "All desired perfections flow from Him" (Aquinas, ST I.6.2).
73. See Aquinas, ST I.4.2.
74. Aquinas, ST I.2.3; I.II.93.1.
75. Aquinas, ST I.II.94.2.
76. Aquinas, ST I.II.95.1.
77. Aquinas, ST I.II.95.1, ad 1.
78. Aquinas, ST I.II.95.1.
79. Aquinas, *De Regno*, in *Aquinas: Political Writings,* R.W. Dyson, ed, (New York: Cambridge University Press, 2002), 43. Aquinas finished writing *De Regno* in 1267 upon the death of the "King of Cyprus" to whom it is dedicated—most likely Hugh II of Lusignan who held

the Dominican order in great esteem. It is likely that it was left unfinished by Aquinas and later completed by Tolommeo of Lucca (Bartolomeo Fiadoni) as part of his larger treatise on governance. See *Aquinas: Political Writings*, xix.

80. See Aristotle, *The Nicomachean Ethics,* J.A.K. Thomson, trans, (London: Penguin Books, 2004), 24.

81. Aquinas, *De Regno*, 43.

82. Aquinas, ST I.II.95.2.

83. Richard Regan, *The Moral Dimensions of Politics* (New York: Oxford University Press, 1986), 43.

84. Aquinas, ST I.II.95.4 and throughout *De Regno*.

85. Aquinas, ST I.II.95.4.

86. I use Thomas Aquinas's masculine gendered language throughout this paragraph in describing his conceptions of government because he did not conceive of women as leaders of governments. I do not agree with him on this point and I am willing to give him the benefit of the doubt that were he writing and thinking today he would concede that women can act as just and competent rulers, but I think to use gender neutral language in describing his ideas on government might be to read something back into the Thomistic text that is not there. In fact I consider it important to acknowledge that Thomas Aquinas did not view women as co-equals with men in this way.

87. Aquinas, ST I.II.95.4.

88. Regan, 44.

89. Aquinas, ST II.II.29.

90. Aquinas, ST II.II.29.1.

91. Aquinas, ST I.II.95.4.

92. Aquinas, ST II.II.40.1.

93. Aquinas, ST II.II.40.1.

94. Aquinas, ST I.II.90.3

95. Aquinas, ST II.II.40.1.

96. Aquinas, ST II.II.40.1.

97. Aquinas, ST II.II.42.2 ad.3.

98. Aquinas, ST II.II.42.2 ad 3.

99. "For even when we wage a just war, our adversaries must be sinning; and every victory, even though gained by wicked men is a result of the first judgment of God who humbles the vanquished either for the sake of removing or of punishing their sins" (Augustine, *City of God*, 693–694).

100. Augustine, *City of God*, 693–694.

101. Langan, 22.

102. Rosemary Radford Reuther, *Sexism and God Talk* (Boston: Beacon Press, 1983), 180.

103. Elshtain, 39.

104. James Turner Johnson, *Morality and Contemporary Warfare* (New Haven: Yale University Press, 1999), 3.

105. Aquinas, ST II.II.40.1 ad. 3.

106. Matthew 10:34.

107. Aquinas, ST II.II.40.1.

108. See Aquinas on tyranny and sedition, ST II.II.42.

109. Cicero, *De Officiis,* 1:11–12, W. Miller, trans., in the Lob Classical Library (Cambridge, MA: Harvard University Press, 1913). Quoted in Mark J. Allman and Tobias L. Winright, *After the Smoke Clears: The Just War Tradition and Post War Justice* (Maryknoll, NY: Orbis Books, 2010), 24.

110. Francisco de Vitoria, *De Indis et de Iure Belli, Relectiones,* Ernest Nys, ed., (Washington, DC: Carnegie Institution, 1917), 187.

111. USCCB, 96.

112. Allman and Winright, 43.

36 Chapter 2

113. See Paulo Emílio Vauthier Borges de Macedo, "The Law of War in Francisco Suárez: The Civilizing Project of Spanish Scholasticism in *Revistada Faculdade de Direito da UERJ*, 2.22 (2012) 19. Open access at http://www.epublicacoes.uerj.br/index.php/rfduerj/article/viewFile/4280/3165.

114. USCCB, 98.

115. de Macedo, 19.

116. USCCB, 98.

117. The introduction to Mark J. Allman's textbook is instructive here. Allman titles the book *Who Would Jesus Kill?* In explaining his choice of title Allman remarks, "War is about killing. One of my greatest frustrations as a professor of war and peace studies is that we often lose sight of this fact." Allman, *Who Would Jesus Kill? War, Peace, and the Christian Tradition* (Winona, MN: St. Mary's Press, 2008), 11.

118. Aquinas, *De Regno*, chapter 4 and ST II.II.42.2 ad. 3.

119. Johnson, *Morality and Contemporary Warfare*, 28.

120. ST II.II.64.7.

121. ST II.II.64.7.

122. The principle of double effect comprises four elements: 1. The object of the action must be right or indifferent in itself; it cannot be intrinsically wrong. 2. The wrong effect, though foreseen, cannot be intended. 3. The wrong effect cannot be the means to the right effect, otherwise it would be intended. 4. There must be a proportionate reason for allowing the evil effect to occur. These elements, applied to a situation of conflict, are meant to operate as an exception-guiding norm to determine whether or not a specific course of action is morally acceptable. As regards warfare, it minimally generates the notion that military force may never be directly and intentionally aimed at civilians.

123. Michael Walzer, *Just and Unjust Wars: A Moral Argument with Historical Illustrations* (New York: Basic Books, 1977), 120.

124. Walzer, 120.

125. See James Turner Johnson, *Morality and Contemporary Warfare*, 119–158.

126. John Finnis, "The Ethics of War and Peace in the Catholic Natural Law Tradition," in *The Ethics of War and Peace: Religious and Secular Perspectives*, Terry Nardin, ed., (Princeton, NJ: Princeton University Press, 1996), 26.

127. James Turner Johnson, *Morality and Contemporary Warfare*, 157.

128. A good deal of the discussion around just peacemaking theory has included a conversation about whether or not it can be considered a form of political realism. See for example Glen Stassen's "The Unity, Realism, and Obligatoriness of Just Peacemaking Theory," and Lisa Sowle Cahill's "Just Peacemaking: Theory, Practice, and Prospects," in *Journal of the Society of Christian Ethics*, 23.1, (2003).

129. This remark appeared in the introduction to the 2nd edition of the text written by Duane K. Friesen, John Langan, S.J., and Glen Stassen, "Introduction: Just Peacemaking as the New Ethic for Peace and War" in *Just Peacemaking: Ten Practices for Abolishing War* (Cleveland, OH: The Pilgrim Press, 2004), 2. The rest of my citations for this topic come from the text's 3rd edition, *Just Peacemaking: The New Paradigm for the Ethics of War and Peace,* Glen H. Stassen, ed. (Cleveland, OH: The Pilgrim Press, 2008).

130. Pamela Brubaker, James B. Burke, Duane K. Friesen, John Langan, S.J., and Glen Stassen, "Introduction: Just Peacemaking as the New Ethic for Peace and War," in *Just Peacemaking: The New Paradigm for Peace and War*, 9.

131. Brubaker et al., 2.

132. Brubaker et al., 2.

133. Brubaker et al., 11.

134. Brubaker et al., 15.

135. Stassen, "New Paradigm: Just Peacemaking Theory," in the *Bulletin of the Council of Societies for the Study of Religion*, 25 (1996), 31.

136. Brubaker et al., 19.

137. Brubaker et al., 19.

138. Brubaker et al., 20.

139. Brubaker et al., 20.

140. Brubaker et al., 21.
141. Brubaker et al., 21
142. Brubaker et al., 21.
143. Brubaker et al., 22.
144. USCCB, 39.
145. Albert Nolan, *Jesus Before Christianity* (Maryknoll, NY: Orbis Books, 2001), 56.
146. Brubaker et al., 24.
147. Brubaker et al., 24.
148. Hollenbach, 23.
149. Second Vatican Council, *Gaudium et Spes,* 78.
150. USCCB, 60.
151. Brubaker et al., 27–28. The emphasis just peacemaking places on community is echoed in the African context as we will see in the discussion of the African communitarian humanist philosophy of *ubuntu* in chapter 4.
152. Consider the important work of John Paul Lederach in this regard. Lederach's thesis of conflict transformation leans heavily on the idea of nourishing relationships across socio-cultural barriers. Lederach, *Building Peace: Sustainable Reconciliation in Divided Societies* (Washington, DC: United States Institute of Peace, 1997).
153. Brubaker et al., 28.
154. Brubaker et al., 30.
155. Brubaker et al., 30.
156. Brubaker et al., 31.
157. Brubaker et al., 31.
158. See Sharon Erikson Nepstad, *Nonviolent Revolutions: Civil Resistance in the Late Twentieth Century* (New York: Oxford University Press, 2011).

Chapter Three

Just Peacemaking Practices for Resisting Oppression

Nonviolent movements and revolutions have been a major feature of the landscape of political resistance in the twentieth and twenty-first centuries. The use of nonviolent strategies has helped to win independence from British colonial powers in India; has overturned authoritarian regimes in Chile, the Philippines, and East Germany;[1] and has ushered in the Civil Rights Act in the United States. Even when they have not succeeded in forcing regime change, nonviolent strategies have nevertheless witnessed to the will of the people in nations like Iran and Burma. Whether one advocates the use of nonviolent methods out of a principled pacifism that rejects the use of armed force altogether, or simply because one believes nonviolence is the most effective means to social transformation, there is no question that nonviolent strategies are a critical component of contemporary revolution.[2]

One of the strengths of just peacemaking theory is that it expands our notion of nonviolent strategies. It offers those who struggle for revolutionary social transformation several categories of practices to further the aim of a just peace *jus ante*—or prior to any consideration of the resort to—armed resistance. "Nonviolent revolution" may often evoke visions primarily of what just peacemaking theorists call "nonviolent direct action": practices like protests, marches, boycotts, and civil disobedience. Indeed, these are crucial components of a nonviolent revolution. But just peacemaking theory insists that nonviolent methods of waging peace also include practices like sustainable development; grassroots organizing; promoting democracy, human rights, and reconciliation; and a variety of forms of international cooperation against injustice. Just peacemaking theory challenges revolutionaries to engage a host of nonviolent strategies, including but not limited to nonviolent direct action, in their efforts to secure greater freedom and justice. Many of these strategies, which should be used *jus ante* armed revolution, can and should also be continued, even if a revolutionary movement comes to the grave conclusion that they must also employ armed resistance. In this way, as I discuss further in the next chapter, nonviolent and armed practices can work in tandem toward the common goal of a just peace.

In this chapter, I explore and analyze a number of nonviolent strategies as they have been defined by just peacemaking theorists and as they were enacted in the struggle against apartheid. The aim here is to advocate the moral responsibility of revolutionary movements to initiate their efforts toward regime change using nonviolent resistance only, and to set up a framework for continuing nonviolent methods of resistance even if the resort to arms becomes necessary. I call this stage of revolution *jus ante* armed resistance to indicate that nonviolent practices should be employed and exhausted *prior* to any consideration of waging armed revolution. I do not mean to indicate that armed revolution is inevitable. Indeed, as I noted above it is possible for a revolution to be won using nonviolent means only, in which case the revolution need not proceed through the next two stages of ethical analysis—*jus ad* and *jus in* armed revolution—and instead can move directly to the *jus post* revolution phase.

Here, drawing on the South African case study, I characterize revolutionary resistance strategies under four of the ten practices of just peacemaking theory: (1) *support nonviolent direct action;* (2) *advance democracy, human rights, and interdependence;* (3) *encourage grassroots peacemaking groups and voluntary associations;* and (4) *strengthen the United Nations and international efforts for cooperation and human rights.* A fifth practice, *foster just and sustainable economic development,* is briefly discussed insofar as it is related to the struggle to establish respect for human rights in a political climate that has often violated them. Finally, a sixth practice—*acknowledge responsibility for conflict and injustice and seek repentance and forgiveness*—was enacted in the South African context via the Truth and Reconciliation Commission *jus post* revolution. The work of reconciliation *jus post* revolution has proven so important for building a just peace that it is discussed at length in chapter 5.

The use of nonviolent just peacemaking strategies brings an oppressed community's grievances to the foreground and invites and pressures those responsible for injustice to negotiate with revolutionaries toward social transformation. Each strategy can contribute to a just revolution in important ways. To demonstrate this, each of the sections below follows a threefold order that accords with my hybrid deductive-inductive method. First, working deductively, I describe the nonviolent strategy as just peacemaking theorists understand it. Second, I posit the importance of the practice for revolution. Third, working inductively I illustrate how the importance of the practice emerges from an analysis of the struggle against apartheid.

Support Nonviolent Direct Action

"Nonviolent direct action" is an umbrella term that encompasses a broad array of strategies including strikes, boycotts, protest marches and demonstrations, acts of civil disobedience, and accompaniment of those exposed to political violence.[3] Practices of nonviolent direct action are the foundation of resistance to injustice. They are morally indispensable for conducting an effective and just revolution and they ought to be employed in a coordinated and confrontational manner against unjust, corrupt, or dictatorial institutions and governments. Just peacemaking theorists argue specifically for the use of nonviolent direct action prior to any consideration of the use of armed force: "The technologies and techniques of nonviolent direct action are . . . evolving in ways that are more powerful and effective . . . The tools have evolved to the point where nonviolent direct action can be considered a norm that must be pursued before violence can be considered as a just last resort."[4] The South African experience illustrates that nonviolent direct action is important for just revolution for at least two reasons: (1) It surfaces tensions inherent in unjust systems so that they can be directly confronted; and (2) it demands broad participation in the revolutionary movement by massive numbers of people, which makes the will of the oppressed clear both to the regime, and to the international community.

The object of nonviolent direct action is not so much to create tension, but publically to expose and directly to confront injustice. Hence, Martin Luther King, Jr. argued: "We who engage in nonviolent direct action are not the creators of tension. We merely bring to the surface the hidden tension that is already alive. We bring it out in the open, where it can be seen and dealt with."[5] Likewise, just peacemaking theorists note that the strategies of nonviolent direct action are meant to confront injustices that are already occurring. For example, in committing civil disobedience by breaking unjust laws, people expose the injustice of the law and simultaneously claim their rights by performing the justice they seek. It is this dynamic of exposure and performance that brings hidden tensions to the surface of a politically unjust situation and confronts them.[6] When African Americans in the Civil Rights Movement sat at lunch counters reserved for whites, they exposed the injustice of segregation, and claimed their right to desegregation and equal treatment by sitting at the whites-only counter; that is, by performing the desegregation they demanded. In this way, civil rights activists illustrated both the injustice of segregation, and the justice and equality they rightly expected. The strategy of civil disobedience "becomes an action that transforms a situation from greater to lesser violence, from greater to lesser injustice."[7] Likewise, by, for example, refusing to buy goods and services that contribute to exploitation, or divesting from companies that benefit from exploitation (boycott); or through noncooperation with unfair labor practices (strike);

nonviolent direct action intentionally confronts injustice, and witnesses instead to a more just order. Surfacing social tension via this process of confrontationally exposing injustice, and claiming and performing justice is critical in contexts that endeavor to hide or mask injustice and the social tension it causes.

In the context of revolution, nonviolent direct action both requires and encourages mass participation. Indeed, it is the necessarily participatory nature of nonviolent direct action that led many members of the African National Congress (ANC), described below, to express a strong preference for confrontational nonviolent methods of resistance.[8] Protest marches and demonstrations involve masses of the population, profoundly and clearly illustrating the will of the majority. Moreover, boycotts are effective when they are large and coordinated; and especially when they include even divestiture in companies that perpetuate or participate in injustice. As part of the nonviolent struggle against apartheid, revolutionaries coordinated major boycotts of companies invested in South Africa with targeted economic sanctions. Just peacemaking theorists call this effort "the most impressive example of global boycott" ever, and argued that these mass, indeed international, boycotts were "crucial in persuading . . . parts of the South African business community of the eventual higher costs of resistance to change."[9] Likewise, strikes, in order to be effective, require the participation of a majority of workers, which is why those who cross the strikers' picket lines are subject to public shaming. The participatory character of nonviolent direct action; the manner in which it mobilizes and empowers masses of people to demand justice from those with power; and the capacity it has to demonstrate the will of the people, all make nonviolent direct action both effective and appealing as an nonviolent revolutionary strategy.

Practices of nonviolent direct action constituted some of the most powerful forms of resistance to apartheid. Masses of people participated in exposing the injustices of apartheid, and claiming their rights. Even during the years of armed resistance, many South Africans continued to perform nonviolent direct action as a way to confront their oppressors. The importance of revolutionary nonviolent direct action for surfacing and confronting tensions and encouraging mass participation emerge from several stages in the struggle against apartheid. First, the development of the ANC into an effective revolutionary organization demonstrates the importance of surfacing and confronting injustice via direct action. Nonviolent direct action must be confrontational to be effective. Second, the organization and performance of the Defiance Campaign reinforce the importance of confrontation and help to illustrate the value of mass democratic participation in revolution.

At its inception in 1912 the ANC was not a revolutionary organization, nor did it embody the kind of nonracial, democratic government it eventually hoped to establish at the national level. It was formed as a response to the all-white, all male parliament established by the Union of South Africa in 1910, and was structured in three tiers. The upper house consisted of hereditary chiefs. A middle tier included males over the age of eighteen who paid an annual membership fee, which funded the organization. The final tier included men who had performed some extraordinary service to the African people and as a result were named honorary members.[10] Originally named the South African Native National Congress (SANNC), the group adopted racialized and gendered policies similar to those of the South African parliament.[11] Its tiered structure and restriction of membership to only males from the "aboriginal races of Africa,"[12] made the organization nondemocratic, patriarchal, and racial. The rationale for an all-male organization was that members wanted to participate in, not overthrow, the male-only national government. "The ANC leaders wanted parity with whites in a parliament consisting of men only at a time when the presence of women in party ranks seemed to be irrelevant to the political struggle for power."[13] At this time, the ANC could not be called a revolutionary organization since it was not actively engaged in attempts to overthrow oppression and establish universal enfranchisement. Rather than revolutionaries, members of the ANC at this time were more reformers.

Its maturation into the largest and arguably most influential political organization in South Africa required transformation in ANC policies. These changes were institutionalized via the organization's 1943 constitution.[14] This new constitution better reflected the revolutionary hopes the ANC had begun to nurture for a nonracial, democratic South Africa. It eliminated both the racial and gender specifications for membership and spurred the formation of the ANC Women's League and the highly influential ANC Youth League (ANCYL), whose membership included three of South Africa's future presidents: Jacob Zuma, Thabo Mbeki, and Nelson Mandela. When the National Party came to power in 1948, with its mandate from the white minority to institute apartheid, the ANC was a more formidable resistance organization that embodied the nonracial democratic government they sought to instantiate at the national level. This suggests an important lesson: revolutionary organizations ought to demonstrate, through their policies, practices, and structure, the type of nation they aim to create.

This structural transformation also engendered procedural and policy changes, especially regarding political tactics. The ANC transitioned toward confrontational nonviolent direct action. The political activity of the ANC in the early twentieth century was sporadic, unorganized, and nonconfrontational. Rather than promoting nonviolent direct action, the ANC occasionally drafted petitions, or formed deputations in an attempt to address grievances with the parliament. These practices were unsuccessful either in generating negotiation with the government, or in drawing widespread attention to the injustices of racial inequality. Indeed, in stark contrast to the government's serious engagement[15] with resistance organizations during the years of confrontational nonviolent direct action, in these early years the ANC was largely ignored by those with political power in South Africa.

The nonconfrontational approach to expressing grievances made the ANC vulnerable to accusations of weakness and ineffectiveness in advancing the cause of human rights. In one of its founding documents, the ANCYL gave voice to these reproaches: "The critics of Congress attribute the inability of Congress in the last twenty years to advance the national cause in a manner commensurate with the demands of the times, to weaknesses in its organization and constitution, to its erratic policy of yielding to oppression, regarding itself as a body of gentlemen with clean hands, and failing to see the problems of the African through the proper perspective."[16] The ANCYL observed that some perceived the ANC to be no more than "a loose association of people who merely react negatively to given conditions, able neither to assert the national will nor to resist it openly."[17] Thus the organization "is compelled to be very vocal against legislation that has harsh effects on the African underdog while it gives no positive lead nor has any constructive program to enforce the repeal of all oppressive legislation."[18] In acknowledging these critics, the ANCYL began a process of revolutionizing its parent organization, making it a model of what it wanted to inculcate at the national level. Moreover, the ANCYL quickly proved itself to be a source of renewed energy and vision for the ANC. The Youth League pledged to "build Congress from within"[19] and vested themselves with "the historic task of imparting dynamic substance and matter to the organizational form of the ANC"[20] so as to attain a nonracial democracy respectful of human rights.[21] The ANCYL understood, better than its parent organization, the importance of confrontational nonviolent direct action for surfacing tensions and promoting mass participation.

Inspired by the ANCYL, the organization prepared itself to mount a more radical and confrontational program of resistance. The "Programme of Action"[22] statement of policy adopted by the ANC in 1949 demanded meaningful participation in the government,[23] and committed the organization both to aggressive fundraising, and to endeavor to "raise the standard of political and national consciousness" within South Africa.[24] The Programme also included a policy of nonviolent direct action: the ANC established a Council of Action with the mandate "to employ the following weapons: immediate and active boycott, strike, civil disobedience, and non-cooperation and such other means as may bring about the accomplishment and realization of our aspirations."[25] Thus, via the Programme and Council of Action, what we now recognize as the just peacemaking practice of nonviolent direct action became official ANC policy for conducting a revolution against apartheid and exposing and confronting its injustices. This is meaningful since just peacemaking theory promotes itself as an inductive theory—that is to say, as one that draws its principles and strategies from the experience of mitigating violence.[26]

While the Programme of Action initiated dozens of acts of resistance, perhaps the most iconic for illustrating how nonviolence seeks to surface and confront tensions, and encourage mass participation was the 1951 Defiance Campaign. The Defiance Campaign represented the fruition of the new ANC policy of employing confrontational nonviolent direct action and it marked the beginning of cooperation among multiple groups in the liberation struggle.[27] The ANC framed the Defiance Campaign as a day of protest and reflection: "It is suggested that, on this day, to mark their general dissatisfaction with their position in this country, the African people should refrain from going to work, and regard this day as a day of mourning for all those Africans who lost their lives in the struggle for liberation."[28] During the Defiance Campaign, thousands of South Africans refused to cooperate with the apartheid regime and its oppressive legislation. They stayed away from work, and instead initiated participatory democracy by making their will known through mass protest. They crossed apartheid's color line by using facilities and amenities reserved for other races. They refused to obey curfew laws, and entered townships reserved for other racial groups. Thus, they exposed unjust laws, performed the justice they sought, and presented themselves peacefully for arrest. As a result of the Defiance Campaign police detained over 8,000 people.[29] Consonant with how nonviolent noncooperation is understood by just peacemaking theorists, the people of South Africa intended "to call attention to widespread . . . injustice [by] . . . making a commitment not to participate, even for a short time, in the structures they wish[ed] to change."[30]

The government's response to the social tension surfaced by the Defiance Campaign was comprehensive, but unfortunately did not result in negotiation. The regime passed legislation which allowed it to authorize States of Emergency[31] and impose harsh penalties—including fines, lashings, and imprisonment—on those convicted of breaking the law in the course of protest.[32] Penalties were more severe for those involved not just in performing civil disobedience, but in organizing it.[33] Organizers of the Defiance Campaign faced prosecution under the Suppression of Communism Act, though "the judge had agreed the charge had nothing to do with communism 'as it is commonly known' and added: 'I accept that you have consistently advised your followers to follow a peaceful course of action and to avoid violence in any shape or form.'"[34] Despite the acknowledgment by the trial judge that the revolutionary movement did not seek to impose communism and employed only nonviolent resistance, Nelson Mandela received a nine month suspended sentence for his role in organizing the Defiance Campaign and he was subsequently placed under banning orders confining him to Johannesburg and restricting his participation in political activity.[35]

Despite these attempts to repress resistance, the revolutionary movement continued to pursue nonviolent direct action to surface tensions and force negotiation. A key example of this dynamic arose in the context of South Africa's declaration of itself as a republic independent from British colonial rule. Black South Africans largely opposed this transition because they feared that the formation of a republic would empower the oppressive regime.[36] Despite this resistance, National Party Prime Minister Hendrik Verwoerd held and narrowly won a 1960 referendum to establish the Republic of South Africa. At the All-In African Conference of 1961 1,400 delegates representing various segments of the South African population opted not to recognize the results of the whites-only referendum, and instead to demand that their voices be heard on the subject of the formation of the republic.[37] This is, again, demonstrative of a revolutionary movement that enacts the change they wish to see in their government: in this case, holding an alternative referendum from the one they had been prevented from participating in at the national level. Nelson Mandela, on behalf of the delegates and in his role as secretary of the National Action Council, wrote to Verwoerd in an attempt to negotiate. He called for "a National Convention representative of all South Africans, to draw up a non-racial and democratic constitution."[38] If the government refused such a convention, the delegates pledged to perform nonviolent direct action. They would "stage country-wide demonstrations" in the form of strikes, protests, and noncooperation.[39] Here we see the revolutionary movement attempting to negotiate with the government, and using nonviolent direct action to pressure the regime to participate in negotiations.

While the revolutionary movement succeeded in mobilizing masses of people for nonviolent direct action, the apartheid regime refused to negotiate and instead engaged in active counter-revolution. "After weeks of raids and arrests—helicopters flying low over their houses at night, flashing on powerful search lights—the non-whites are in a harassed state. The disclosure that the police are going into the townships on Monday to hustle the residents out to work has sent a ripple of apprehension throughout the country."[40] Despite these tactics sixty percent of workers in Johannesburg and Pretoria, and up to seventy-five percent in Port Elizabeth refused to work.[41] With the advent of confrontational nonviolent direct action, ordinary South Africans were becoming increasingly politically active, claiming their right to participation in their government, surfacing and confronting the tensions of racial injustice, and placing enormous pressure on the apartheid regime to negotiate.

It is not accidental that just peacemaking theory, which as has been said, employs an inductive method drawing from history the best practices for establishing justice and peace without resort to force, references the South

African struggle against apartheid in its explanation and promotion of nonviolent direct action.[42] Nonviolent direct action was the foundation of the revolutionary struggle against apartheid, and as I demonstrate in the following chapter, the practices of nonviolent direct action were used even alongside eventual armed resistance. These practices were crucial for surfacing and confronting the injustices of apartheid, and inviting mass participation in the revolution. Nonviolent direct action, as just peacemaking theorists rightly point out, ought to be considered normative for any revolution which seeks to be just.

Advance Democracy, Human Rights, and Interdependence

As a component of just peacemaking theory advancing democracy, human rights, and interdependence applies to both international and intranational relations. Just peacemaking theorist Bruce Russert defines a democracy as "a country in which nearly everyone can vote, elections are freely contested, the chief executive is chosen by popular vote or an elected parliament, and civil rights and civil liberties are substantially guaranteed."[43] With regard to international relations, Russert argues that countries that fit this description rarely fight wars against one another because of "normative constraints on conflict between democracies."[44] Specifically, democratic governments are, at least in theory, accountable to their citizens via institutionalized electoral and legislative processes.[45] From this Russert concludes, "The leaders of two democracies, knowing each other's incentives to choose carefully, will be reluctant to get into war with each other. A dictator ... has the opportunity to enrich self and cronies by a successful war and runs less risk of being overthrown in a losing fight by being able to forcefully suppress popular opposition."[46] Similarly, democracies would in theory have intranational mechanisms in place for the peaceful resolution of internal conflict, i.e., citizens' differing perspectives on social and legal questions are dealt with by discussion and debate. Compromises are arrived at through electoral and judicial processes rather than through resort to force. Admittedly, this is a potentially rosy view of Western democracy where well-funded special interest groups sometimes wield disproportionate power and influence over discussions and debates, as well as over elected officials and the compromises they broker. Nevertheless, in general just peacemaking theory holds that advances in democracy with the institutionalization of human rights and efforts toward international economic interdependence protect and enhance both intrastate peace and an international order that seeks global peace.

Since revolutions, by definition, seek "liberation from oppression" and "the constitution of freedom,"[47] and since democracies, for Russert "substantially guarantee" at least civil-political human rights, "advancing democracy and human rights" is an especially important practice for revolutionary movements to inculcate. Indeed, historically campaigns for human rights have been linked to efforts to establish democratic governments, including in South Africa.[48] The South African context illustrates the importance of inculcating democratic processes and a commitment to human rights within the revolutionary movement itself. The South African struggle against apartheid suggests that institutionalizing democracy and human rights as part of the revolution becomes meaningful not just for promoting its success in overthrowing a dictatorial regime, but also in previsioning the just peace that revolutionaries seek to establish. Thus, revolutionaries have both an opportunity and an obligation to establish the contours of the justice they seek. As much as is possible, just revolutionaries should operate with the kinds of participatory mechanisms and respect for human rights that they wish to inculcate at the national level. Here was see a linkage of *jus ante* armed revolution—or the revolution that is nonviolent—and *jus post* revolution. How participation and human rights are previewed and institutionalized by the revolutionary movement can impact the post-revolutionary transition to a more just government. A commitment to human rights *jus ante* armed revolution will also be important for movements that find themselves compelled to take up arms, since, as we will see in the next chapter, *jus in* armed revolution requires a basic commitment to the human dignity of one's adversaries even in the midst of fighting.

Viewed broadly, the entire anti-apartheid struggle was one of advancing democracy and human rights. The revolution sought to overturn a despotic regime notorious for human rights abuses and replace it with a constitutional democracy.[49] In this way, the South African revolution struggled to engender a more just peace in South Africa throughout and by virtue of the entire movement against apartheid. Still, there are discreet events and policies within the period of nonviolent resistance through which the people of South Africa specifically previsioned the nonracial participatory democracy characterized by respect for human rights that they sought via revolution. Foremost among these was the adoption of the Freedom Charter as the guiding document of the resistance movement. Both the document and the process by which it was ratified provide examples of how revolutionary movements can institutionalize mass participation and a commitment to human rights. This prepares the citizenry to participate in a national government and sets the foundation for human rights and a future just peace.

The Freedom Charter was a constitution and declaration of human rights for all South Africans. Its overarching theme is the demand for a just, nonracial government by the people of South Africa. The famous preamble reads: "We, the people of South Africa, declare for all our country and the world to know: That South Africa belongs to all who live in it, black and white, and that no government can justly claim authority unless it is based on the will of the people."[50] A primary concern of the charter then is to promote a democratic South Africa in which "every man and woman shall have the right to vote . . . regardless of race, colour, or sex" and "all bodies of minority rule . . . shall be replaced by democratic organs of self-government."[51] The Freedom Charter is thus a document of revolution: it aspires toward liberation from an authoritarian regime and transformation to a participatory government.

Along with its demand for democracy, the Freedom Charter articulates a vision for human rights. It declares ten categories of human rights, which can be grouped under the headings of civil-political rights,[52] social-economic rights, and cultural rights.[53] This comprehensive declaration of human rights provides a model for other revolutionary movements that want to prevision the nation they wish to build.

There are four categories of civil-political rights declared in the Freedom Charter. First, the foremost right, from which all other rights listed in the charter flow, is the people's right to govern themselves. This includes the right to vote, to run for office, and to participate meaningfully in government.[54] A second category of civil-political rights concerns equality under the law and the rights of those convicted of crimes. Here, the drafters of the Freedom Charter insist on a fair judiciary "representative of all the people," and a police force and army open to all South Africans, and the abolition of discriminatory laws.[55] Moreover, under a regime where political imprisonment was commonplace, the Freedom Charter insists that imprisonment should be used for "serious crimes against the people," and rejects the use of capital punishment.[56] Instead the charter makes an option for restorative, rather than retributive, justice by calling "re-education, not vengeance" the goal of the criminal justice system.[57] Third, under a call for "equal human rights" the Freedom Charter calls for freedom of speech, assembly, religion, and the press. Here also is listed a right to privacy, and a right to travel freely. Finally, the fourth category of civil-political rights claims a right to peace, national security, as an independent nation that also "respects the rights and sovereignty of all nations."[58] Peace and security are understood to be derivative of justice and based on "upholding the equal rights, opportunities, and status" of all persons. Thus the Freedom Charter suggests that revolutionaries issue a robust call for civil-political human rights so as to inculcate a respect for political participation and human dignity.

The Freedom Charter also declares six sets of social-economic and cultural human rights.[59] The declaration of these rights is a repudiation of the economic practices and policies of both the colonial powers that drove many black South Africans into poverty, and the apartheid policies that kept them impoverished. It should also be noted that while there has certainly been some progress made in forwarding these social-economic human rights in South Africa since its liberation from apartheid, there is still far to go in instantiating the kind of economic justice envisioned by the Freedom Charter. Moreover, many of the social-economic and cultural human rights declared by the Freedom Charter are key to establishing a just peace in a revolutionary context.

First, the charter demands public ownership of the "national wealth of the country,"[60] including de-privatization of gold and diamond mines. Tied to this is the right to choose one's own profession, and the responsibility of the state to regulate industry toward the common good. In its demand for public ownership of all natural resources, referring specifically to "the mineral wealth of [the] country,"[61] the Freedom Charter illustrates widespread dissatisfaction with South Africa's gold and diamond industries. Mining has been a potent symbol of the colonial exploitation of African states. While the physically demanding labor of mining was exclusively the work of black South Africans, profits were enjoyed by a small fraction of white entrepreneurs.[62] Miners were subjected to poor working conditions and earned meager wages. The charter demands a reversal of these exploitative practices and a transition toward industry in service to the common good.

Second, the charter calls for fair distribution of the land in order to "banish famine and land hunger."[63] Under apartheid over eighty percent of South African land was owned by the white minority[64] while the remaining population was forced to live in overcrowded townships or "homelands." Blacks did not own farmland, but worked as migrant farmworkers, earning low wages. The radically uneven distribution of land served to keep black South Africans in a state of both poverty and dependence upon white landowners, and as such fomented revolutionary spirit. Rejecting the homeland strategy and the monopolization of land, the Freedom Charter avers that "all shall have the right to occupy land wherever they choose."[65] It abolishes race-based restrictions on land ownership and calls for land to be re-divided amongst those who work it.[66]

The third category of social-economic rights involves workers' rights. The charter declares "the right and duty of all to work" and to social assistance for the unemployed. It presents a progressive vision of worker rights and benefits including a forty-hour work week, paid leave, including sick days and maternity leave, a "national minimum wage," and the right to form labor unions. It demands gender equality among workers, including equal pay for equal work.[67] Finally, it calls for the abolition of child labor, "compound labor"—or the practice of forcing migrant mine workers to live in highly regulated compounds—and the "tot" system, which partially paid vineyard workers with alcohol.[68]

A fourth category of social-economic and cultural rights demands "houses, security, and comfort."[69] It displays a concern for the general health, wellbeing, and fulfillment of human beings. In a land of poverty emblematized by seas of corrugated tin shacks, it calls for decent housing and basic security within one's home. "Slums shall be demolished, and new suburbs built where all have transport, roads, lighting, playing fields . . . and social centres."[70] The charter ties this call for housing and safe neighborhoods to a general right to have human health supported by access to "plentiful food," "rest, leisure," a "preventative health scheme . . . run by the state,"[71] that pays particular attention to the vulnerable. Here, revolutionaries present and demand a just government whose primary concern is care for the common good.

These initial four categories of social-economic and cultural rights point to another just peacemaking practice: "Foster just and sustainable economic development." As a just peacemaking strategy, the call to "foster just and sustainable economic development" is based on three basic arguments. First, true peace does not consist only in the absence of conflict, but rather in a state of human flourishing dependent upon justice. Second, despair, disorder and unrest are often the result of economic depression and the lack of "chance to earn a useful livelihood."[72] Severe economic inequality and injustice foments violence.[73] Such are the conditions that often lead to the formation of revolutionary movements. Third, "the absence of sustainable development, and impediments to it, are often bitter fruits of human greed, sin, violence and injustices."[74] Thus, lack of sustainable development is not ethically neutral. It points to social injustices that ought to be countered and remedied. By demanding that South Africa's mineral wealth benefit all of its people; by arguing for redistribution of land; by declaring that industry and manufacturing ought "to be controlled to assist the well-being of the people,"[75] the Freedom Charter concurs with the "basic developmental goals"[76] of just peacemaking. Namely, "providing all people with access to resources and opportunities necessary to full human flourishing, and protecting the rights of weaker people . . . as they try to escape situations of dependence and poverty."[77] Thus, while the Freedom Charter is most felicitously understood as an expression of democracy in support of human rights, it shows how a comprehensive vision of human rights can contribute to a just peace also by its commitment to sustainable economic development. Since revolutions are often waged in situations of economic inequality or depression, the practice of generating sustainable economic development becomes particularly salient.

Finally, the charter declares a right to education. The charter views education as a highly important aspect of cultural rights. The notion of a right to culture has been vastly important in formerly colonized nations. Declaring a right to culture is an acknowledgment of the threat that colonialism poses to traditional, indigenous values, languages, and customs. Staving off this threat is also tied to a right to inculturated education. The charter espouses free, compulsory education for all children, and insists that "the aim of education shall be to teach the youth to love their people and their culture . . . the colour bar in cultural life, in sport, and in education shall be abolished."[78] While the apartheid regime might have claimed to respect a right to culture through its plan of segregated homelands, the philosophical roots of this segregation in white supremacy, and the regime's insistence that education be provided in Afrikaans undermined this claim.[79] Under these circumstances the social-economic and cultural right to education was steeped in a right to understand one's own cultural context and heritage.

Cultural rights are more explicitly declared in the Freedom Charter's demand for equal rights not just for individuals but also "for all national groups and races."[80] This reflects both the communitarian anthropology of most South Africans—the sense that persons receive their full humanity from their community[81]—and the fact that the discriminatory policies of apartheid were viewed as a threat not only to individual South Africans but also to whole cultures. The charter claims the right of "all people . . . to use their own languages and to develop their own folk culture and customs" in a society where "groups shall be protected by law against insults to their race and national pride."[82] In its concern for cultural rights, the Freedom Charter thus anticipated the African [Banjul] Charter on Human and Peoples' Rights, adopted by the Organization of African Unity in 1981.[83]

Besides the vision that it presents of human rights, the Freedom Charter was ratified by a democratic process: the Congress of the People. In this way, again, South African revolutionaries demonstrate the importance of previsioning the governmental practices and policies that the revolutionary movement seeks to enact at the national level. The Congress of the People endeavored to unite and increase interdependence among disparate racial groups and organizations in the struggle. The importance of this cannot be underestimated in a nation made up not only of several racial groups, but also of varying ethnicities. Historically in South Africa, different ethnic groups had been at odds. This fact bolstered the regime's case for distinct "homelands" for each ethnic group, and "separate development" not only for whites and blacks, but also among blacks—Zulus developing and living separately from Xhosas, Xhosas developing separately from Tswanas, and so forth. The regime used the common colonial tactic of exploiting historical animosities between various ethnicities to drive wedges between Africans and solidify their own power. The Congress of the People aimed to overcome those same animosities and bring South Africans together in revolutionary struggle. Thus, the Congress of the People represents one way that South African revolutionaries implemented the mechanisms of democracy that they sought to instantiate nationally.

Organized by the ANC, the South African Indian Congress (SAIC), the Congress of Democrats (COD), and the South African Coloured People's Organization[84] (SACPO), the Congress of the People was itself an expression of democracy and participation including elected representatives from all of South Africa's diverse population groups. The meeting was attended by nearly three thousand delegates. Intentionally chosen to mirror proportionally the country's general population, over two thousand delegates were black, over three hundred were Indian, over two hundred were Coloured, and approximately 112 were whites who had joined the struggle and fought against their own racial group's domination and exploitation of others. These delegates adopted the Freedom Charter via a democratic process of ratification. The charter became the guiding document of the South African revolution, previsioning the kind of South Africa that revolutionaries sough to establish.

As a vision for human rights, ratified by an inclusive democratic process, the Freedom Charter is an example *par excellence* of the just peacemaking practice of advancing democracy and human rights in an intrastate framework. The South African context illustrates the importance of this just peacemaking practice for just revolution. It reminds revolutionaries to articulate a vision of the nation that they are struggling for—one which, for South Africans, included institutionalized respect for human and peoples' rights; and to inculcate this vision as much as possible within the revolutionary movement itself. This just peacemaking practice can thus breathe fresh life into the what has no doubt become a clichéd proposition—Mahatma Gandhi's exhortation that we must "be the change" we wish to see in the world. Likewise, revolutionary movements must "be the change" by previsioning the justice and participation that they desire to establish.

Encourage Grassroots Peacekeeping Groups and Voluntary Associations

Just peacemaking theorists urge us to encourage grassroots peacemaking groups and voluntary associations. Duane K. Friesen considers this task, in part, as one of building "moral communities that can form people of character" and "that nurture a commitment to a social vision."[85] Since in the previous section on the Freedom Charter I argued that revolutionaries have a responsibility to articulate and embody a vision of the societies they want to inculcate nationally, revolutionaries will also want to encourage grassroots organizations for supporting and sustaining that vision. Friesen argues that the task of building a just peace requires "institutions of civil society" that "can form people morally willing to commit their energies to just peacemaking because they believe it is right in and of itself."[86] Underpinning the notion that grassroots peacekeeping ought to be encouraged is a belief that ordinary people can become political actors through their participation in collective advocacy on behalf of peace and justice. In this way, the strategy of encouraging grassroots peacekeeping groups is intimately related to the strategy of supporting nonviolent direct action. Emphasis is placed less on the activity of centralized governments or powerful leaders, and more on ordinary people that are empowered to carry out nonviolent direct action toward social transformation. Moreover, these ordinary agents of political transformation can sustain "concern and interest [for a cause] when the media and world opinion are unaware, forget, or flit about from one thing to the next."[87] Grassroots peacekeeping organizations are typically stable and committed to justice in their communities, in part because of their proximity to the injustice that needs correction.

There are at least two key ways in which the struggle against apartheid evidenced the importance of the just peacemaking practice of encouraging grassroots peacemaking organizations. First, the South African Council of Churches illustrates the role that religious organizations can play in empowering people to engage in nonviolent direct action. Second, the implementation of the M-Plan by the ANC demonstrates the importance of maintaining a grassroots network for organizing nonviolent direct action when the leadership of a revolutionary movement has been suppressed such that they are unable to carry out their activities publically without facing severe repression. Thus, both the South African Council of Churches and the M-Plan reinforce the important role that grassroots organizations have in supporting nonviolent direct action, which remains the foundation of revolutionary resistance against oppression.

The South African Council of Churches is an association of Christian churches that promotes social justice. It brings together dozens of Christian denominations "to teach, prophesy, rebuke and correct the wrongs that seek to define society."[88] In its efforts to sustain a grassroots network of Christians committed to a just and peaceful South Africa, SACC "maintains links between . . . South African Churches and the worldwide community."[89] In this way SACC represents precisely the kind of "network of interlocking groups of people at a grassroots level"[90] that just peacemaking theorists seek to encourage. The activities of SACC in the midst of apartheid affirm the important role that churches, as grassroots organizations, can have in just revolutionary movements. Moreover, a review of the SACC's activities can encourage and exhort churches and religious organizations directly to get involved in struggles against oppression.

Rooted in the conviction that Christian spirituality generates Christian social activism, SACC was a formidable opponent of apartheid. "Our belief is that a relevant and authentic spirituality cannot but constrain us to be involved, as we are involved, in the socio-political realm," declared Archbishop Desmond Tutu, Secretary General of SACC from 1978–1985.[91] "It is precisely our encounters with Jesus in worship and the sacraments, in Bible reading and meditation, that force us to be concerned about the hungry, about the poor, about the homeless, about the banned and detained, about the voiceless whose voice we seek to be."[92] SACC took a public stand against apartheid and instead supported the idea of a South Africa where people of all races would be reconciled to one another.[93]

SACC was grounded in a biblical hermeneutics of liberation from oppression. The organization included multiracial churches but not the whites-only, Afrikaner-dominated Dutch Reformed Church of South Africa, which attempted to provide a theological and scriptural justification for apartheid.[94] Instead, Tutu promoted a theology of emancipation. He declared SACC to be a "Christian organization with a definite bias in favor of the oppressed and exploited in our society."[95] Drawing on the Biblical accounts of Exodus and the Hebrew prophets, as well as Jesus as one who "sets God's children free from bondage,"[96] Tutu avers that SACC stands with the oppressed in seeking, not just an "ethereal" emancipation from personal sin, but social and political transformation in human history. In colorful language Tutu argues that Jesus does not promise "pie in the sky when you die . . . He knew that people want their pie here and now, today and not in some future tomorrow."[97] Tutu's theology is unwavering in its support for those who endeavor to liberate themselves from oppression.

As a network of grassroots organizations, SACC was instrumental in supporting and promoting nonviolent direct action against apartheid. As an example of the capacity of grassroots movements to "generate the kind of perseverance that is needed so that a just peace can emerge over generations,"[98] Friesen notes that "Bishop Desmond Tutu and the South African Council of Churches were in the forefront in advocating nonviolence in the struggle in South Africa."[99] Specifically, SACC sought to support individuals under banning orders, and their families;[100] to advocate against the practice of banning;[101] to support political prisoners and their dependents;[102] and to provide legal services for those arrested and detained in the course of protest.[103] As an organization, SACC was committed to noncooperation with injustice, arguing that "South African Churches are under an obligation to withdraw as far as that is possible from cooperation with the State in all those areas in the ordering of our society where the law violates the justice of God."[104] Thus SACC demonstrates the way in which religious organizations, as networks of interlocking groups of people at the grassroots, can and should help sustain a revolutionary cause and support nonviolent resistance against oppression.

In an effort to protect and sustain their power, dictatorial regimes find ways to suppress popular revolutionary movements. The apartheid regime banned individuals and organizations, detained and imprisoned revolutionaries, and drove resistance leaders into exile. Such attempts at suppression ought to be anticipated by the leadership of revolutions, and grassroots networks ought to be intentionally and meticulously encouraged by revolutionary leaders in order to sustain nonviolent direct action in the wake of counterrevolutionary suppression.

Grassroots organizing became pragmatically necessary in South Africa as the ANC and other resistance organizations faced government suppression of the struggle. South African historian and former anti-apartheid activist Raymond Suttner notes that "the M-Plan" for organizing ordinary South Africans to promote social change, "was prompted by a belief that political conditions were becoming more repressive."[105] Anticipating becoming a banned organization itself, leaders of the ANC devised a plan for how it could promote grassroots revolutionary resistance from underground. In order to continue to plan and organize nonviolent direct action with mass participation, the ANC needed to evolve into an organization with more grassroots leadership. "Broadly speaking," remarked ANC leader Joe Matthews, "the idea is to strengthen the organization tremendously. To prepare for the continuation of the organization under conditions of illegality by organizing on the basis of a cell system."[106] This cell system, named the "M-Plan" after its implementer, Nelson Mandela, restructured the ANC and set up a complex system for communication. Those involved in the struggle at the grassroots would receive information from intermediaries between them and ANC leaders who were underground or in exile.[107] Mid-level leaders, or "stewards" could communicate quickly and effectively to both the ANC elite leadership and to the grassroots. In his autobiography, Nelson Mandela describes the organization of the M-Plan:

> The smallest unit was the cell, which in urban townships consisted of roughly ten houses on a street. A cell steward would be in charge of each of these. If a street had more than ten houses, a street steward would take charge and the cell stewards would report to him. A group of streets formed a zone directed by a chief steward, who was in turn responsible to the secretariat of the local branch of the ANC. The Secretariat was a subcommittee of the branch executive, which reported to the provincial secretary . . . every cell and street steward should know every person and family in his area, so that he would be trusted by the people and would know whom to trust. The cell steward arranged meetings, organized political classes and collected dues. He was the linchpin of the plan.[108]

Swift communication amongst the levels of people would enable the ANC to continue to recruit members, collect dues, and organize mass resistance actions without the need for formal meetings, announcements, and literature.[109] Mandela and the ANC's focus on developing mid-level leaders as conduits between upper leadership and the grassroots is evocative of the work of John Paul Lederach who views the development and resourcing of mid-level leaders as crucial to peace-building and the social transformation of conflict.[110]

The implementation of the M-Plan for empowering ordinary people to continue to engage in political resistance even in the midst of suppression and repression offers numerous important lessons for revolutionary movements. It demonstrates that revolutionary leaders must anticipate the regime's counter-revolutionary activity and plan for this accordingly. Moreover, it makes evident the significance of revolutionary leadership that is flexible and humble. Leaders must be able to trust and empower others, and to delegate tasks, so that a struggle against oppression is one of the whole people, not just an elite few. The ANC was doubtless a hierarchical organization, but nevertheless it was committed to and capable of developing leadership at mid and grassroots levels. Empowering ordinary people in this way ensured that nonviolent direct action continued even when the leaders of the revolution were banned, in prison, or exiled.

In conversation with the just peacemaking practice of encouraging grassroots peacekeeping groups, the South African context illustrates that just revolutions ought not underestimate the importance of empowering ordinary people. The work of SACC highlights the role that churches and religious organizations have in promoting liberation by supporting nonviolent direct action with financial and legal assistance for those who take on the burden of civil disobedience. Noncooperation with an unjust regime has greater impact as ordinary individuals unite in networks of grassroots resistance organizations, grounded in a liberating faith experience. Moreover, the implementation of the M-Plan demonstrates that it is necessary to anticipate suppression of the popular struggle. The continuation of organized nonviolent direct action must be thoroughly planned for, as much as possible, in advance of severe repression. Revolutionaries must devise systems for continuing to empower the resistance of ordinary people under the conditions of counter-revolution. The need for the institutionalization of grassroots resistance, via organizations like the SACC and the implementation of the M-Plan belies any impression that successful revolutions are primarily spontaneous outbursts. Indeed, they are more often deliberate, shrewdly plotted, and organized movements.

Strengthen the United Nations and International Efforts for Cooperation and Human Rights

In a world that is increasingly socially, economically, and politically interconnected, just peacemaking theorists encourage us to *strengthen the United Nations and international efforts for cooperation and human rights.* "An approach to just peacemaking," argues Michael Joseph Smith, "must encourage . . . international developments for the pacific settlement of . . . conflicts. In the most basic terms this means support for the United Nations, associated regional international organizations and nongovernmental organizations (NGOs) so that, collectively, we can develop the capacity to identify, prevent, and if necessary, intervene in conflicts within and between states that threaten basic human rights."[111] Just peacemaking theorists recognize that the UN is not currently strong enough to meet the global needs for peacekeeping.[112] Nevertheless, they are confident in its ability, given adequate support, to coordinate international responses to crises. They reject attempts to besmirch or diminish the UN, and instead argue that the UN "remains the only institution capable of sustained peacekeeping operations, and it provides the only genuinely international forum for considering, authorizing, and legitimizing multilateral action."[113] Indeed, Smith contends that the UN's efficacy in dealing with apartheid, including declaring it a threat to peace, "brought about a gradual expansion of legitimate international concern in matters that states had traditionally treated as domestic affairs."[114] Likewise, Louis Henkin cites the UN coordination of sanctions against apartheid as revealing "a major rent . . . in the cloak of sovereignty due to this idea of human rights."[115]

Indeed, a growing international consensus regards state sovereignty as a value contingent in part upon a government's willingness and ability to protect its own citizens. This conditional understanding of state sovereignty is meant to apply precisely in cases of grave human rights violations that endanger peace. In urging the international community to strengthen the United Nations and international efforts for cooperation and human rights, just peacemaking theory supports this consensus. The international norm known as the "Responsibility to Protect" (R2P)[116] commits the international community first to prevent mass violations of human rights: we are encouraged to "address both the root causes and direct causes" of intrastate conflict that puts civilian populations at risk.[117] If prevention does not succeed; if a state is unable or unwilling to protect its citizens against large scale loss of life and other mass violations of human rights; then the international community has a "responsibility to react,"[118] that is to intervene to protect human beings. This intervention can be nonmilitary or military, depending on the circumstances of a given conflict. To guide the international community in discerning whether or not military intervention is justified, R2P adapts the criteria of the just war tradition. Much attention has been paid to analyzing the ethics of military intervention, or "reaction," as part of a responsibility to protect. Less attention, however, has been paid to R2P's suggestions for nonmilitary forms of intervention, or "reaction." R2P supports the use of monitored and targeted sanctions including arms embargoes and the withdrawal of military cooperation and support; financial sanctions that target particular individuals, groups, activities, and/or resources; no fly zones; and diplomatic restrictions that target elites including closure of embassies, travel restrictions, and isolation from international organizations.[119]

Recent scholarship in ethics and international studies has shown that economic sanctions are not morally neutral, and have in several situations caused more harm than good to civilian populations. Sanctions can be a deeply problematic tool for coercing dictatorial and so-called rogue regimes.

The devastating effects of economic sanctions in the 1990s on Iraq's population compels political philosopher Joy Gordon to question seriously the moral legitimacy of sanctions. Comparing sanctions to siege-warfare, Gordon cogently argues that sanctions cause "foreseeable" and "*direct*" harm to those who are, in Just War doctrine, supposed to be exempt from warfare."[120] She therefore rejects the use of sanctions—which she argues can be a form of violence—as a legitimate tool of nonmilitary coercion. "The situation in Iraq," Gordon contends, "compels us to reexamine the moral basis of economic sanctions."[121] Gordon concedes that "the case of South Africa made [sanctions] seem quite attractive. The Black population of South Africa itself—the population most likely to be harmed by economic sanctions—called for sanctions against South Africa as an act of international solidarity."[122] However, Gordon suggests that South Africa is an exceptional case, and that sanctions typically cause severe suffering to ordinary citizens. She warns that "situations where outside sanctions actually help erode the internal legitimacy of the state, such as in South Africa, are infrequent. In South Africa . . . the external sanctions imposed on the country were accompanied by extensive political activity toward democracy inside South Africa."[123] Thus, while acknowledging the importance of economic sanctions for ending apartheid, Gordon views South Africa as a lone exception to the rule that sanctions are fundamentally unethical. This suggests that the international community ought not come to the aid of revolutionaries by imposing economic sanctions against dictatorial regimes.

In response to Gordon, however, George A. Lopez acknowledges that there are grave concerns regarding economic sanctions, but he suggests that these illustrate a need to "build real refinements in sanctions policy that will work."[124] Lopez counters that South Africa is not the only positive example of sanctions. The dismantling of the white minority regime in Rhodesia, and Libya's extradition of suspects in the bombing of a Pan Am airliner over Lockerbie also provide successful examples of the use of sanctions.[125] While Gordon argues that sanctions are an unethical means, Lopez counters that sanctions can and should be designed to minimize harm to civilians: "The impact of Gordon's analysis must be a renewed and steadfast commitment to develop sanctions that do not have as their goal the crippling of the general economy, or as their unintended consequences the further devastation of the lives of the poor and vulnerable of the society."[126]

Debates surrounding the ethical validity of sanctions have prompted the development of "smart" sanctions designed to target those responsible for objectionable policies and practices. For Lopez, "smart" sanctions would include many of those considered by R2P: "asset freezes and other financial measures . . . arms embargos and bans on travel and international meetings targeted specifically at elites."[127] Moreover, sanctions as they would apply specifically in situations of just revolution would be accompanied by "extensive political activity"[128] toward democracy, or other more participatory forms of governance that Gordon notes as having been important for determining the success of international sanctions against South African apartheid.

International cooperation in an intrastate revolution is important for several reasons. First, the international community is reciprocally responsible for recognizing the legitimacy of one another's governments. Insofar as nation states recognize one another as legitimate, they agree to normalized international relations with one another. But nation states also have the power to engage in noncooperation—on a massive scale—with states that they deem illegitimate. It is thus in the interests of a just revolutionary movement to use this function of the international community to their advantage by demonstrating the illegitimacy of the oppressor regime to the international community; and likewise to demonstrate their own legitimacy as a revolutionary movement. Second, once a regime is viewed by the international community as illegitimate revolutionaries can work with cooperative forces for additional measures—such as targeted sanctions—to help the revolution succeed. Nonviolent, responsible, international "reactions" can have real and important effects in assisting and supporting intrastate revolutionary movements that are already employing other practices of just peacemaking.

The South African case study illustrates that well-planned, coordinated, and targeted sanctions can be an international form of support for nonviolent resistance in the context of a just revolution. It is helpful when revolutionaries themselves, who have the primary responsibility for claiming their own rights, request that the international community impose sanctions.[129] Moreover, as a pragmatic matter, revolutionaries may find that certain nations or groups that are more familiar with their experience of injustice may be able to advocate effectively with the rest of the international community for the imposition of sanctions, or policies of divestment.

It is important to remember that South African revolutionaries themselves raised global opposition to apartheid by issuing an urgent appeal for international sanctions. Z.K. Matthews, an ANC leader and a professor at Union Theological Seminary, used his position in New York to draw the attention of the United Nations to the Defiance Campaign. While Matthews faced resistance in the still-segregated United States, the UN nevertheless established a Commission on the Racial Situation in South Africa.[130] The commission issued several reports over the following years culminating with the establishment of the United Nations Special Committee Against Apartheid. This committee subsequently declared apartheid "a threat to peace"[131] and called on the international community to employ economic sanctions against South Africa. Likewise, inside South Africa in the early 1960s a revolutionary policy on behalf of sanctions was drafted by the All-In African Conference, in which delegates approved a resolution calling "upon democratic people the world over to impose economic and other sanctions against the government" of South Africa.[132] During his travels throughout Africa in the years immediately following the All-In African Conference, Nelson Mandela repeated this request, and heralded those nations that were already imposing a "boycott of South African goods and . . . economic and diplomatic sanctions against South Africa."[133] That the request for sanctions came from South Africans themselves strengthened its force.

The South African case also illustrates the point made by those who formulated the *Responsibility to Protect* that allies closer to the situation of crisis may be more helpful in the fight to impose sanctions. "It is generally the case that countries within the region are more sensitive to the issues and context behind the conflict headlines."[134] These regional powers are "more familiar with the actors and personalities involved in the conflict, and have a greater stake in overseeing a return to peace and prosperity."[135] When revolutionaries and the UN first called for sanctions against apartheid, the South African regime's major trading partners in the West voted against implementation, while several decolonized African nations chose to impose them. These states were intimately familiar with the politics of colonialism and post-colonialism, and had a clear personal stake in opposing white supremacy. They strongly supported a position of solidarity with South African revolutionaries.[136]

The campaign to impose sanctions and encourage divestment continued into the next decades. Following international outrage at the death in police custody of Black Consciousness Movement leader Steve Biko in 1977, the United Nations imposed a mandatory arms embargo on South Africa.[137] As violent repression increased throughout the next decade, the campaign for sanctions and divestment intensified. In 1986 the U.S. legislature, over and against a veto by President Ronald Reagan, passed the Comprehensive Anti-Apartheid Act, which prohibited South African imports, and made new investment in South Africa illegal.[138] As the major economic powers of the West supported resistance to apartheid, sanctions began to have real effects on the South African economy, leading many South African business elites to reject the policies of apartheid. Historians generally credit sanctions as a major contributing force in South Africa's social transformation.

In terms of international assistance in intrastate revolution, the South African case study shows that revolutionaries should consider courting non-militaristic international interventions *jus ante* armed revolution, and when necessary and possible alongside the revolutionary movement's own armed resistance *jus in* armed revolution. Ethicists, diplomats, political scientists, and peace keepers are right to question and reject economic sanctions that have devastating effects on civilian populations.[139] Nevertheless, the success of sanctions in the South African context points to need to find creative ways for the international community to resist authoritarian regimes in solidarity with internal protest.

VIOLENT REPRESSION IN SOUTH AFRICA

Had the apartheid regime responded to nonviolent resistance with repressive legislation, arrests, and court proceedings, the revolutionary movement would likely have continued to espouse a nonviolent struggle, using only practices of what we now call the just peacemaking theory. Unfortunately, apartheid repression became increasingly violent. This violence initiated a transition in the revolutionary movement from the use of nonviolent tactics only, to the use of a combination of armed and nonviolent resistance, which I call the tandem approach and discuss further in chapter 4. Two events characterize apartheid's growing violent response to peaceful resistance: the Sharpeville Massacre and the subsequent State of Emergency.

Although the Sharpeville Massacre was not the first time police had killed demonstrators, its sheer brutality and demonstration of the South African Defense Force's (SADF) willingness to use violence against unarmed civilians shocked and sparked outrage in South Africa and around the world. The massacre was a response to a protest organized by the Pan Africanist Congress (PAC), a resistance organization and political rival of the ANC, in which 5,000–7,000 people refused to carry their government-issued pass books and presented themselves peacefully at the building housing Sharpeville's municipal offices. The group was unarmed and expected to be arrested. Instead, police officers opened fire on the crowd. Approximately 69 people were killed and 180 others wounded. Doctors' reports document 30 shots entering people from the front while at least 155 entered from the back, presumably as civilians fled.[140] In the immediate aftermath of this attack resistance organizations continued to practice nonviolent direct action in protest.[141]

While Prime Minister Verwoerd and other National Party leaders originally dismissed the shooting as symptomatic of unrest on the continent in general, they quickly retreated from this position, instead declaring a national State of Emergency.[142] The State of Emergency was characterized by a massive show of military force. "Verwoerd's determination to withstand the challenge was captured in his admonition to white South Africans to 'stand like walls of granite because the survival of a nation is at stake.'"[143] Thus, the police and military forces geared up "as though for an imminent civil war."[144] Leaders of the ANC, the PAC, and even South Africa's trade unions were arrested, detained, and subsequently banned, and media was strictly censored.[145] Thousands of additional people were detained. "The military was used to support the police in the townships, turning them into armed camps . . . Through all this detained activists continued to die mysteriously in police custody."[146] In defiance of the violent repression, people around the country, and the world, continued to demonstrate peacefully against the actions of the South African government.

Meanwhile the ANC was beginning to reevaluate its strategy of using only nonviolent tactics. After forty years of peaceful resistance, ANC leaders began to consider whether or not they had come upon what the just war tradition calls "the last resort." The massacre at Sharpeville had illustrated—horrifically—that nonviolence would not, in the case of South Africa, ensure a bloodless revolution.

CONCLUSION

Demonstrating redoubtable discipline and patience, resistance organizations led the majority of South Africans through decades of nonviolent resistance. The government's violent response neither detracts from the ways in which these practices are effective, nor proves that they ought not to be attempted. South African revolutionaries set the foundation of resistance through nonviolent direct action. Using marches, strikes, and boycotts they illustrated the role that nonviolent direct action can play in a just revolution, surfacing social tensions and demonstrating the will of the people. South Africans worked to advance democracy and human rights within both the movement and the nation as a whole. Thus they demonstrated how just revolutions ought to prevision the participation and respect for human rights that revolutionaries wish to inculcate at the national level. The ANC strengthened grassroots and mid-level leadership so as to empower ordinary people to work for social transformation, illustrating the importance of anticipating a regime's counter-tactics and mobilizing the whole population for nonviolent revolution. Finally, South African revolutionaries advocated for and accepted international cooperation in the struggle. The efficacy of international support for the struggle against apartheid testifies to the need for revolutionaries and the international community to work together creatively to find ways to assist and support those who seek to liberate themselves from oppression. South African political resistance against apartheid attests that just peacemaking practices ought to comprise the first stage of any just revolution against oppression. Revolutionaries have a moral responsibility to begin with nonviolent strategies *jus ante* armed revolution. If oppression can be rooted out using nonviolent measures then armed resistance is neither necessary nor ethical.

Thus, nonviolent just peacemaking strategies bring a number of strengths to those seeking ethically and effectively to overturn an illegitimate government. They expose and confront the injustices of a regime, and encourage broad democratic participation in political resistance. They prevision a government dedicated to respecting human rights and inculcate into the revolutionary movement itself the participatory mechanisms that the revolution seeks to instantiate at the national level. They empower ordinary people to become politically engaged against injustice through collective action. They seek out the cooperation of the international community in declaring an authoritarian regime to be illegitimate, sanctioning its oppressive activities, and thereby working together for positive social transformation. Moreover, these nonviolent practices demonstrate a reverence for human life, and a hope that oppression can be overcome without loss of life. Such a commitment to the value and dignity of human life carries moral authority and can win allies in the work to end oppression. While, in the following chapter, I will argue for the possibility of ethical armed revolt, it is crucial to note that these strengths are a result of nonviolent resistance and cannot be replaced by armed resistance. A revolution that too hastily takes up arms will find it difficult to reap the benefits of the kind of carefully planned and implemented nonviolent just peacemaking practices witnessed by the struggle against apartheid.

NOTES

1. For an excellent analysis on the use of nonviolent resistance in these three revolutions see Sharon Erikson Nepstad, *Nonviolent Revolutions: Civil Resistance in the Late 20th Century* (New York: Oxford University Press, 2011).

2. For more on the effectiveness of nonviolent resistance see Erica Chenoweth and Maria J. Stephan, *Why Civil Resistance Works: The Strategic Logic of Nonviolent Conflict* (New York: Columbia University Press, 2011).

3. For a full explanation of each of these practices see Cartwright and Thislethwaite, "Support Nonviolent Direct Action," in *Just Peacemaking: The New Paradigm for the Ethics of Peace and War*, Glen H. Stassen, ed., (Cleveland, OH: The Pilgrim Press, 2008).

4. Cartwright and Thislethwaite, 56.

5. Martin Luther King, Jr., "Letter from a Birmingham Jail" (1963). Available at http://www.africa.upenn.edu/Articles_Gen/Letter_Birmingham.html.

6. For more on the relationship between civil resistance and performance see Dwight Conquergood, *Cultural Struggles: Performance, Ethnography, Praxis*, E. Patrick Johnson, ed. (Ann Arbor, MI: University of Michigan Press, 2013); Norman K. Denzin, "The Call to Performance," *Symbolic Interaction*, 26.1 (2003): 187–207; Stanley Hauerwas, *Performing the Faith: Bonhoeffer and the Practice of Nonviolence* (Grand Rapids, MI: Brazos Press, 2004); and W.J.T. Mitchell, "Image, Space, Revolution: The Arts of Occupation," *Critical Inquiry*, 39 (2012): 8–32.

7. Cartwright and Thislethwaite, 43.

8. Bill Sutherland and Matt Meyer, *Guns and Gandhi in Africa: Pan-African Insights on Nonviolence, Armed Struggle, and Liberation* (Asmara, Eritrea: Africa World Press, 2000), 156.

9. Cartwright and Thislethwaite, 45.

10. Harold Jack Simons, *Struggles in Southern Africa* (New York: St. Martin's Press, 1997), 115.
11. The organization changed its name to the African National Congress (ANC) in 1923.
12. Simons, 115.
13. Simons, 115. Nelson Mandela later acknowledged sexism in the nascent ANC and argued that men should accept responsibility for sexist stereotyping that excluded women from the political movement. As a point of interest, women were perhaps more revolutionary and confrontational than their male counterparts during this period in South African history. As early as 1913 women in the Orange Free State, led by Charlotte Maxeke, organized a major protest against monthly housing permits in segregated areas. Some 600–800 people marched in the original protests. As a result of the energy around these resistance actions, Maxeke organized the Bantu Women's League, which sent a delegation directly to Prime Minister Botha to discuss grievances regarding the permits. The permit law was abolished in 1920.
14. The ANC constitution is available at http://www.sahistory.org.za/archive/constitution-anc-0.
15. I do not mean to suggest here that the government *negotiated* with resistance organizations during this period, but it certainly *engaged* them in the sense that it attempted to repress resistance in a variety of ways. This indicates that the use of confrontational nonviolent direct action succeeded in drawing attention to the revolutionary cause.
16. ANCYL, "Manifesto" (1944) in Nelson Mandela, *The Struggle is My Life* (New York: Pathfinder Press, 1986), 16.
17. ANCYL, 17.
18. ANCYL, 16–17.
19. ANCYL, 17.
20. ANCYL, 24.
21. "The goal of all political organization and action is the achievement of true democracy," wherein, "all nationalities and minorities would have their fundamental human rights guaranteed in a democratic constitution." ANCYL Executive Committee, "Basic Policy Document," (1948) in *The Struggle is My Life*, 21. It is interesting to note here the language of human rights. The ANCYL released this policy statement in 1948, at the same time the United Nations adopted the Universal Declaration of Human Rights. Thus the ANCYL demonstrates not only its commitment to the cause of freedom in South Africa, but also its keen awareness of world trends and events and how the South African struggle might fit into a global agenda for peacemaking through the recognition of human rights.
22. The spelling reflects the British colonial influence on South African English. For the "Programme of Action," see *The Struggle is My Life,* 28–30.
23. At this time Africans were theoretically "represented" in the parliament through the "Natives Representative Council" which consisted of unelected whites.
24. "Programme of Action," 29.
25. "Programme of Action," 29.
26. "Just peacemaking theory . . . focuses on what in fact works to prevent wars in real history, based on empirical reality" (Pamela Brubaker, James B. Burke, Duane K. Friesen, John Langan, S.J., and Glen Stassen, "Introduction: Just Peacemaking as the New Ethic for War and Peace," in Stassen, 12).
27. The Defiance Campaign was implemented in response to apartheid's "Unlawful Organizations Bill"—the legislation that would eventually evolve into the "Suppression of Communism Act." This legislation attempted to stifle dissent by characterizing it as a product of foreign communism. "Walter Sisulu, a founding member of the ANC Youth League . . . pointed out that although appearing to be aimed against communists, the bill was designed to suppress the struggles of all oppressed peoples. The whites were determined to keep Africans in a state of permanent subordination, which the ANC would resist by all the means at its disposal" (Simons, 118). Thus the legislation would define "communism" in the broadest possible terms with the intention of catching all resistance to the regime in its net. Organizations participating in the Defiance Campaign included the ANC, South African Indian Con-

gress, the African Political Organization, and the Communist Party. The Defiance Campaign thus also represents the beginning of the Congress Alliance, a coalition of several resistance organizations that worked together in the South African revolution.

28. ANC National Executive Committee, "ANC Statement" (1950), *The Struggle is My Life*, 31.

29. William Beinart, *Twentieth Century South Africa* (New York: Oxford University Press, 2001), 154.

30. Cartwright and Thistlethwaite, 49.

31. The Public Safety Act, 1953.

32. The Criminal Laws Amendment Act, No. 8, 1953.

33. Simons, 118.

34. "Introduction," *The Struggle is My Life*, 3.

35. Banning was a common tool of the apartheid regime. It targeted key individuals in the resistance movement to keep them from participating in assemblies, making speeches or publically discussing politics, and traveling nationally or internationally.

36. In his letter on the subject to Prime Minister Verwoerd, Nelson Mandela wrote that Black South Africans "feared that under this proposed Republic your Government, which is already notorious the world over for its obnoxious policies, would continue to make even more savage attacks on the rights and living conditions of the African people." Nelson Mandela, "First letter from Nelson Mandela to Hendrik Verwoerd." The full text of this letter is available at http://www.sahistory.org.za/archive/document-9-first-letter-nelson-mandela-hendrik-verwoerd.

37. "Introduction" to *The Struggle is My Life*, 5. See also All-In African Conference, "Resolutions" (1961), *The Struggle is My Life*, 97–98.

38. Nelson Mandela, "First letter from Nelson Mandela to Hendrik Verwoerd."

39. Nelson Mandela, "First letter from Nelson Mandela to Hendrik Verwoerd."

40. *Observer,* (May 28, 1962), quoted in *The Struggle is My Life,* 6.

41. "Introduction," *The Struggle is My Life,* 6.

42. Cartwright and Thistlethwaite, 45.

43. Bruce Russert, "Advance Democracy, Human Rights, and Interdependence," *Just Peacemaking: The New Paradigm for the Ethics of Peace and War,* 119.

44. Russert, 120.

45. Russert, 120.

46. Russert, 120.

47. Hannah Arendt, *On Revolution* (New York: Penguin Books, 1990), 35.

48. Russett, 122. Russert offers several examples of this linkage including in revolutionary and resistance movements in Korea, Taiwan, Poland, East Germany, South Africa, Czechoslovakia, and throughout Latin America (122).

49. The constitution of the new South Africa includes a firm commitment to human dignity and to a broad diversity of human rights.

50. National Action Council, "The Freedom Charter," in *The Struggle is My Life,* 50.

51. "The Freedom Charter," 51.

52. In *Claims in Conflict* (New York: Paulist Press, 1979), David Hollenbach enumerates as among civil-political rights, rights to "freedom of religion, speech and assembly, the right to be secure in one's person and property, and the rights of *habeas corpus* and to due process of law" (13). For the *International Covenant on Civil and Political Rights* see http://www.refworld.org/pdfid/3ae6b3aa0.pdf.

53. For Hollenbach these include "the right to work and to choose professions . . . the right to material security, including the right to protection of health . . . right to education and housing" (21). For the *International Covenant on Economic, Social, and Cultural Rights* see http://www.refworld.org/docid/3ae6b36c0.html.

54. "The Freedom Charter," 51.

55. "The Freedom Charter," 52.

56. "The Freedom Charter," 52.

57. "The Freedom Charter," 52.

58. "The Freedom Charter," 53.

59. The prominence of social-economic and cultural rights in "The Freedom Charter" further confirms David Hollenbach's thesis that "there appears . . . to be more of a causal link between economic deprivation and the denial of rights to political participation, freedom from arbitrary arrest and torture, freedom to organize labor unions, etc . . . ." (192). It also confirms Meghan J. Clark's arguments about the importance of participation for integrating civil-political and economic-social human rights. See "Integrating Human Rights: Participation in John Paul II, Catholic Social Thought and Amartya Sen," *Political Theology* 8.3 (2007).
60. "The Freedom Charter," 51.
61. "The Freedom Charter," 51.
62. For more on the conditions of South African mines at this time see Beinart, 25–34.
63. "The Freedom Charter," 51.
64. Beinart, 10.
65. "The Freedom Charter," 52.
66. "The Freedom Charter," 52.
67. "The Freedom Charter," 52.
68. See footnote on page 52 of *The Struggle is My Life*.
69. "The Freedom Charter," 53.
70. "The Freedom Charter," 53.
71. "The Freedom Charter," 53.
72. David Bronkema, David Lumsdaine, Rodger A. Payne, "Foster Just and Sustainable Economic Development," *Just Peacemaking: The New Paradigm for the Ethics of Peace and War*, 135.
73. Pope Francis recently made this argument in *Evangelii Gaudium*, 57.
74. Bronkema, Lumsdaine, and Payne, 135.
75. "The Freedom Charter," 50.
76. Bronkema, Lumsdaine, and Payne, 135.
77. Bronkema, Lumsdaine, and Payne, 135.
78. "The Freedom Charter," 53.
79. Since the end of the regime in the early nineties, the importance of cultural heritage has been recognized by the democratic government. In my conversations with South African school children I learned that South Africa has eleven official languages. Children are taught their own tribal language, as well as English, and another additional language which they elect from the remaining nine official languages. Respecting the diversity of cultures within the nation of South Africa has been a key aspect of the attempt to build post-apartheid reconciliation.
80. "The Freedom Charter," 51.
81. For more on the communitarian anthropology of much of Southern Africa see Julius Gathogo, "African Philosophy as Expressed in the Concepts of Hospitality and Ubuntu," *Journal of Theology for Southern Africa*, 130 (2008), 39–53; Mluleki Mnyaka and Mokgethi Motlhabi, "The African Concept of Ubuntu/Botha and its Socio-Moral Significance," *Black Theology*, 3.2 (2005), 215–237; and Anna Floerke Scheid, "Interpersonal and Social Reconciliation: Finding Congruence in African Theological Anthropology," *Horizons*, 39.1 (2012), 27–49.
82. "The Freedom Charter," 51.
83. The full text of the African [Banjul] Charter of Human and Peoples' Rights is available at http://www.achpr.org/instruments/achpr/.
84. National Action Council, "Call to the Congress," *The Struggle is My Life*, 48.
85. Duane K. Friesen, "Encourage Grassroots Peacekeeping Groups and Voluntary Associations," in *Just Peacemaking: The New Paradigm for the Ethics of Peace and War*, 202.
86. Friesen, 203.
87. Friesen, 211.
88. See South African Council of Churches at http://www.sacc.org.za/pages/about.html.
89. Desmond Tutu, "Address to the Provincial Synod of the Anglican Church in Southern Africa," *The Rainbow People of God: The Making of a Peaceful Revolution*, John Allen, ed., (New York: Image Doubleday, 1994), 35.
90. Friesen, 201.
91. Tutu, 30.
92. Tutu, 30–31.

93. Tutu, 35–36.
94. See John Allen's editorial remarks in *The Rainbow People of God*, 25.
95. Tutu, 36.
96. Tutu, 37.
97. Tutu, 29.
98. Friesen, 210.
99. Friesen, 210.
100. Tutu, 33.
101. Tutu, 35.
102. Tutu, 33.
103. Tutu, 34.
104. Quoted in the South Africa Council of Churches Statement to the Truth and Reconciliation Commission, 2.5. Available at http://web.uct.ac.za/depts/ricsa/trc/sacc_sub.htm.
105. Raymond Suttner, "The African National Congress (ANC) Underground: From the M-Plan to Rivonia," *South African Historical Journal*, 49 (2003), 130.
106. Tim J. Juckes, *Opposition in South Africa: The Leadership of Z.K. Matthews, Nelson Mandela, and Stephen Biko* (Santa Barbara, CA: Praeger Publishers, 1995), 83.
107. Suttner cogently notes that "The literature on underground activity in South Africa is very limited: mainly pages or chapters of biographies or autobiographies, usually of leaders. There is a limited range of writings of underground workers below the level of national leadership" (124).
108. Nelson Mandela, *Long Walk to Freedom* (Boston, MA: Back Bay Books, 1995), 145.
109. Suttner also notes that one function of the ANC, enabled by the M-Plan, while it was underground was "of a welfare nature," including providing assistance to the families of detainees, and legal support for those charged with political offenses. Eventually, after the onset of armed struggle, the M-Plan also functioned as a means of recruiting people to serve in the ANC's armed wing, *Umkhonto we Sizwe* (143).
110. See John Paul Lederach, *Building Peace: Sustainable Reconciliation in Divided Societies* (Washington, DC: United States Institute of Peace, 1997), especially Part II.
111. Michael Joseph Smith, "Strengthen the United Nations and International Efforts for Cooperation and Human Rights," *Just Peacemaking: The New Paradigm for the Ethics of Peace and War,* 166.
112. Smith, 173.
113. Smith, 173.
114. Smith, 170–171.
115. Louis Henkin, "That 'S' Word: Sovereignty, and Globalization, and Human Rights, Et Cetera," *Fordham Law Review,* 68.1 (1999): 4–5.
116. The International Commission on Intervention and State Sovereignty (ICISS), *The Responsibility to Protect* (Ottowa: International Development Research Center, 2001).
117. Smith, 174.
118. ICISS, Chapter 4.
119. For a full list of measures short of military action see ICISS, 4.3–4.9.
120. Joy Gordon, "Economic Sanctions, Just War Doctrine, and the 'Fearful Spectacle of the Civilian Dead,'" *Crosscurrents,* 49.3 (1999), 392. Italics in the original.
121. Gordon, 388.
122. Joy Gordon, *The Invisible War: The United States and the Iraq Sanctions* (Cambridge, MA: Harvard University Press, 2010), 5.
123. Joy Gordon, "Economic Sanctions," 390.
124. George A. Lopez, "More Ethical Than Not: Sanctions as Surgical Tools: Response to 'A Peaceful, Silent, Deadly Enemy,'" *Ethics and International Affairs,* 13 (1999): 144.
125. Lopez, 145.
126. Lopez, 147.
127. Lopez, 148. For more on smart sanctions see David Cortright and George A. Lopez, eds., *Smart Sanctions: Targeting Economic Statecraft* (New York: Rowman and Littlefield Publishers, 2002). See also Gary Clyde Hufbauer, Jeffery J. Schott, Kimberly Ann Elliot, and Barbara Oegg, *Economic Sanctions Reconsidered,* 3rd edition (Washington, DC: Peterson

Institute for International Economics, 2007). It is also worth noting that Gordon clarifies that what she rejects are sanctions that target whole economies, and not "smart" sanctions that target individuals and their assets (Joy Gordon, "Reply to George A. Lopez's 'More Ethical Than Not,'" *Ethics and International Affairs,* 13 [1999]: 149).

128. Gordon, "Economic Sanctions," 390.

129. However, Lopez points out that it may not always be reasonable to expect that populations under severely repressive governments will be able to voice their desire for sanctions as international assistance. To require members of a repressed population to call for sanctions may be "to condemn those citizens as being the regime's next targets" (147).

130. Scott Thomas, *The Diplomacy of Liberation: The Foreign Relations of the African National Congress Since 1960* (London, UK: Tauris Academic Studies, 1996), 5. For a good analysis of U.S. policy and apartheid see Audie Klotz, "Norms Reconstituting Interests: Global Racial Equality and U.S. Sanctions against South Africa," *International Organization,* 49.3 (1995): 451–478.

131. Smith, 171.

132. All-In African Conference, "Resolutions" (1961), *The Struggle is My Life,* 99.

133. Nelson Mandela, "ANC Address at Pan-African Freedom Conference" (1962), *The Struggle is My Life,* 124.

134. ICISS, 6.32.

135. ICISS, 6.32.

136. Among the first to apply sanctions against apartheid were Ethiopia, Somalia, Sudan, and the West African nation then called Tanganyika. See Mandela, "ANC Address at Pan-African Freedom Conference," 124.

137. See John Allen's editorial comments in *The Rainbow People of God,* 15–16.

138. See "United States: Comprehensive Anti-Apartheid Act of 1986," 26 I.L.M. 77 (1987). Available at http://www.gpo.gov/fdsys/pkg/STATUTE-100/pdf/STATUTE-100-Pg1086.pdf.

139. For example, R2P notes that non-military forms of intervention can be "blunt and often indiscriminate weapons and must be used with extreme care to avoid doing more harm than good—especially to civilian populations . . . Sanctions that target leadership groups and security organizations responsible for gross human rights violations have emerged as an increasingly important alternative to general sanctions in recent years, and efforts to make such sanctions more effective have drawn increasing attention" (4.5).

140. Simons, 129.

141. For a full analysis of this event see Tom Lodge, *Sharpeville: An Apartheid Massacre and Its Consequences* (New York: Oxford University Press, 2011).

142. The Public Safety Act of 1953 allowed the government to declare states of emergency in which all parliamentary and judicial processes could be suspended.

143. Chris Alden, *Apartheid's Last Stand: The Rise and Fall of the South African Security State* (London: MacMillan Press Ltd, 1996), 18.

144. Simons, 131.

145. Simons, 131.

146. Juckes, 157.

Chapter Four

The Just War Tradition and Revolution

In the previous chapter I discussed the practices of just peacemaking theory in conversation with the program of nonviolent resistance against South African apartheid as a way to generate strategies for *jus ante* armed revolution. In this chapter, I turn to the possibility of ethical armed resistance against repressive regimes, inducing and deducing principles for *jus ad* and *jus in* armed revolution. My task here is to examine the just war tradition not from the perspective of powerful nation states or society's dominant classes, but instead from the perspective of oppressed peoples. Viewed in this way "from below," the just war tradition might be transformed to provide principles to guide a just armed revolution. These revised understandings of the just war criteria allow for, but also limit and restrain, armed resistance as a moral response to severe repression. In keeping with my hybrid inductive-deductive method, in each section I begin by stating the manner in which a particular just war criterion must be revised to apply to just revolution, and then I demonstrate how the South African context illustrates that particular revision. I focus first on the *jus ad bellum* criteria of just cause, legitimate authority, right intention, last resort, and reasonable hope of success, and second on the *jus in bello* criteria of proportionate means, and noncombatant immunity. I close the chapter by describing and noting the value of the "tandem approach" to revolution, which emerges from an exploration of the South African struggle against apartheid. The tandem approach may be useful both in promoting just revolutions elsewhere, and evaluating revolutionary activity around the globe.

JUS AD ARMED REVOLUTION

Just Cause

The first criterion of just cause seemingly requires little revision in a revolutionary context. In thinking about reasons to take up arms, the just war tradition holds that the only just cause for waging war is to counter "grave wrongs and injustices"[1] in order to establish peace. For Aquinas this meant that force can only be used for some good reason, which James Childress describes as protection of the innocent from unjust attacks, restoring rights wrongly denied, and establishing a just order.[2] Good reasons such as these are also necessary in justifying armed revolution. It is not enough to be displeased with how a particular political party or politician is managing a particular political situation. Instead, coupled as it must be with the criteria of last resort and proportionality, just cause suggests that the injustice we seek to rectify is so severe; that it creates a socio-political situation that is so discordant, that despite the inevitable chaos and disorder that come from violence, war, or in this case, armed revolution, it is the only viable means left to secure the telos of a just peace. Because, according to our working definition, revolutionary activity is directed against oppression and toward "the formation of a new body politic, where the liberation from oppression aims at . . . the constitution of freedom,"[3] it may even more fully manifest the just war tradition's sense of just cause as one that threatens a just peace than typical interstate wars do. All three of Childress' "good reasons" are often operative in contexts of oppression and repression. Nevertheless, I would like to suggest that the South African context fleshes out the meaning of just cause for the ethics of revolution. Specifically it illustrates that just cause in a revolutionary context manifests as the necessary self-defense of a people against an internal threat posed by their own government. This internal threat may include one, or an overlapping combination of three types of violence: (1) Degrading violence manifest as daily attacks on human dignity that aggregate into an oppressive sense of shame and humiliation; (2) Structural violence that leaves devastating effects on human dignity and violates the rights of the population; (3) Assault in the form of direct repressive violence. In cases of just revolution—whether nonviolent or armed—revolutionaries are often resisting and defending themselves and their communities against one or more of these forms of violence.

International law commonly understands just cause for war as tied to necessary defense of one's nation against an external enemy, or in coalition with allies against external enemies.[4] Historically, the just war tradition has been conceived of largely as a means of restraining interstate conflict. The South African struggle against apartheid illustrates, however, that in the context of revolution, our understanding of just cause must be adapted to deal with the self-defense of a people against their own government. Under the apartheid regime the majority of South Africans endured one or more of these types of violence that, when coupled with the other *jus ad bellum* criteria, are justifiably met with self-defensive armed resistance. When a people seeks to justify their defense of self against their government they ought to be able to point to these or similar forms of violence as a just cause for revolutionary action.

First, black South Africans suffered a regular barrage of indignities. These constant humiliations constituted in an essential way the oppressive regime that was apartheid. The legislation described in chapter 1 demonstrates this atmosphere of degradation: much of black South African life was subject to unjust laws, which decreed where black South Africans would live, what types of jobs they could hold, whom they could marry, what type of education they would receive, and whether they were allowed to be in areas outside of their "homelands" at any given time. A striking example of the indignity and humiliation black South Africans endured was the pass book requirement. Under the apartheid regime, all black South Africans were required to carry with them at all times a set of official papers called a pass book. These contained information as to one's racial classification, one's employment, and one's designated homeland. To enforce the pass laws in the face of civil disobedience, the regime resorted to humiliating tactics, which marred the human dignity of all South Africans. During his tenure as president of the ANC, Jacob Zuma described government enforcement: "Flying squads, pick-up vans, troop carriers, and mounted police are all abroad irritating and exasperating Africans by indiscriminately demanding passes [and] handling them in an insulting and humiliating way."[5] Nelson Mandela similarly averred, "Pass laws . . . render any African liable to police surveillance at any time. I doubt whether there is a single African male in South Africa who has not at some stage had a brush with the police over his pass."[6] Likewise, the humiliation regularly endured by South Africans prompted Albert Nolan, a theologian and anti-apartheid activist, to write, "It is not so easy for the average black person in South Africa to get through life without spending some time in prison for some offence or another. Apart from the extraordinary number of laws that you could transgress or be suspected of transgressing at any time, you are in constant danger of detention without trial for resisting or being suspected of resisting the system."[7] Laws that restricted movement, relationships, and associations, coupled with the threat of arrest and detention, created a culture of oppression and degradation in South Africa that provides just cause for resistance. Peace is gravely threatened in a society that systematically ridicules its own citizens.

The apartheid system itself points to the second form of violence against which people may choose to defend themselves: structural violence. Medical anthropologist and human rights activist Paul Farmer describes structural violence as "social arrangements that put individuals and populations in harm's way. The arrangements are *structural* because they are embedded in the political and economic organization of our social world; they are *violent* because they cause injury to people."[8] The structures of apartheid did substantial mental and physical injury to countless people in the form of poverty, unemployment, preventable illness, and premature and preventable death. In the late 1980s South African Archbishop Desmond Tutu described apartheid as a system that was "inherently violent," marked by policies that "uproot over three million people, disrupting stable communities, demolishing habitable dwellings, destroying schools, churches, small businesses and clinics. These people are dumped in poverty-stricken resettlement camps and their children are made to starve, not because there is no food in South Africa, but in order to satisfy government ideology . . . This is legalized, structural violence."[9] Structural violence causes malnutrition, hunger, disease, and in many cases, death. It is a form of violence that is rightly resisted, and in extreme cases coupled with the other criteria for a just revolution, may justify armed self-defensive revolutionary activity.

Finally, the clearest form of violence against which a people may consider armed resistance as a form of self-defense is direct repressive assault. This is violence inflicted on persons or communities as punitive retribution for and/or to discourage political activity against a regime. In the South African context direct repressive assault was manifest in multiple forms and was a constant threat, especially to those involved in political resistance. It included the taking of political prisoners, lengthy detention without trial, torture, maiming, threats upon one's life or one's family, and killing.[10] The Sharpeville Massacre, which I described in more detail in chapter 3, may be the most prominent example of direct repressive violence in the South African context. In March, 1960, during a nonviolent demonstration against pass laws, police opened fire on unarmed protesters killing over sixty and wounding nearly 200 others. Following the massacre, the government declared the first of several national "States of Emergency," which included broad leeway to repress nonviolent protest and crush agitation for social change.[11] The event served as a pivot point in the struggle against apartheid because it led leaders in the ANC to begin to debate the possibility of initiating armed resistance.[12] While government-initiated massacres of civilians are perhaps the most obvious and intense form of direct repressive assault, it is important to note that less pronounced smaller repressive incidences, or a buildup of repressive violence over time, including the use of States of Emergency to justify the repression, may be more common.

All three of these forms of violence—degradation, structural violence, and direct assault—are just causes for self-defensive resistance. They are social forms of violence which overlap at times, and which preclude a just peace. When coupled with the additional *jus ad bellum* criteria, this violence provides justification for armed resistance. It should be emphasized, however, that a just cause alone is not sufficient grounds to wage either war or armed revolution. In discussing critiques of the just war theory, Mark Allman notes that "in practice the just cause principle reigns supreme. Political rhetoric and popular opinion often reduce the entire JWT [just war theory] to the just cause principle."[13] This is a misuse of the just war tradition that I would seek to avoid in developing a theory of just revolution. Absent the presence of additional *jus ad bellum* criteria including last resort, right intention, and legitimate authority a just cause alone warrants nonviolent action, but does not allow for the initiation of armed revolutionary resistance.

Legitimate Authority

The second revised just war criterion that emerges from the South African struggle against apartheid is an alternative conception of what constitutes legitimate authority. As I already suggested in chapter 2, the criterion of legitimate authority can be particularly dicey for understanding the just war tradition in terms of armed revolutionary force because historically the tradition has been biased in favor of the *de facto* ruler. Augustine, for example, held that since God is the source of all power and authority, any given leader must have received his power from God and is therefore divinely ordained to rule. Echoing Jesus's testimony to Pontius Pilate,[14] Augustine states, "No one can have any power but what is given him from above. For there is no power but of God, who either ordains or permits."[15] On the surface, this traditional understanding would seem to discount any revolutionary group from being a legitimate authority simply because they do not wield this kind of official power. However, multiple theological and political traditions espouse the notion that a governing authority forfeits its legitimacy when it fails to safeguard justice or attacks the common good. If a legitimate authority is one who cares for the community and promulgates laws which are intended for the good of the community, as Thomas Aquinas argued,[16] then an illegitimate authority is one who disregards the needs of the community and promulgates laws that disrupt the common good. Instead of seeing itself as invested with the responsibility to care for the common good, an illegitimate regime favors the interests of a few. Thus Aquinas contends that "a tyrannical government is not just, because it is directed, not to the common good, but to the private good of the ruler."[17] Such a government will use political and coercive power, which is meant to uphold the common good and serve the public, to maintain these private interests. Under oppressive circumstances that constitute just cause and that meet the obligations of last resort, considered below, the question arises: who has the moral authority to depose an illegitimate government and to establish a just peace? Who is vested with authority to wage armed revolution? Three principles emerge from the South African struggle that can enable us to recognize the legitimate authority or authorities[18] in a revolutionary context. Legitimate authority (1) encourages the already emerging political participation of all for the sake of the common good, (2) enjoys the support of the broader population, and (3) controls and limits violence in the face of a regime which uses violence with impunity to maintain power. This final principle illustrates how legitimate authority is wed in the revolutionary context to the criterion of mirco-proportionality: legitimacy depends, in part, on using force in a proportionate manner to help decrease overall violence and free the majority of the people to continue nonviolent resistance.

First, a legitimate authority in the context of revolution is one who encourages emerging political participation and demonstrates care and concern for the common good. Indeed, participation acts as a bulwark to protect the common good against those who would abuse power. Emphasis on participation as promoting the common good is founded on the traditional political theology espoused by Thomas Aquinas, for whom attention to the common good defined political legitimacy. As we saw in chapter 2, Aquinas favored monarchical rule and he held that a virtuous monarch was the true legitimate authority. While some theorists argue that Aquinas's political theology was more democratic than we sometimes acknowledge,[19] he did not reflect extensively on how participation by the populace in the structures of government might affect the common good. More recently however, with the evolution of modern democratic states and Catholic social thought, Christian theology generally accepts the idea that participation in the structures which govern our lives is a human right.[20] Indeed, Meghan J. Clark argues that participation is intimately tied to the protection of human rights and the integration of civil-political and economic-social human rights. For Clark, the way that people are empowered to participate in society forms an "integral background" to the common good.[21] It is generally with the persistent violation of a people's right to participate that a government's legitimacy is called into question because participation promotes and helps to define the common good.[22]

It is appropriate to note here that to recognize a connection between legitimacy and the right to participation is not to suggest the imposition of Western style parliamentary or representative democracy on a nation or group which does not desire it. As we saw in the previous chapter, in the context of revolution, people are already choosing to participate, indeed oftentimes at great threat to their personal well-being, and are thus demonstrating a desire for participation. In the South African context there was mass political participation through strikes, protests, boycotts, and membership in political parties, even ones which had been banned. This participation will also be important later as we consider the North African and Middle Eastern nations affected by recent revolutions in the Arab Spring. In his memoir detailing the influence of social media on the Egyptian revolution, Wael Ghonim describes not only online participation as a force for revolutionary change, but also dozens of protests and rallies against the Mubarak regime. As in South Africa, the participants in the Egyptian revolution were subject to severe consequences including torture, and threats to their lives and the lives of their family members.[23] To argue that the legitimate authority supports participation is not to impose democracy from without, but rather to recognize how the participation that people are already engaged in is being supported or thwarted within a particular state.

Writing in the South African context, Charles Villa-Vicencio reminds us that governments "can never be theologically accepted as self-legitimating."[24] In other words, there must be some standard external to the government itself by which its legitimacy can be measured and judged. While care for the common good is a legitimate authority's most basic task, broad participation by the population in the structures of governance can provide an external standard for evaluating whether or not a given government has the common good as its primary goal. Citing the principle of the common good, the South African *Kairos Document* noted that apartheid's "mandate," since it served only the interests of the minority and only a minority could participate in it, "is by definition hostile to the common good of all people."[25] Legitimate authority can thus be recognized by its commitment to the participation of all, for the sake of the common good. Under apartheid, the majority of South Africans were denied the right to political participation in their government, which was therefore viewed as having "no democratic mandate" from that majority.[26] The ANC, on the contrary, encouraged universal political participation through the organization of nonviolent direct action against the illegitimate regime. The contrast between the regime's insistence on denying participation and the ANC's insistence on participation as a human right further highlights in this case the illegitimacy of the apartheid government and the genuine legitimacy of what were often referred to as South Africa's leaders in exile.[27] Through organizing mass participation, made up of the people of South Africa, the ANC promoted the common good and began to act as the legitimate authority in the midst of an illegitimate regime.

A legitimate public authority can be further defined by its intentions toward the public. A positive intention fulfills a mandate from the people, who therefore view the legitimate authority as serving their interests. Anyone, or group, proposing to overthrow a despotic regime must listen to the people and heed their voices, building revolutionary action on the desires of the wider community. This principle can be deduced from Aquinas's democratic leanings in the *Summa*[28]: "The directing of anything to the end," that is, the common good, "concerns him to whom the end belongs," the community of people.[29] Since the common good belongs to the whole community, the approval of the community is necessary to establish a legitimate public authority, whose task is to protect and promote the common good. Thus the consent of the people remains critical to the identification of a public authority vested with the moral power to conduct armed resistance.

The ANC demonstrated itself as a leader of the broader South African population in multiple ways. Under apartheid over 70 percent of South Africans were systematically excluded from the official political process.[30] Those who opposed apartheid argued that the people should make the country "ungovernable"[31] through use of strikes, boycotts, and other forms of protest. However, they were not simply anarchists. Rather, they were open to being governed by organizations in which they had a substantial participatory role, such as the ANC. This dynamic between the leaders of the revolution and other participants in it, led Buti Tlhagale to argue that "recognized leaders of the oppressed masses are the legitimate authority to lead the masses in revolt against the perpetrators of injustice."[32] In other words, organizations like the ANC partially derived their authority from the fact that they were viewed by the broader population as the legitimate leaders. The ANC, including its armed wing *Umkhonto we Sizwe*, acted in concert with the will of the people. Describing the ANC's turn to armed resistance, Malusi Mpumlwana remarked, "Black political opinion recognizes the resistance movement as doing a necessary duty of national defense against the self-imposed onslaught of government machinery."[33] Furthermore, the support enjoyed by the ANC is evidenced by the ferocity with which the government attacked its leadership, by the consistent persecution of its members,[34] and most impressively by their overwhelming political victory in the first South African democratic elections in 1994.

Finally, the legitimate authority in a revolutionary context uses force to pursue justice rather than to maintain its own power. Authority is diminished when it uses violence purely to maintain itself, or to maintain privileges that result from its position of power. Villa-Vicencio points out that "the moral legitimacy of a regime suffers in direct proportion to the violence employed to maintain law and order."[35] When the law and its coercive power is used to subvert the interests of the majority, to promote only the interests of a minority, or to secure privileges for a majority at the expense of a minority, then it violates the common good and loses the quality of legitimacy. Indeed, the UN has recently recognized this idea in its groundbreaking document *The Responsibility to Protect*. The writers of this document argue that when sovereign states use coercive power to violate the human rights of their own people—particularly in the form of genocide, ethnic cleansing, and crimes against humanity—they forfeit their sovereignty, and the global community has a responsibility to intervene.[36] Moreover, if a regime cannot maintain order without violence against its own population, it reveals that the broader population does not accept it as legitimate.

Through the just war tradition, Christian political theory has generally recognized a state's right to use force to defend itself, to maintain order, and to pursue a just peace.[37] Coercive power can be morally licit, but the role of the authority is to control, limit, and restrain violence. A legitimate public authority must be dedicated to the common good and therefore should regulate the use of force to promote order and justice. In a revolutionary context, freedom fighters may not use force indiscriminately and still be considered champions of a just revolution. This limitation is consonant with the just war theory broadly speaking: "Traditionally just war theory was intended to limit war between nations, and as a theory of just revolution it should legitimately be used in the same restraining manner."[38] The task of the legitimate authority is to limit and control violence so as to establish a just peace.

The legitimate revolutionary authority thus cares for the common good, and therefore encourages the political participation which emerges in a revolutionary context. Its commitment to the common good is evidenced by its support from the people who participate in shaping a vision of the common good. It uses coercive force only to pursue a just peace. What begins to emerge, then, is a synthesis wherein the criteria of legitimate authority, last resort, and proportionality converge in a revolutionary context. The legitimate authority uses violence only as a last resort. In the face of an illegitimate regime that uses violence with impunity, a legitimate revolutionary authority limits its use of force in accordance with principles of proportionality.

Right Intention

In the just war tradition, right intention refers to the motivation of those involved in making decisions about whether or not to engage in warfare. In my discussion of right intention in chapter 2, I noted that Augustine used the notion of right intention as a means of reconciling killing in war with the biblical mandate to love one's enemies. Augustine viewed love as crucial to right intention in warfare, since, for him, rightly ordered love is necessary for peace.[39] This conception of right intent has generated critique since it is counterintuitive, (i.e., one is not inclined to kill those whom one loves). One is not likely to be motivated by love to kill one's enemies.[40] Moreover, it does not correspond to many soldiers' actual experiences with war: they do not normally express feelings of love for those whom they are ordered to kill, nor are they encouraged by superiors to feel love for those whom they are under direction to kill.[41] Thomas Aquinas adapted the notion of right intent by shifting the focus of intentionality from love to justice. Those initiating war must intend to promote the common good through the establishment of a just peace. In this way right intention and just cause are very intimately related. Just causes are those which severely disrupt peace and justice, and a right intention is one that hopes to restore them.

An analysis of the South African struggle against apartheid yields at least one adjustment of the criterion of right intention as it has generally been understood in the just war tradition. Right intention in the context of revolution includes the intent of those who choose to employ armed resistance, as a last resort, and in accordance with a just cause, to effect eventual reconciliation with their oppressors.[42] Because reconciliation was so central to conflict resolution in South Africa via the Truth and Reconciliation Commission (TRC), the topic will be taken up more thoroughly in the next chapter; nevertheless, some comment on reconciliation will be helpful here. Whether discussing justice in the aftermath of either war or revolution, reconciliation is an important tool for staving off cycles of retaliation and revenge. Thus, any manner of conceiving a just peace must include some attention to reconciliation so as to secure that peace in a meaningful, long-lasting, and sustainable manner. An intent to reconcile is especially important given the historical tendency of victors to continue cycles of violence, punishing the vanquished with a vengeance that perpetuates feelings of enmity and hatred, and can lead to further violence. The South African struggle against apartheid illustrates that a desire for reconciliation *jus post* revolution means thoughtfulness about and planning for reconciliation both *jus ad,* and as we shall see in the section on proportionality below, *jus in* armed revolution. Reconciliation thus represents a point of intersection between these various stages of a just revolution.

The ANC demonstrated an intent to reconcile post-revolution even in the period prior to armed revolution, as they began to consider if and how to engage in armed resistance. Leaders understood that those who tear down a corrupt order must replace it with a new, just order[43] and that attempting to build a just peace would necessitate efforts at post-conflict reconciliation. Even as he began to consider the turn to armed resistance, Nelson Mandela expressed concerns that unless armed resistance was organized and directed by the ANC as a legitimate authority, it would break out spontaneously, and be directed against civilians. This, he feared, would increase racial hostility in a way that would generate cycles of retaliation and revenge, and that might even foment civil war. Mandela reveals that the intent of the ANC when it authorized the formation of its armed wing, *Umkhonto we Sizwe,* was to implement limited and controlled armed resistance that would make the possibility of future reconciliation amongst the people of South Africa more, not less, auspicious.[44]

The notion that right intention for armed revolution includes reconciliation is important to Christian ethics for at least two reasons. First, it incorporates realistically Augustine's concern for love of enemies into the motivation for armed resistance in a way that has been difficult to do for interstate warfare. Second, it points to the need for armed revolutionaries to maintain an ethical stance toward their enemies, particularly encouraging them to resist the temptation to exact vengeance and dehumanize their oppressors.

Right intention as reconciliation has the capacity and flexibility to begin to integrate love of enemies into an ethic of just revolution. I, like many just war theorists who analyze conflict in the shadow of Augustine, am hesitant to understand right intent as love of enemies for the reasons indicated above. Instead I am more comfortable with the Thomistic conception that understands intention in warfare as directed toward justice and peace as the advancement of the common good. Nevertheless the South African struggle against apartheid suggests that including a motivation of love for enemies in the criterion of right intent *jus ad* armed revolution may be reasonable and even helpful, if love is envisioned as the ongoing intent of those who use force as a last resort, and in accordance with a just cause, to effect eventual reconciliation with those whose policies and ideologies they resist. In the case of armed revolution then, "love of enemies" becomes less abstract, less likely to occupy only the requirements of a "higher" Christian life that need not be enacted in the fallen circumstances of the world.[45] Instead, right intent understood as intent to reconcile promotes respect for the human dignity of one's oppressors. Thus reconciliation will tie right intention very firmly to proportionate means since just armed revolutionaries will judge the proportionality of tactics based in part on the degree to which they inhibit the possibility of post-revolutionary reconciliation.

Second, conceiving of right intention as reconciliation may act as a check on potentially unethical responses to violent repression. Intent to reconcile restrains and reins in motivations of vengeance or the impulse to return harm for harm. Understanding oneself as motivated by the goal of future reconciliation with one's enemies may curb action based on these impulses, even if a desire for vengeance may be a normal human response to victimization.[46] To reconcile with one's enemies is, in part, to forgo vengeance. It involves a kind of insistence on the fundamental human dignity of one's oppressors, even in the face of their inhumane actions, and even as they refuse to afford one the same dignity. The tendency to demonize those against whom one fights is thus restrained by the intent to reconcile, and it is transformed instead into a struggle to humanize the enemy. Thus, right intention for revolution reminds those engaged in planning and implementing armed resistance that the enemy is a human being with whom they intend to be in a relationship, of some sort, after armed hostilities cease.

Last Resort

The principle of last resort restrains states from waging war unless all non-military options for establishing or reestablishing a just peace have been explored and exhausted. Likewise a just revolution must begin with nonviolent methods and only proceed to the use of armed resistance as a last resort. There are at least two principles governing last resort in a revolutionary context that can be derived inductively from South Africa's struggle against apartheid. An oppressed people have reached the point of last resort if (1) all forms of democratic, nonviolent resistance have been outlawed and/or met with violent repression, and (2) the regime shows no intention of deescalating its repressive practices and instead demonstrates that it views dissenting citizens as opponents to be defeated or eliminated.

During the national State of Emergency following the massacre at Sharpeville, the apartheid regime made all democratic, nonviolent forms of protest illegal. Nelson Mandela remarked that "By resorting to these drastic methods the government had hoped to silence all opposition to its harsh policies."[47] The ANC had been practicing legal forms of nonviolent protest since its inception, whether in the less confrontational manner of letter writing campaigns or the more confrontational manner of strikes, marches, and boycotts. Following the Sharpeville Massacre, to participate in protests of any kind—indeed, even to claim simple membership in many political organizations—was to commit civil disobedience, and the government responded to civil disobedience and black political participation with severe repressive violence. The ANC and the Pan-Africanist Congress (PAC), another political organization that fought to represent black South Africans,[48] were made illegal via a blanket ban.[49] Their organizers were forced underground. Marches and strikes were crushed with intense force. For example, in South Africa's Western Cape Province "strike action . . . brought industry to a standstill,"[50] so that it seemed as if South African workers were succeeding through the use of nonviolent resistance. However, the regime was determined not to tolerate dissent. "It took the police four days of continuous brutality to break the strike. They used sticks, batons, guns, and Saracen armoured cars to comb the townships and force men back to work."[51] Through its liberal use of repressive violence, the government thus created a precarious situation: an oppressed and justifiably angry populace, who had clearly demonstrated a will to participate in governing structures had no legal outlet for dissent and political participation.

It was under these circumstances that members of the ANC formed *Umkhonto we Sizwe,* "Spear of the Nation" (MK). MK became the armed wing of the ANC, dedicated to defending the people of South Africa from the apartheid regime. MK's founding document proclaims: "The time comes in the life of any nation when there remain only two choices: submit or fight . . .

The government policy of force, repression, and violence will no longer be met with nonviolent resistance only! The choice is not ours; it has been made by the Nationalist government, which has rejected every peaceable demand by the people for rights and freedom and answered every such demand with force and yet more force!"[52] The South African context illustrates an unmistakable connection between a government's use of repressive violence and the initiation of armed resistance. Villa-Vicencio affirms this point: "The politics of resistance and revolutionary struggle in South Africa cannot be understood apart from the criminalization of meaningful democratic political protest."[53] Responding to nonviolent protest with repressive violence forces an oppressed people against the rock of last resort.

Last resort is further evident when a repressive regime illustrates no intention of deescalating violence, and indeed begins to perceive its own people as enemies who must be defeated, or even eliminated. This not only represents a clear violation of the criterion of noncombatant immunity, as we shall see below; it also illustrates that the regime is willing to sacrifice the fundamental humanity of those it oppresses in order to perpetuate itself. Under such circumstances armed resistance becomes self-defense, connecting the criterion of last resort to that of just cause. Last resort is reached if a government shows no intention of scaling back force once order is achieved, but instead increases it until all dissent is eliminated. Thus a repressive regime's domestic policy resembles less a pursuit of the common good and more a military strategy of opposition to a foreign enemy.

Further illustrating the difference between a legitimate state's use of force to maintain order versus an illegitimate regime's use of force to maintain its own power, the apartheid regime developed plans to squash dissent through heightened militarization.[54] It enlisted civilians to assist in its efforts at repression and prepared its military forces for war. The government sent troops for training in then Portuguese-controlled Mozambique. It built up the size of its army, navy, air force, and police. Additionally, "road blocks [were] being set up all over the country. Armament facilities [were] being set up in Johannesburg and other cities. Officers of the South African army . . . visited Algeria and Angola where they were briefed exclusively on methods of suppressing popular struggles."[55] By all accounts, the South African regime was not aiming for the common good or even for social order, let alone preparing for negotiation or de-escalation of the conflict. Instead, it focused its energies on more intensive efforts at repression. It was not attempting to keep order, but to defeat, militarily, an opponent—South Africa's own native peoples.

In this context where the government sought to wage war against the majority of its own people, the ANC concluded that it had reached the last resort and that nonviolent measures must be coupled with limited and measured armed resistance. Led by the ANC, South Africans had used peaceful tactics for some forty years, several of which were marked by the use of concentrated, confrontational nonviolent strategies. Beginning with the Sharpeville Massacre, the government responded to peaceful protest not with negotiation or an expansion of legal political participation for the majority, but with direct repressive violence. Through its criminalization of participation, its habitual use of violence in the face of nonviolent resistance, and its demonstrated intent to wage greater violence against a citizenry it saw as enemies, the South African apartheid regime "persuaded large sections of the oppressed community seriously to consider revolutionary violence as the only option available for effective political transformation."[56] Indeed, the oppressed had been left with little choice but to accept oppression or to take up arms. Thus the South African context reveals that armed resistance should not be taken up impetuously. Nevertheless, when a program of nonviolence is consistently met with violent repression, and the state sees dissenters as opponents to be defeated militarily, the situation regrettably becomes one of last resort. As the just war tradition allows for the use of defensive armed force against an aggressor state, the oppressed have a moral option to use limited armed resistance as a means of self-defense against a repressive regime.

Reasonable Hope of Success

In the contemporary just war theory the criterion of reasonable hope of success is meant to prevent the resort to warfare when it is unlikely or improbable that force will enable the establishment of a just peace. This criterion is related to the notion that there must be a proportionate reason for going to war: the threat to peace and justice must be so severe that it outweighs the inevitable damage that will be done by war. This principle of macro-proportionality asks us to determine that a situation would be worse if we were not to engage in war; and coupled with last resort, suggests that war is the only means for establishing peace. In a related way, reasonable hope of success presumes that war is so destructive that it should not be fought unless we can expect to win. In addition to discouraging nations from fighting futile wars, reasonable hope of success also functions to encourage leaders and military strategists to be clear about the overall goals of a war and of particular missions in wars, since it is impossible to know if one can reasonably expect to win unless it is clear what constitutes victory.

Given that revolutionaries will often be far less powerful than the apparatuses of state that they oppose, reasonable hope of success may appear to be one of the criteria of the just war tradition that mitigates strongly against the notion of just revolutionary activity. However, the South African context suggests that some amendment and deepening of our conception of reasonable hope of success is necessary for understanding how this criterion ought to function for the ethics of revolution. First, we need a retrieval of the original context of this criterion in Francisco Suárez's political thought on war. Second, it is helpful to deepen our understanding of hope in the midst of oppression through an examination of theologies of hope that emerged in the context of the struggle against apartheid.

As we saw in chapter 2, we owe the presence of the criterion of reasonable hope of success in the just war tradition initially to the Spanish theologian Francisco Suárez. Suárez's understanding of this idea, however, is considerably more nuanced than how the criterion is often imagined to function today. A retrieval of this nuance makes this criterion highly applicable for revolutionary ethics. Indeed, Suárez's original intent was to moderate this principle as it had been expressed by fellow theologian Tommaso de Vio Cajetan. According to Suárez, Cajetan, in his commentary on Thomas Aquinas's *Summa Theologiae,* argued that "for a war to be just, the sovereign ought to be so sure of the degree of his power, that he is morally certain of victory."[57] In responding to, and indeed revising Cajetan's principle, Suárez argues that there are at least three reasons why "this condition [of certitude] does not appear to me to be absolutely essential."[58] First, Suárez avers that the kind of certitude of success Cajetan desires is "almost impossible of realization."[59] Second, it is often not in the interest of the common good to put off recourse to war until certitude of success is demonstrable. Finally, in perhaps the most important reason, given our concern for the ethics of revolution, Suárez states, "If the conclusion [of Cajetan] were true, a weaker sovereign would never declare war upon a stronger, since he is unable to attain the certitude which Cajetan demands."[60] Suárez's intention then in promoting reasonable hope of success was to moderate or temper the more strict need for certainty advocated by Cajetan. Certainty of success is impossible, and necessitating it prevents those who are weak from opposing the injustices of those who are strong. The implications for the ethics of revolution are rather clear. The weak, when they are subject to grave injustices that threaten peace, ought not be prevented from taking up arms against the strong simply because success is uncertain.

Indeed it is possible to glean from Suárez a kind of endorsement for armed resistance when there is a just cause requiring defense. Suárez did not universally reject the possible justice of wars of aggression or war viewed as purely punitive as we generally do today.[61] At the same time, he strongly supported the Thomistic notion that the duty of the authority is to care for the common good. He thus considered wars in defense of the common good to be at times mandatory.[62] Thus in explaining the notion of reasonable hope of success, Suárez argues, "If the expectation of victory is less apt to be realized than the chance of defeat, and if the war is offensive in character, then in almost every case that war should be avoided. If, [on the other hand] the war is defensive, it should be attempted; for in that case it is a matter of necessity, whereas the offensive war is a matter of choice."[63] Thus Suárez suggests that wars of defense are less subject to the criterion of reasonable hope of success than aggressive or punitive wars; or, in other words, that in matters of defense of life and community, which as I argued above are necessary to the criterion of just cause for armed revolutionary activity, force can, and even sometimes should, be used even if, as Suárez says, "victory is less apt to be realized than . . . defeat."[64]

This exposition on Suárez's understanding of reasonable hope of success is not meant to discount its value as a just war criterion, but rather to bolster its value as a criterion for just revolution. Indeed, in that it limits and restrains warfare, and encourages leaders to develop clear objectives and missions, this criterion is a key component of the ethics of the just war theory. Moreover, contemporary just war theorists are, like Suárez, generally aware of the impossibility of perfect certitude of success; that is why we speak of "hope" or "probability"—or as Suárez himself put it "preponderance" (likelihood) of success rather than certainty. The U.S. Bishops themselves note that "this is a difficult criterion to apply" and that "at times defense of key values, even against great odds, may be a 'proportionate' witness."[65] For the ethics of revolution we should retrieve Suárez's original conception of this criterion: it was meant as an attempt to temper Cajetan's desire for certainty of success; it was primarily a restraint against wars of choice and punishment; but it was not an absolute prohibition against defensive force in situations where there was a just cause, even if it seems as though success is less than probable. This emphasis on the moral necessity of defense is echoed centuries later by the U.S. Bishops's suggestion that "success" may sometimes need to be defined as witness to critical values.

The second adaptation of reasonable hope of success for revolutionary contexts involves how we understand hope itself. The South African context can be rather helpful in exploring the meaning and value of hope in the midst of repression and revolution since hope was an explicit subject of theological conversation and debate during the struggle against apartheid. An examination of these discussions generates two principles of revision for this criterion: (1) the oppressed themselves are the subjects of hope, thus they are in the best position to determine whether their hopes for liberation and justice are sufficiently "reasonable," and (2) the object of a reasonable hope is liberation from sinful injustice.

In *Civil Disobedience and Beyond: Law, Resistance, and Religion in South Africa,* written during perhaps apartheid's most repressive decade (1980s), Charles Villa-Vicencio argues that people who are not involved in the struggle against apartheid are in no position to tell those enduring violent repression whether or not the criterion of last resort has been met.[66] Villa-Vicencio contends that those who are subject to violent government repression, who are in danger of losing their lives or their loved ones, are in the best position to determine whether there are additional nonviolent measures that can and should be taken prior to initiating armed resistance. Those people who bear the brunt of the state's violence as a consequence of their resistance are both practically and morally best equipped to declare whether or not a last resort threshold has been passed. My contention is that this line of reasoning extends also to the criterion of reasonable hope of success. Only those who are actually enduring degrading violence, structural violence, and repressive assault are in a position to declare whether or not their hopes of defending themselves against this violence are reasonable.

The second principle of revision for understanding hope in the midst of oppression emerged via discussions among anti-apartheid Christians about the theology of hope as it relates to oppression and violence. There are at least two key documents in these discussions worth attending to. One was generated by the Southern African Catholic Bishops Conference (SACBC), and the other by a group of scholars and activists known as the Kairos theologians. Similarly to Villa-Vicencio's *Civil Disobedience and Beyond*, both of these documents were produced at the height of South Africa's mid-1980s State of Emergency. Both documents dealt explicitly with hope as a theological concept of serious importance for South Africans in the midst of their socio-political crisis. The major difference in the theologies of hope developed in these two documents concerns how they understand hope's object. The Southern African bishops determine that the object of hope is unity; the Kairos theologians, rooted in the experience of the oppressed people, argue that the object of hope is justice, which is a prerequisite for building unity, peace, and reconciliation.

At the height of the systematic repressive violence of apartheid, the South African bishops boldly argued that the subject of Christian hope is unity in the body of Christ. Given that the essence of apartheid is separation, or disunity, this was indeed an audacious, and potentially powerful theological claim. Hope, the bishops argue, is a matter of life and death— "we cannot live without some form of hope."[67] Christian hope, specifically, is hope for unity, even amongst those considered enemies. The bishops hold up the example of Jesus who prayed that his disciples "may . . . be one."[68] Thus, the Christian faith, the bishops contend, "is all about being one in Christ. It is all about Christians forming a new society, a society based on service to others, rather than the desire to dominate."[69] In this way, the bishops suggest that hope seeks to end destructive social divisions. The bishops could have been stronger and clearer in explicitly naming the oppressors as the ones who foment disunity through unjust structures and policies; in other words, they might have more clearly named social injustice, perpetrated by oppressors, as the barrier to social unity. However, they do rightly demand that "hope will, first of all, lead the privileged among us to work for the freedom of our brethren."[70] People of privilege whose social and economic interests in maintaining the status quo foment the very discord that unity seeks to dissolve must be called to account.

The bishops' document focuses heavily on sacrifice, especially the sacrifice expected of those who resist oppression. They argue that Jesus "knew well the price that had to be paid for [unity] to exist. He paid the first installment Himself—a crucifixion inflicted on Him because the love he preached and practiced was too demanding."[71] This emphasis on necessary sacrifice in order to achieve unity may be a problematic message to those already enduring humiliation, structural violence, and even direct assault at the hands of the state. Here, the price of reconciliation with enemies is literally presented as crucifixion. This might suggest that those who suffer violent repression ought to expect and even accept the violence of the state, as the cost, not of justice, but of unity. Indeed, the bishops contend, "It is not easy to suffer and, above all, die for being one with those who have oppressed you. But that is precisely what Jesus calls us to do."[72]

It may be this theology which elevates sacrificial violence inflicted on the oppressed as a means to their unity with the oppressor that prompted the development of South African liberation theology, and its understanding of hope. Liberation theologies, such as the work of Albert Nolan and of the Kairos theologians, emphasize instead God's will to free those who suffer injustices.[73] In these theologies, those who willingly sacrifice themselves do so for the cause of justice and freedom more so than unity. Unity, or reconciliation, becomes a possibility only after the oppressor attends to justice. Consider that Albert Nolan's interpretation of the cross and crucifixion diverges profoundly from the bishops'. As Nolan argues, "Unfortunately . . . Christian Churches have tamed and domesticated the cross. It has become a symbol of love and self-sacrifice . . . The cross was a gruesome instrument of torture and punishment . . . Jesus was one of the oppressed struggling to free all who suffered under the yoke of repression."[74] Jesus's death on the cross was, for Nolan, less a sought after means to sacrifice himself for unity than the unjust and repressive consequence of his resistance to oppression, and his life lived in liberative praxis on behalf of the poor and vulnerable.

The Kairos Document is a theological reflection condemning apartheid, and a call to resistance that is rooted in hope for justice. Many of the themes and ideas presented in *The Kairos Document* resonate in other repressive socio-political situations. The method used to develop the document ensured that the oppressed themselves voiced their experiences and collaborated in forming a response to apartheid from the perspective of Christian ethics. A group of over thirty ordinary lay people, theologians, and Church leaders who wanted to address the growing crisis of violent repression initiated a process of theological reflection. Over the course of several discussions, initial drafts of the document were developed and then these were widely disseminated across South Africa to elicit a broad range of feedback. "Everybody was told that this was a people's document which you can also own even by demolishing it if your position can stand the test of biblical faith and Christian experience in South Africa."[75] The response was tremendous, illustrating a strong desire for theological reflection among the oppressed on their personal experience of degrading, structural, and direct violence. The result is a South African liberation theology that is thoroughly rooted in the experience of the oppressed themselves.

A major theme of the document is hope. Whereas the South African bishops argued that the object of hope is unity, the Kairos theologians contend that it is justice. Indeed, *The Kairos Document* explicitly rejects the idea that unity may be achieved in a situation of oppression without explicit prior attention to justice: "It would be quite wrong to try to preserve 'peace' and 'unity' at all costs, even at the cost of truth and justice and, worse still, at the cost of thousands of young lives."[76] Moreover, the Kairos theologians admit that what they call "Church theology" is attentive to justice. However, they suggest that the Churches advocate for *"the justice of reform*, that is to say, a justice that is determined by the oppressor . . . that is offered to the people as a kind of concession."[77] This kind of justice is not sufficient to address problems of structural violence. "It has not worked and it never will work."[78]

Instead, Christian hope—which the Kairos theologians view as a mandate of the faith—is a deep desire for the Reign of God, a political community marked by "goodness and justice and love" where "tyranny and oppression cannot last."[79] This hope for justice is not primarily eschatological: "We believe that God is at work in our world turning hopeless and evil situations to good so that his 'Kingdom may come' and his 'Will may be done on earth as it is in heaven.'"[80] Christian hope is hope not only for salvation from death, but also for justice in this life, on earth. Their Christian faith leads the Kairos theologians to view the Reign of God as an inevitability, but one that will require intensification of resistance to sin and evil. *The Kairos Document* affirms the possibility of morally legitimate armed resistance[81] because it may be the case that "there is no other way to remove the injustice and oppression."[82] Here hope prioritizes justice, with unity, peace, and reconciliation flowing from justice.

What these discussions of hope in the midst of the struggle against apartheid reveal is that for the criterion of reasonable hope of success to be meaningful for just revolution, our theology of hope must be thoroughly rooted in the context of repression. Thus a "reasonable" hope must be allowed to be any hopes for liberation from injustice. Hope for the Reign of God, free from sin and its destructive effects, is constitutive of the Christian faith. Without hope for justice Christianity fails to be meaningful in a context of oppression. Moreover, while they differ on acceptable forms of resistance, both the South African bishops and the Kairos theologians agree that hope requires resistance. Indeed resisting degrading, structural, and direct violence may be the only truly reasonable response to it. This resistance should always begin nonviolently, but it may—in concert with a just cause, as last resort, undertaken proportionately, with a right intention, and directed by a legitimate revolutionary authority—also involve armed force.

JUS IN ARMED REVOLUTION

Proportionate Means

Once the legitimate authority within a just revolutionary movement has determined that it has reached the point of last resort, and has decided to implement armed resistance, it must consider the question of means. In the just war tradition this involves adherence to the criterion of proportionate means, which functions *in bello* to restrict the weaponry and tactics of warfare to avoid unnecessary harm. Thus, having determined under what circumstances an oppressed people have the right to defensive armed resistance, I turn now to the question of proportionate means for this resistance.

We can glean from the South African context a threefold rule of proportionality in a just revolution. This rule prioritizes the resolution of conflicts in such a way that the possibility of post-revolutionary reconciliation—in accordance with right intention—is left open: (1) armed resistance should be graduated, beginning with those means that intend to incur no loss of life, (2) opportunity for negotiation should be offered regularly, and (3) armed resistance should escalate to forms that include loss of life only as is necessary to promote negotiation, and to decrease overall violence. This last principle is bolstered by three reasons, considered below, as to how armed resistance may function to decrease overall violence in an oppressive context.

The legitimate revolutionary authority should begin armed resistance with the intent to incur no loss of human life whatsoever. Armed resistance should only escalate to acts of killing if the oppressive regime continues to repress the people and refuses to negotiate a just peace and enfranchise the entire population to participate legally and meaningfully in the political life of the society. Thus proportionality in the revolutionary context demands that armed resistance be slowly graduated as is necessary to force negotiation and to leave open the possibility of post-revolutionary reconciliation.

In concert with its commitment to minimize the loss of human life, Nelson Mandela commanded MK "to start with the form of violence that inflicted the least harm against individuals: sabotage."[83] MK targeted various government installations, including administration buildings, post offices, and electrical and railway facilities.[84] Implicitly acknowledging the importance of a slow escalation of armed resistance, Mandela remarked that he hoped sabotage would "bring the government and its supporters to its senses before it [was] too late, so that the government and its policies [could] be changed before matters reach[ed] the desperate state of civil war."[85] Note the goal of the just revolutionary who employs armed resistance: The aim is not to bring enemies to their knees, but rather to create "a climate of urgency that would emphasize the necessity of a negotiation process."[86] For Mandela the gradual escalation of armed resistance, beginning with less devastating acts of force, left open the possibility of eventual reconciliation because it "offered the most hope for future race relations."[87]

When acts of sabotage did not succeed in promoting negotiations, the ANC escalated to guerrilla tactics. The initial attempts at forcing negotiation through guerrilla warfare occurred in the late 1960s when MK forces attempted to enter South Africa through then Rhodesia in what are known as the Wankie and Sipolilo campaigns.[88] Fighting between MK and Rhodesian and South African Defense Forces was valuable in highlighting weaknesses in MK's strategies and organization, including the necessity of further mobilizing mass support.

As part of a gradual escalation of armed resistance, in the 1980s, MK resumed sabotage but with more serious consequences, and accepting the possibility of loss of life. Explosions occurred in and around power plants, military bases, and government buildings. "Extensive structural damage was caused . . . a number of military personnel were killed and a number of civilians were also killed."[89] This escalation of armed tactics "reflected a shift away from symbolic military actions,"[90] toward more intense armed struggle, but the initiation of tactics that would include loss of life was not taken up lightly. Speaking for the ANC, Chris Hani implicitly expressed a commitment to the just war tradition's principle of double-effect, referred to in chapter 2, in considering micro-proportionality: "We further accepted that some civilians might be caught in the crossfire. Apartheid was definitely at war with our people and we understood that in a situation of war some casualties, though unintended, might be unavoidable. But we remained emphatic that we would not deliberately choose white civilians."[91] Thus, Hani illustrates that in a just revolution, like a just war, the means of armed resistance must be proportionate and civilians must never be intended as direct targets.

Mindful of the *jus ad bellum* commitment of right intention for a just peace marked by post-conflict reconciliation, revolutionaries must attend carefully to the notion of a gradual escalation of armed resistance as crucial to fulfilling the requirement of proportionate means. As shown above, this priority of using only what force is necessary to promote peace and justice, indeed limiting and restraining the use of force, is one of the factors that makes an authority legitimate.

The ANC's commitment to a gradual escalation of armed force can be most clearly seen by comparing *Umkhonto we Sizwe* to *Poqo,* the armed wing of the Pan-Africanist Congress. *Poqo* means "pure" or "alone."[92] Its name emphasized the PAC's understanding of the movement against apartheid as being the particular struggle of black South Africans to the exclusion of other racial groups, an ideology not shared by the ANC. Despite serious failures of some individuals, as an organization the ANC generally displayed both patience and discipline in the face of the apartheid regime. It might be argued that *Poqo* represented those South Africans who, perhaps justifiably, could no longer be patient when confronted with apartheid's horrors. *Poqo* was the first resistance organization in South Africa to use killing as a revolutionary means. Contrasting *Poqo* with the ANC, South African theologians Allan Boesak and Alan Brews note, "There were those who from the initiation of the armed struggle acted with less restraint . . . [*Poqo*] because of its more militant ideology, was less controlled than *Umkhonto*."[93]

The ANC, on the contrary, conceived of the movement against apartheid as a "protracted struggle."[94] The gradual escalation of armed resistance fit well with this notion. For the ANC, revolution was understood as a lengthy endeavor requiring intense patience and discipline. In the title of his autobiography, Nelson Mandela describes the work for freedom as a "long walk." It is significant that it is a walk, not a race. There is no running or rushing the just revolution. A commitment to a just peace marked by reconciliation is a commitment to gradual escalation, with ongoing opportunities for negotiation and an end to violence.[95]

Through the use of gradually escalating acts of armed resistance and a standing invitation to negotiation, the just revolutionary seeks to decrease the overall violence within a given conflict situation. This goal may sound counterintuitive: take up arms to decrease violence. Yet, we must bear in mind not only the armed resistance of the revolutionaries but also the violence of the oppressive regime, including the degradation, structural violence with its attendant serious consequences, and direct repressive assaults.[96] Thus restricted armed resistance against an illegitimate government can become a moral option when it is used by a legitimate authority with a right intention, as a last resort to decrease overall violence and establish a just peace.

The limited use of armed resistance in a revolutionary context may help decrease overall violence for three reasons. First, proportionate armed resistance conducted by a legitimate authority as a last resort can control and limit violent resistance and thereby increase the possibility of post-conflict reconciliation. Second, armed resistance can provide a sign of hope to oppressed people who are then less likely to respond with spontaneous, undisciplined acts of violence. Third, proportionate armed resistance can relieve ordinary noncombatants of the burden of violence and free them to continue nonviolent strategies.

First, the ANC understood itself as invested with a grave responsibility to limit violence. The ANC turned to armed resistance reluctantly, only after all other options had failed.[97] Under the ANC's leadership initial acts of armed resistance were calculated to limit the loss of human life. In initial debates about the use of revolutionary armed force, Nelson Mandela argued that unless the ANC led the nation in armed resistance, spontaneous civilian violence would erupt. "Many people were already forming military units on their own," Mandela asserted.[98] "Unless responsible leadership was given to canalize and control the feelings of the people, there would be outbreaks of terrorism which would produce an intensity of bitterness and hostility between the various races of this country."[99] Thus Mandela suggested that should the ANC control and limit armed resistance, (i.e., "canalize and control the feelings of the people"), this redirection would actually prevent terrorism and potentially decrease spontaneous violent acts. Moreover, "responsible leadership" that can control and limit violence and provide an alternative to civilian-formed terrorist cells offered more hope for future reconciliation between South Africa's disparate racial groups, which, as we have already seen is a necessary vision for the ethics of *jus ad* armed revolution. The *jus in* armed revolution criterion of proportionality thus links back to the *jus ad* criterion of right intention, and forward toward *jus post* revolution.

Again, a comparison of the ANC's armed wing, MK, to the Pan-Africanist Congress's armed wing, *Poqo* is helpful to illustrate the point that just revolutionaries should seek to use armed resistance to limit overall violence. While the ANC revered planning, organization, and discipline, the PAC encouraged spontaneous acts of civil disobedience and violent resistance. "The PAC approach was characterized by the belief that all they had to do was provide the spark and the fire would automatically catch alight . . . . The ANC on the other hand, held that even the spontaneous responses of the masses require careful direction."[100] To endeavor to decrease overall violence in the context of armed revolution means that the legitimate authority should exercise disciplined and restrained armed resistance. Indeed, as we have seen, doing so is part of what makes an authority legitimate.

Second, armed struggle can decrease overall violence when it functions as a sign of hope to the oppressed. Given the dictatorial nature of the apartheid regime and its disproportionate and brutal response to nonviolent dissent, noncombatants felt the need for a means of self-defense. In their desperation, people were becoming more willing to employ violence to defend themselves and "violence [had] increased where responsible leadership had been prevented from fulfilling its role" of limiting and regulating the use of force.[101] In the midst of this volatile situation, Boesak and Brews note that oppressed

South Africans began to view MK as their defense force.[102] Since they now had legitimate defenders employing armed resistance on their behalf, ordinary civilians were less likely to feel the need to initiate violent acts themselves. MK provided a common defense, which was "a welcome sign of hope" for the real possibility of liberation from injustice for black South Africans.[103]

Third, armed resistance instituted by a legitimate authority as a last resort can decrease overall violence because it relieves noncombatants of the burden of violence and frees them to continue nonviolent resistance. Reassured that a trained, armed force with concern for the common good was acting on their behalf, the vast majority of South Africans were free to continue to participate in the revolution through nonviolent means. They continued to organize marches, strikes, boycotts, and other forms of civil disobedience. They continued to organize international pressure against the illegitimate regime. These nonviolent methods were crucial to toppling the apartheid government and should be encouraged by the leadership of revolutionary movements. Additionally, the continuation of these nonviolent measures bolstered the ANC's moral authority and thus ensured continued support from a number of churches and foreign governments. By taking on the role of armed defenders, MK freed the rest of the ANC and the majority of South Africans from the onus of armed resistance, instead allowing them to concentrate on nonviolent resistance toward the goals of liberation and reconciliation. Working in tandem, both armed and nonviolent strategies can shorten the duration of the revolution, decrease desperate resorts to terrorism, and hasten an end to the repressive regime without spiraling into a protracted and more violent civil war.

MK showed restraint in its use of force and thus demonstrated a keen implicit understanding of the just war tradition. The leadership of MK seemed to comprehend that simply because the struggle had arrived at the point of last resort did not mean that just any acts of armed resistance were acceptable. Indeed, Joseph Lelyveld, a former foreign correspondent for the *New York Times,* once suggested that the ANC ought to be considered among the world's least effective liberation movements. This comment prompted Charles Villa-Vicencio to note the restraint with which the ANC carried out armed resistance. Villa-Vicencio remarked, "If efficacy is measured in terms of violence (and one would hope not) this may well be true!"[104] What is notable, however, is that history suggests that the ANC, in terms of its limits on the use of armed force, has been among the most effective liberation movements as it brokered a transition to democracy that was as peaceful as South Africa's was and that left open the possibility of post-conflict reconciliation. The ANC was focused on the common good of the entire people. By pursuing proportional armed resistance designed to provoke negotiation and eventually lead to a state that would allow for the participation of everyone, the ANC demonstrated itself time and again as a legitimate authority. The relatively peaceful transition to democracy suggests that the ANC's approach is not only politically effective but also morally licit. This approach reveals key principles that can be employed by other movements of political resistance toward social transformation.

The criterion of proportionate means thus takes on a robust role in the context of just revolution. It demands that armed resistance be implemented gradually, always inviting the regime to negotiate. It seeks to limit loss of life and decrease overall violence in order to promote future reconciliation between enemies. Keeping in mind the goal of reconciliation, proportionality requires that revolutionary armed resistance never exceed that which is needed to force dialogue with repressors because any more force would subvert the goal of reconciliation. As a legitimate form of defense in which civilians can place their hope, proportionate armed resistance can decrease spontaneous violence. In this spirit of hope, noncombatants are freed to continue their participation in the form of nonviolent resistance which works together with armed resistance toward the goal of a just peace.

Noncombatant Immunity

In the just war theory, the criterion of noncombatant immunity functions to protect civilians, as much as possible, from the effects of war. It prohibits direct intentional targeting of civilians, and, in general, of purely civilian infrastructure. Understanding how this criterion functions for revolutionary ethics requires analyzing it from two angles: first from the perspective of the regime's activity in repressing a popular uprising, and second from the perspective of how armed revolutionaries ought to proceed in carrying out resistance. The first angle yields two points: (1) A despotic regime is illegitimate and therefore may not justly use force. Its only morally licit option is to relinquish power. (2) Presuming a regime will not hand over power, it nevertheless has a clear responsibility to distinguish between combatants, or armed revolutionaries, and noncombatants; and to treat captured combatants in accordance with the standards dictated by international law.

Throughout the discussion of *jus ad* armed revolution criteria, I noted that a despotic regime which finds itself under justified attack by armed revolutionaries has already engaged in violence against civilian noncombatants. It is largely a regime's violent and repressive activity against its own citizens that satisfies criteria such as just cause and last resort for the ethics of revolution. What must first and foremost be acknowledged, then, in understanding how the criterion of noncombatant immunity functions for revolutionary ethics, is that the predominant reason that armed resistance can be considered in the first place lies in a regime's disregard for the sanctity of human life; its perpetuation of degrading, structural, and direct repressive violence, often including the torture, maiming, and killing of civilians. South African apartheid provides dozens of harrowing examples of direct assaults against civilians both prior to and during the initiation of armed resistance by MK; from the Sharpeville Massacre, to the death in police custody of Black Consciousness Movement founder, Steve Biko, to the killings of protesters during the Soweto Uprisings, to the regular detention and torture of political prisoners.[105]

No person, whether a combatant or a civilian, may legitimately be targeted by a tyrannical regime that maintains its power against the will of the people and at their expense. The fundamental illegitimacy of a despotic regime extends to its activities of suppressing the popular struggle of the people to participate in their own governing structures. Such a regime has no moral recourse other than to negotiate a transition of power that acknowledges the people's desire to participate in the political process in a normalized manner. Tyranny may not morally defend itself using force. Thomas Aquinas's statements on sedition remain some of the clearest on this point. Sedition is sinful because it is opposed to the unity and peace of a people, manifest in the common good.[106] By definition, however, tyranny is directed "not to the common good, but to the private good of the ruler."[107] While Aquinas does not use the term "revolution," action to overcome such a regime is also not characterized as sedition. Instead, "the tyrant rather . . . is guilty of sedition, since he encourages discord and sedition among his subjects, that he may lord over them more securely; for this is tyranny, being conducive to the private good of the ruler, and to the injury of the multitude."[108] Since it is illegitimate, indeed seditious, a tyrannical regime cannot morally use force. Coercive force, for Thomas Aquinas and for the just war tradition generally speaking, is the prerogative only of a *legitimate* authority.

Obviously, however, many regimes will refuse to concede that they are indeed illegitimate. The apartheid regime characterized those who took up arms in resistance to tyranny as "terrorists" and viewed itself as just in using the coercive and violent power of the state to curb what they viewed as treasonous activities.[109] In a situation where a regime does not acknowledge its own illegitimacy, it is still morally and legally bound by the criterion of noncombatant immunity. The question then becomes how to distinguish combatants from noncombatants in revolutionary resistance. Using the via negativa, combatants are *not* persons whose activities only include supporting, politically, ideologically, or even materially (via financial or other resources), the efforts of armed resistance. Michael Walzer makes this point quite clearly in his discussion of guerrilla warfare: "Even when he sympathizes with the goal of the guerrillas, we can assume that the average citizen would rather vote for them than hide them in his house . . . the services [the people] provide [to guerrilla soldiers] are nothing more than the functional equivalent of the services civilians have always provided for soldiers."[110] In a just revolution, it is the structure of political life that is to blame for civilian support of armed resistance, and it thus is this structure that must change. There is no justification for killing civilians who support armed resistance politically, ideologically, or materially. To echo Walzer, they would rather participate in a normal political process than feed and shelter armed defenders. Moreover, persons engaging in nonviolent resistance but not armed resistance are never legitimate targets. Nonviolence marks one as an opponent of a regime, not a combatant.

A final note on how the criterion of noncombatant immunity ought to function for regimes who view themselves as legitimate despite a massive popular revolutionary campaign involves how the government ought to treat captured agents of armed resistance. Again Walzer's work on guerrilla warfare is instructive here. He contends that "any significant degree of popular support entitles the guerrillas to benevolent quarantine customarily offered prisoners of war."[111] In such cases, the people demonstrate that they view revolutionaries as their legitimate leaders. The popular support of the people functions as a moral safeguard (if not a physical one) against their abuse in custody. Indeed, to torture or execute agents of armed resistance in a just revolution is to further compromise a despotic regime and to further illustrate its illegitimacy.

The second angle from which the criterion of noncombatant immunity must be explored for revolutionary ethics is from the perspective of those conducting armed resistance. Here, the South African context generates three principles for how armed revolutionaries must implement noncombatant immunity in a just revolution: (1) Armed resistance ought to be declared so that combatants make themselves known; (2) As in a just war, armed resistance must not directly and intentionally target civilians; (3) Related to number two, organizations of armed resistance should investigate and police their own agents if abuses are alleged and/or if there is evidence that abuses have occurred.

Armed revolution, like war, must be declared so that armed revolutionaries acknowledge themselves to be combatants and assume the risks involved in combat. A declaration of armed resistance satisfies a moral norm: it mitigates, to a degree, the criticism Walzer levies against combatants who aim to deceive their opponents by hiding among and pretending to be ordinary civilians so as to use civilian life, not only to mask armed activities, but also as a platform for launching them.[112] It also provides a vehicle for revolutionaries to state their grievances, to give the reasons for their resort to force, and to propose the conditions under which they would discontinue armed resistance. Thus in declaring the resort to force, armed revolutionaries explain the revolutionary cause publically, to the community of nations, and may even draw desirable international support. In South Africa, after decades of nonviolent tactics, MK coupled their initiation of the use of force with a clear declaration of armed resistance. The first acts of sabotage "were accompanied by the distribution of the Umkhonto we Sizwe manifesto."[113] The document declared the onset of armed resistance and stated that "*Umkhonto we Sizwe* will be at the front line of the people's defense. It will be the fighting arm of the people against the government and its policies of race oppression."[114] The distribution of the manifesto allowed the ANC to state the grievances of the people and make their demands clear to the regime. The declaration cites racial oppression, the use of violent repression against unarmed protesters, and the escalation of military training for the purposes of countering protesters as grievances.[115] It laments that the situation in South Africa has arrived at the last resort of armed resistance, and makes clear the people's demands for "the abolition of white supremacy and the winning of liberty, democracy and full national rights and equality for all the people of this country."[116] In declaring themselves in this way armed revolutionaries acknowledge themselves as combatants against injustice, in favor of a just peace.

The second and third requirements of noncombatant immunity for a just revolution are related. Armed revolutionaries may not carry out direct, intentional attacks on civilians. To do so is both unethical and validates the charge of "terrorism" that may be brought against revolutionaries by a tyrannical regime. As discussed above in the section on proportionality, armed resistance should be graduated, beginning with those methods that intend to incur no loss of life, and should escalate to acts that include killing only insofar as it becomes necessary to force negotiation and a transition of power. Acts of direct, intentional killing should never be carried out against civilians, even those who support politically, ideologically, or materially, a regime. Likewise, any enemy combatants or prisoners detained by armed revolutionaries ought to be afforded the humane treatment demanded in the conventions of international law.

Finally, armed revolutionaries should investigate and hold responsible their members who do commit violations of human rights. This requirement is demonstrated by the ANC's decision to initiate two truth and reconciliation commissions to investigate allegations of abuse by prisoners in ANC detention facilities during the years of armed struggle against apartheid. While these detainees were not noncombatants, the actions of the ANC nevertheless demonstrate the importance of investigating and holding responsible members of the revolutionary movement for violations of human rights and international law. Priscilla B. Hayner, program director for the International Center for Transitional Justice, notes that "the African National Congress (ANC) is the only example of an armed resistance group that independently established a commission to investigate and publically report on its own past abuses."[117] The initial Commission of Enquiry into Complaints by Former African National Congress Prisoners and Detainees was held in 1992. Its seventy-four page report of abuses inflicted on detainees was made public by the ANC. "Nelson Mandela accepted collective responsibility on behalf of the leadership of the ANC for 'serious abuses and irregularities' that had occurred, but insisted that individuals should not be named or held personally accountable."[118] Nevertheless, problems with the first commission prompted the development of a second—the Commission of Enquiry into Certain Allegations of Cruelty and Human Rights Abuse Against ANC Prisoners and Detainees by ANC Members—held in 1993.[119] The ANC accepted the "general conclusions" of the commission[120] and these experiences prompted the ANC to call for a national truth commission to investigate abuses and violations of human rights on all sides of the South African conflict. This call would eventually be answered by the establishment of the Truth and Reconciliation Commission.[121]

Even though these commissions dealt largely with abuses committed not against civilians but against detainees who were at least presumed to have been enemy combatants, they nevertheless point to the need for revolutionary movements to respect human rights in the form of noncombatant immunity. They provide a model for other resistance organizations in that they express the importance of investigating and acknowledging responsibility for wrongs committed. Highlighting responsibility in this way epitomizes the criterion of noncombatant immunity that ought to characterize a just revolution.

The criterion of noncombatant immunity, when it is respected in accordance with the principles I have outlined, thus functions in a revolutionary context to shield civilians from both the violence of the regime and of armed resistance. It requires that a clear distinction between combatants and noncombatants be respected by both the regime and freedom fighters. For the regime, this involves accepting norms of international law insofar as nonviolent protesters are not viewed as legitimate targets; and captured combatants are treated in accordance with their basic human rights. For revolutionaries, it will involve a declaration of armed resistance that functions to acknowledge themselves as combatants, who are willing to assume the risks of combat. In addition, it requires that revolutionary movements hold themselves to the highest standards of the protection and promotion of human rights by investigating and acknowledging abuse of these rights in their own ranks.

THE TANDEM APPROACH

Having highlighted both strategies for waging nonviolent revolution and principles to guide armed revolution, I turn now to what I have been calling "the tandem approach" to revolution that emerges from the South African context. The "tandem approach" refers to the simultaneous use of both nonviolent and armed revolutionary strategies against an oppressive regime. The South African context illustrates that in a revolution that seeks to be just, there are at least three reasons why it is important to try to continue to organize and practice nonviolence resistance even after the initiation of limited graduated armed resistance.

First, nonviolent strategies even alongside armed resistance may help hasten an end to repressive regimes, especially when they divide the regime's forces and its capacity to engage revolutionaries. The tandem resistance of MK guerrilla tactics and the Soweto Uprisings provide an example of this dynamic. In 1976, the Soweto Uprisings reignited nonviolent direct action in South Africa after a period in which the severe repression of the regime had been somewhat successful in squelching nonviolent dissent. Soweto is the largest black township in Johannesburg, South Africa's largest city. In response to severe poverty, rising unemployment, and inequalities in education for black students, including the "introduction of Afrikaans, 'the language of the oppressor,' as a teaching medium for some subjects,"[122] the South African Students' Movement (SASM) launched a successful boycott of Soweto schools, followed by a demonstration in June 1976. Police repression of the demonstration led to more than 150 deaths and unleashed over a year of nonviolent resistance against the regime.[123] Prior to the uprising, the struggle against apartheid had largely shifted to areas outside of South Africa, as the South African Defense Forces engaged MK fighters on the border with then Rhodesia (now Zimbabwe).[124] The Soweto Uprisings forced the regime to conduct repression on two fronts—both at the border in its response to armed struggle, and internally in its response to nonviolent struggle. While it would take another fourteen years before the regime would begin to negotiate with the ANC, the Soweto Uprisings nevertheless signaled that the regime would not remain in power indefinitely. Apartheid could not last under the pressure of armed resistance, nonviolent resistance, and international economic intervention in the form of sanctions and divestiture. Indeed, in the case of the struggle against apartheid, one could also argue that nonviolent resistance in the form of international economic pressure constituted a third front on which the apartheid regime had to defend itself. These multiple sources of resistance and dissent both provide cover for those engaged in armed resistance and make it difficult for a regime to maintain normal governing activities.

Second, specifically from the perspective of Christian social ethics, nonviolent resistance in principle stresses the ideal of social and political transformation without recourse to killing and as such testifies to the inherent dignity of the human person, made in the image and likeness of God, whose fundamental right to life generally ought not be violated. Unfortunately, as both the South African context and the more recent revolutions across the Middle East have made abundantly clear, this ideal is not often met, even in revolutions that have not resorted to the use of armed force. Targeting and killing of nonviolent protesters has been a feature of these revolutions, and at times a catalyst for armed resistance. Nevertheless, when the bulk of internal resistance to a regime is nonviolent, as was the case in the South African revolution, the dignity of the human person is rightly emphasized by those who seek liberation. Moreover, the emphasis on human dignity through the use of nonviolent resistance lends a sense of moral authority to the revolution and its leaders, which can draw the attention of the international community and elicit assistance in the cause.

Third, nonviolent practices provide a meaningful role for noncombatants in revolutionary struggle, and indeed as we saw above, they help to clarify who may be considered combatants and who may not. Both the South African experience and the Arab Spring revolutions demonstrate that ordinary people often want to participate in revolutionary action against their oppressors. This desire for participation is itself a signal toward democracy and human rights that bodes well for peacebuilding and governance *jus post* revolution. Still, armed resistance, while it can be morally licit in accordance with the principles I have discussed, is not an activity that the majority of people are able to participate in, especially not in a way that allows for the disciplined and limited use of force. On the other hand, all persons can find ways to participate in some form of nonviolent resistance against oppression, and this nonviolent activity marks them as *opponents* to the regime as opposed to *combatants*.

The ways in which nonviolent just peacemaking practices were used, even alongside armed struggle, in the South African revolution indicates the great value of nonviolent practices for those currently resisting despotic regimes. Even in revolutionary situations that have arrived at the point of "last resort" and have chosen to implement armed resistance, nonviolent strategies can work in tandem with armed ones to divide a regime's focus and hasten its demise, to testify to the dignity of human life, and to give all people who want to participate a role in resisting the regime, while clearly marking them as noncombatants.

CONCLUSION

I have argued that Christian ethicists can draw principles from the South African struggle for understanding the just war theory "from below." When viewed in the context of repression the traditional criteria of the just war theory—just cause, legitimate authority, right intention, last resort, reasonable hope of success, proportionality, and noncombatant immunity—function both to justify the use of force by an oppressed people enduring gross violations of human rights, and also to limit and restrain the use of revolutionary force. This theory of just revolution thus constitutes a Christian ethics of armed resistance against tyranny.

A tandem approach to revolution, where nonviolent and armed strategies work together simultaneously, can provide hopeful prospects for overcoming oppression toward peace and justice. The South African revolution illustrates that a tandem approach that includes nonviolent strategies and limited armed resistance in accordance with revised just war principles can contribute to the goal of a just peace. While some may claim that despotism and repression make just peacemaking approaches seem naïve and unsustainable, the South African example illustrates that it is exactly in these situations that the nonviolent practices of just peacemaking theory are indispensable. Working together with armed resistance, the strategies of just peacemaking theory act as a palpable reminder that the goal of all armed force is a just peace, and that impulses toward revenge or disproportionate violence must be resisted in favor of eventual reconciliation. In revolutionary situations, the broad array of nonviolent practices of just peacemaking theory become the primary way that most individuals resist the regime. Thus while I advocate a repressed people's right to armed resistance, I also argue that nonviolent strategies remain crucial to overcoming oppression. Indeed, it may be the case that the nonviolent strategies of just peacemaking theory are primary in struggles against despotism and armed strategies are secondary, acting only to supplement the practices of just peacemaking so as to force negotiation toward social transformation.

NOTES

1. Mark J. Allman and Tobias L. Winright, *After the Smoke Clears: The Just War Tradition and Post-War Justice*(Maryknoll, NY: Orbis Books, 2010), 38.

2. James Childress, "Just War Criteria" in *War or Peace,* T.A. Shannon, ed., (Maryknoll, NY: Orbis Books, 1980), 40.

3. Hannah Arendt, *On Revolution* (New York: Penguin Books, 1990), 35.

4. Allman and Winright, 40. It should be noted that under the norm of "the responsibility to protect" recent international law also views as potentially legitimate a multilateral military intervention aimed at protecting people from genocide or gross violations of human rights. See The International Commission on Intervention and State Sovereignty, *The Responsibility to Protect* (Ottawa: International Development Research Center, 2001), 4.19–4.24.

5. William Beinart, *Twentieth Century South Africa* (New York: Oxford University Press, 2001), 158. Beinart is quoting from Deborah Posel, *The Making of Apartheid 1948–1961* (New York: Oxford University Press, 1991).

6. From Nelson Mandela's second court statement during the Rivonia Trial, 1964. Available in Nelson Mandela, *The Struggle Is My Life* (New York: Pathfinder Press, 1988), 180.

7. Albert Nolan, *God in South Africa* (Grand Rapids, MI: Wm. B. Eerdmans Publishing Co., 1988), 57.

8. Paul Farmer, Bruce Nizeye, Sara Stulac, and Salmaan Keshavjee, "Structural Violence and Clinical Medicine," PLoS Med 3(10), e449. DOI: 10.1371/journal.pmed.0030449 (2006). Emphasis in the original. Open access available at http://www.plosmedicine.org/article/info%3Adoi%2F10.1371%2Fjournal.pmed.0030449#s2.

9. Desmond Tutu, "Freedom Fighters or Terrorists?" in *Theology and Violence: The South African Debate*, Charles Villa-Vicencio, ed., (Grand Rapids, MI: Wm B. Eerdmans Publishing Co., 1988), 74.

10. There are multiple resources that attest to these forms of repression in the South African context. Especially important is the report of South Africa's Truth and Reconciliation Commission available at http://www.justice.gov.za/Trc/report/index.htm. Another text that gives voice to the victims of repressive assault and other forms of violence during the apartheid era is Antjie Krog's *Country of My Skull: Guilt, Sorrow, and the Limits of Forgiveness in the New South Africa* (New York: Three Rivers Press, 2000).

11. Beinart, 166.

12. For a full analysis of this event see Tom Lodge, *Sharpeville: An Apartheid Massacre and Its Consequences* (New York: Oxford University Press, 2011).

13. Mark J. Allman, *Who Would Jesus Kill: War, Peace, and the Christian Tradition* (Winona, MN: St. Mary's Press, 2008), 196. See also Daniel M. Bell, Jr., "Just War and Counterinsurgency: Discriminating Force," *Christian Century* (August 7, 2013), 22.

14. John 19:11.

15. Augustine, *Contra Faustum*, XXII.75. Available at http://www.newadvent.org/fathers/1406.htm.

16. See Thomas Aquinas, *Summa Theologiae*, I.II 90.3 and 4. Translated by Fathers of the English Dominican Province. Available at http://www.newadvent.org/summa/.

17. Aquinas, II.II.42.2 ad 3.

18. It is possible that there may be more than one authoritative group working together toward the goal of a just peace.

19. See James M. Blythe, "The Mixed Constitution in Aquinas," *Journal of the History of Ideas* 47.4 (1986): 547–565.

20. See *Compendium of the Social Doctrine of the Church*, Pontifical Council for Justice and Peace, ed. (Washington DC: United States Conference of Catholic Bishops, 2005), 189–191.

21. Meghan J. Clark, "Integrating Human Rights: Participation in John Paul II, Catholic Social Thought and Amartya Sen," *Political Theology* 8.3 (2007), 302.

22. Consider the importance of the principle subsidiarity in Catholic social thought. Subsidiarity promotes participation in the structures which most intimately affect our lives, largely because it is believed that those who are most affected by a given institution or situation have the most invested in its well-being or outcome and are thus best equipped to shape it in accordance with the common good.

23. Wael Ghonim, *Revolution 2.0* (New York: Houghton, Mifflin, Harcourt, 2012). Moreover, Al Jazeera English's senior political analyst, Marwan Bishara, in his book on the Arab Spring describes activism and participation as major features of the revolutionary movements in Libya, Syria, Tunisia, and Yemen (Marwan Bishara, *The Invisible Arab: The Promise and Peril of the Arab Revolution* [New York: Nation Books, 2012]).

24. Charles Villa-Vicencio, *Civil Disobedience and Beyond: Law, Resistance, and Religion in South Africa* (Grand Rapids, MI: Wm. B. Eerdmans Publishing Co., 1990), 106.

25. The Kairos Theologians, *The Kairos Document*, 4. Available at http://www.sahistory.org.za/archive/challenge-church-theological-comment-political-crisis-south-africa-kairos-document-1985.

26. Malusi Mpumlwana, "Legitimacy and Struggle," in *Theology and Violence: The South African Debate*, 91.

27. See for example Mpumlwana, 95.

28. I use the word "leanings" because I do not intend to suggest that Thomas Aquinas was an advocate of the modern democratic state. Nevertheless, James M. Blythe cogently argues that Aquinas supported a "mixed constitution" (James M. Blythe, "The Mixed Constitution in Aquinas," *Journal of the History of Ideas* 47.4 [1986], 547–565). Most revealing perhaps is Aquinas's description of "the best form of government" which "is to be found in a city or kingdom in which one man is placed at the head to rule over all because of the preeminence of his virtue, and under him a certain number of men have governing power also on the strength of their virtue; and yet a government of this kind is shared by all, both because all are eligible to govern, and because the rulers are chosen by all. For this is the best form of polity, being partly kingdom, since there is one at the head of all, partly aristocracy, insofar as a number of persons

are set in authority, partly democracy, this is government by the people, insofar as the rulers can be chosen from the people, and the people have a right to choose their rulers" Aquinas, I.II.105.1.

29. Aquinas, I.II.90.3.

30. Tutu, 77.

31. See for example Mpumlwana, 90.

32. Buti Tlhagale, "Christian Soldiers," in *Theology and Violence: The South African Debate*, 85.

33. Mpumlwana, 96.

34. Indeed, Tlhagale argues that in situations of oppression, a repressive regime will attack emerging leaders with the direct intention of incapacitating those in whom the people place their trust and hope. Tlhagale remarks, "if . . . violent struggle does not seem to have any distinct leadership it is because the leadership is not allowed to survive for long in public" (85). This suggests that one way to recognize the legitimate authority, the one who is supported by the broader population, is to watch for who is being attacked by the illegitimate authority. Who is being banned, imprisoned, or even killed?

35. Villa-Vicencio, *Civil Disobedience and Beyond: Law, Resistance, and Religion in South Africa*, 102.

36. The International Commission on Intervention and State Sovereignty, *The Responsibility to Protect* (Ottawa: International Development Research Center, 2001).

37. Pope John Paul II summarized this way of thinking succinctly when discussing the Fifth Commandment, "You Shall Not Kill," in his 1995 encyclical *Evangelium Vitae:* "Yet from the beginning, faced with the many and often tragic cases which occur in the life of individuals and society, Christian reflection has sought a fuller and deeper understanding of what God's commandment prohibits and prescribes . . . Legitimate defense can be not only a right but a grave duty for someone responsible for another's life, the common good of the family or of the State." Pope John Paul II, *Evangelium Vitae*, March 25, 1995. Available at http://www.vatican.va/holy_father/john_paul_ii/encyclicals/documents/hf_jp-ii_enc_25031995_evangelium-vitae_en.html.

38. Villa-Vicencio, *Civil Disobedience and Beyond: Law, Resistance, and Religion in South Africa*, 95.

39. Recall Lisa Sowle Cahill's description of Augustine's thinking here: "Ordered love is the essence of peace." *Love Your Enemies: Discipleship, Pacifism, and the Just War Theory* (Minneapolis, MN: Fortress Press, 1994), 75.

40. Cahill notes that for Augustine, "It is an act of love to restore the peace by using violence; in his mind it is even an act of love toward the object of the violence" (75).

41. The series of interviews conducted by PBS Frontline is instructive on these points. See http://www.pbs.org/wgbh/pages/frontline/shows/heart/themes/prep.html. The interview with Lt. Col. David Grossman (U.S. Army, Retired) is particularly important for a contemporary understanding of right intention in warfare. Grossman suggests that in order to kill their enemies in war, soldiers must "overcome . . . [physiological] resistance" to killing "through operate conditioning, to make killing a condition reflex." The idea that killing in warfare must be made reflexive calls into question the entire notion that a soldier is killing *with intention* in warfare at all, since reflex is the opposite of intentionality. The physiological likelihood that soldiers, in a moment of battle, are killing based on instinct makes it that much more important that higher ranking officers and military strategists give orders and make plans with an eye to peace and justice, so that soldiers can depend on their superiors to have had a right intention when ordering them to carry out killing that is, for them, reflexive in situations of battle.

42. There is already some precedent for this adjustment within the just war tradition. The U.S. Bishops argue that "Right intention is related to just cause—war can be legitimately intended only for the reasons set forth . . . as a just cause. During the conflict, right intention means pursuit of peace and reconciliation, including avoiding unnecessarily destructive acts or imposing unreasonable conditions." USCCB, *The Challenge of Peace: God's Promise and Our Response* (May 3, 1983), 95. Available at http://www.usccb.org/upload/challenge-peace-gods-promise-our-response-1983.pdf

43. Villa-Vicencio, *Civil Disobedience and Beyond*, 71.

44. See Nelson Mandela's second court statement at the Rivonia Trial (1964), available in *The Struggle is My Life,* 161–181, especially 162.
45. Cahill, 56.
46. Indeed, Martha Minow suggests that "through vengeance we express our basic self-respect." *Between Vengeance and Forgiveness: Facing History After Genocide and Mass Violence* (Boston, MA: Beacon Press, 1998), 10.
47. Nelson Mandela, "ANC Address at Pan-African Freedom Conference 1962" in *The Struggle is my Life*, 127.
48. The Pan-Africanist Congress (PAC) was a political organization which splintered off of the ANC over ideological differences. The PAC strongly felt that the struggle for freedom in South Africa ought to be the work of Africans and rejected the ANC's multi, or even nonracial approach. They "espous[ed] a militant Africanism," (Beinart, 166). The PAC had organized the protest at Sharpeville and was critiqued for its hasty, less disciplined, and less organized approach. The PAC remains a political party in today's democratic South Africa, though it has declined in popularity over the last fifteen years, evidenced by its having lost seats in the South African parliament.
49. Beinart, 166.
50. Thomas Lodge, *Black Politics in South Africa Since 1945* (Johannesburg, South Africa: Ravan Press, 1983), 223. Quoted in Villa-Vicencio, *Civil Disobedience and Beyond,* 52.
51. Villa-Vicencio, *Civil Disobedience and Beyond,* 52.
52. "Umkhonto we Sizwe Manifesto, 1961" in Nelson Mandela, *The Struggle is My Life*, 122–123. Exclamation points in the original.
53. Villa-Vicencio, *Civil Disobedience and Beyond,* 87.
54. "Scores of citizens' forces and commando units were mobilized in the big towns. Camps were established at strategic points; heavy armed vehicles carried equipment . . . helicopters hovered over African residential areas and trained searchlights on houses, yards, lands, and unlit areas. Hundreds of white civilians were sworn in as special constables, hundreds of white women spent weekends shooting at targets. Gun shops sold out of their stocks of revolvers and ammunition. All police leave was cancelled . . . Police vans patrolled areas and broadcast statements that Africans who struck work would be sacked and endorsed out of town." Nelson Mandela, "ANC Address at Pan-African Freedom Conference, 1962" in *The Struggle is My Life,* 127.
55. Mandela, "ANC Address at Pan-African Freedom Conference," 130–131.
56. Villa-Vicencio, *Civil Disobedience and Beyond,* 87.
57. Francisco Suárez, *The Three Theological Virtues: On Charity,* Disputation XIII: On War, trans. Gladys L. Williams, Ammi Brown, and John Waldron, with revisions by Henry Davis, (London: Oxford University Press, 1944), 822.
58. Suárez, 822. Brackets in original translation.
59. Suárez, 822.
60. Suárez, 822.
61. It is arguable that what Suárez calls a "war of aggression" differs from how we understand the term today. See Suárez, 803–804: "Even when war is aggressive it is not an evil in itself, but may be right and necessary . . . such a war is often necessary to a state, in order to ward off acts of injustice and to hold enemies in check . . . we have to consider whether the injustice is, practically speaking, simply about to take place; or whether it has already done so, and redress is sought through war. In the second case, the war is aggressive." Here Suárez seems to categorize punishment as aggression. Today we often do the opposite, subsuming punishment, or "response to an act of aggression," under defense (see Allman, 195). Thus we would not generally characterize only force in the face of imminent attack as defense, while characterizing force as a response to an attack already carried out as aggression, as Suárez seems to do. Today, force both in the case of imminent attack, and as a response to an attack, would be viewed as defensive. Preventative war, understood as "an attack launched in response to a future (and uncertain) threat," remains controversial among just war scholars (this definition is taken from Kenneth R. Himes, "Invervention, Just War, and U.S. National Security,"

Theological Studies, 65 (2004): 148. The most recent Iraq War has raised considerable questions regarding the justice or injustice of preventative warfare (i.e., the Bush Doctrine), much of which Himes summarizes helpfully.

62. Suárez, 802.
63. Suárez, 823. Brackets in original translation.
64. Suárez, 823.
65. USCCB, 98.
66. Villa-Vicencio, *Civil Disobedience and Beyond,* 96.
67. SACBC, "On Christian Hope in the Current Crisis" (May, 1986), 2. Available at http://www.sacbc.org.za/wp-content/uploads/2013/05/PASTORAL-LETTER-ON-THECHRISTIAN-HOPE-IN-THE-CURRENT-CRISIS.pdf.
68. SACBC, 2. Quoting John: 17:21.
69. SACBC, 2
70. SACBC, 3.
71. SACBC, 2.
72. SACBC, 3.
73. See Albert Nolan's *God in South Africa,* and *Jesus Before Christianity*, 3rd edition (Maryknoll, NY: Orbis Books, 2001). *The Kairos Document* is available at http://www.sahistory.org.za/archive/challenge-church-theological-comment-political-crisis-south-africa-kairos-document-1985.
74. Nolan, *God in South Africa,* 58–61.
75. *The Kairos Document*, preface.
76. *The Kairos Document*, 3.1.
77. *The Kairos Document*, 3.2.
78. *The Kairos Document*, 3.2.
79. *The Kairos Document*, 4.
80. *The Kairos Document*, 4.
81. See section 3.3 which is a critique of what *The Kairos Document* calls "Church Theology" and its emphasis on nonviolence without serious social analysis of the meaning and forms of violence in an oppressive context.
82. *The Kairos Document*, 4.
83. Nelson Mandela, *Long Walk to Freedom* (Boston, MA: Back Bay Books, 1995), 282.
84. Villa-Vicencio, *Civil Disobedience and Beyond,* 53.
85. Quoted in Allan Boesak and Alan Brews, "The Black Struggle for Liberation: A Reluctant Road to Revolution" in Villa-Vicencio, *Theology and Violence,* 59.
86. Boesak and Brews, 59.
87. Boesak and Brews, 59.
88. See Janet Cherry, *Spear of the Nation: South Africa's Liberation Army* (Athens, OH: Ohio University Press, 2011), especially chapter 3.
89. Rocky Williams, "South African Guerrilla Armies: The Impact of Guerrilla Armies on the Creation of South Africa's Armed Forces," *ISS Monograph Series,* 127 (2006), 26–27.
90. Williams, 27.
91. Chris Hani, "ANC and Armed Struggle" quoted in Williams, 27.
92. Boesak and Brews, 61.
93. Boesak and Brews, 61.
94. Boesak and Brews, 61.
95. Consider Boesak and Brews' comment that "Mandela envisioned a process of conversation and concession in which the black majority would gradually attain greater participation in central government in a unitary South Africa" (59). Mandela, acting as the leader of MK, intended the South African struggle to culminate not in a revolutionary bloodbath, but rather in revolutionary negotiation. It is important to note that this indeed is what happened. The handover of power in South Africa was ultimately a lengthy process of negotiation between Nelson Mandela and then Prime Minister F.W. de Klerk. Both men received the Nobel Peace Prize in 1993 "for their work for the peaceful termination of the apartheid regime, and for laying the foundations for a new democratic South Africa." See Nobelprize.org at http://www.nobelprize.org/nobel_prizes/peace/laureates/1993/.

96. For a good model of the social analysis of violence see Rollo May, *Power and Innocence: A Search for the Sources of Violence* (New York: W.W. Norton, 1972). Malusi Mpumlwana systematically applies this model to violence during the era of apartheid in his essay "Legitimacy and Struggle" in *Theology and Violence* (93–96). Further analysis and description of structural versus other forms of violence in South Africa during the struggle against apartheid can be found in *The Kairos Document*, 3.3; in Desmond Tutu's essay "Freedom Fighters or Terrorists?" in *Theology and Violence* (74); and Boesak and Brews' essay "The Black Struggle for Liberation: A Reluctant Road to Revolution," also in *Theology and Violence* (64–65).

97. Numerous sources confirm the ANC's reluctance to employ armed resistance including interviews with ANC leaders and ANC archives. When nonviolent civil disobedience was met with repression (such as the Sharpeville Massacre), Nelson Mandela called for armed resistance saying, "There are many people who feel that it is useless and futile for us to continue talking peace and nonviolence to a government whose response is only savage attacks on unarmed and defenseless people." He later remarked, "There was a great deal of resistance [to the use of force] from the [ANC] leadership but . . . the government had left us with no other alternative" (Transcript, *Mandela: An Audio History* [Joe Richman, Radio Diaries and Sue Johnson, Radio Diaries, 2004], "All Things Considered" NPR: Broadcast April 26–30, 2004).

98. Mandela, *Long Walk to Freedom,* 271.

99. Nelson Mandela's court statement at the Rivonia trial, 1963, in *The Struggle is My Life,* 162.

100. Boesak and Brews, 55.

101. Boesak and Brews, 63

102. Boesak and Brews, 63.

103. Boesak and Brews, 63.

104. Villa-Vicencio, *Civil Disobedience and Beyond,* 98. Parenthetical and exclamation points in the original.

105. The seven volume report of South Africa's Truth and Reconciliation Commission is an excellent, if deeply disturbing, resource for describing incidences of repressive violence under the apartheid regime. The full report is available at http://www.justice.gov.za/Trc/report/index.htm.

106. Aquinas, II.II.42.2.

107. Aquinas, II.II.42.2.ad 3.

108. Aquinas, II.II.42.2 ad 3.

109. Tutu, 71.

110. Michael Walzer, *Just and Unjust Wars: A Moral Argument with Historical Illustrations,* 4th edition, (New York: Basic Books, 2006), 185.

111. Walzer, 185. Walzer goes on to state in a parenthetical, "unless they are guilty of specific acts of assassination or sabotage, for which soldiers, too, can be punished." Again I would use the Thomistic argument that the tyrannical regime is ultimately responsible for these acts in that by their oppression they foment these forms of armed resistance. "Punishment" in such a case, if it is applicable at all, would have to be dealt with rather delicately, perhaps in a similar fashion to how such activities were dealt with in the Truth and Reconciliation Commission.

112. Walzer, 183. Walzer's example here is of a group of French Resistance "disguised as peaceful peasants" (177). After France had surrendered to German forces during World War II, this group, pretending to be harvesting potatoes, ambushed and killed a passing group of German soldiers who had presumed them to be noncombatant civilians. The Resistance soldiers used deception to achieve a surprise "of a kind virtually impossible in actual combat. It derived from what might be called the protective coloration of national surrender, and its effect was obviously to erode the moral and legal understandings upon which surrender rests" (177). Walzer is rightly concerned that when guerrilla soldiers—or as is becoming a greater concern today, terrorists—intentionally quarter with civilians the effect is to erode the distinction between civilians and combatants, and thus the moral and legal protection of noncombatants. In general, anti-guerrilla, or anti-terrorism efforts should endeavor to separate guerrilla soldiers or terrorists from civilians. However, for our purposes here, it is important to remember that

108 *Chapter 4*

Walzer also argues that if guerrillas truly have a level of popular support that makes it impossible to separate them from civilians, then "a moral argument can be made . . . [that] the anti-guerrilla war can then no longer be fought—and not just because, from a strategic point of view it can no longer be won. It can no longer be fought because it is no longer an anti-guerrilla war but an anti-social war, a war against an entire people . . . " (187). This characterization almost certainly applies to the situation of revolution in South Africa, and likely to many other situations of revolution as well. Repression against popular revolution more nearly resembles Walzer's notion of an "anti-social war" than an "anti-guerrilla war."

113. "Umkhonto we Sizwe Manifesto, 1961" in Mandela, *The Struggle is My Life,* 122.

114. "Umkhonto we Sizwe Manifesto, 1961," 123.

115. "Umkhonto we Sizwe Manifesto, 1961," 123.

116. "Umkhonto we Sizwe Manifesto, 1961," 123.

117. Priscilla B. Hayner, *Unspeakable Truths: Facing the Challenge of Truth Commissions* (New York: Routledge, 2002), 60.

118. Hayner, 61.

119. Hayner, 63.

120. Hayner, 64.

121. Hayner, 64.

122. Beinart, 237.

123. Beinart, 237.

124. See South African Democracy Education Trust, *The Road to Democracy in South Africa, Volume 1 1960–1970* (Cape Town, South Africa: Zebra Press, 2004), 488, 534, 654–655, and 659. *Umkhonto we Sizwe* had allied itself with the Zimbabwe African People's Union (ZAPU) forces attempting to liberate Zimbabwe (then Rhodesia) from Ian Smith's minority white government. MK had hoped to infiltrate South Africa through the border at Rhodesia.

Chapter Five

Restorative Justice for the Common Good

The last two chapters dealt with *jus ante* armed revolution, and *jus ad* and *in* armed revolution. The final phase of just revolution to investigate is *jus post* revolution. In nations emerging from histories of oppression some form of transitional justice[1] is necessary for dealing with the past such that it does not dictate a compromised future. Transitional justice will be necessary regardless of whether a revolution has been nonviolent, armed, or has employed a tandem of both since it facilitates social transformation away from the oppressive context that fomented revolution and toward greater justice as the foundation for a peaceful future.

One key emerging aspect of transitional justice that arose in the South African context exemplifies another practice of the just peacemaking theory: *acknowledge responsibility for conflict and injustice and seek repentance and forgiveness*; however for several reasons I did not deal with this practice for just peacemaking with the others in chapter 3. This is decidedly a *post* conflict practice. Acknowledging responsibility, and pursuing forgiveness and repentance presumes prior conflict. Moreover, this practice, as I illustrate below, cannot effectively take place unless the injustice of political oppression has already been dealt with. Thus it is necessarily a post-revolutionary practice, since revolution, by definition, seeks liberation from political injustices. To say it is a post-revolutionary practice does not negate its value as a just peacemaking strategy, though. Indeed, the pursuit of forgiveness, repentance, and ultimately social reconciliation is crucial in post-conflict situations precisely because it staves off new cycles of violence: retaliation and revenge that occur when historical animosities are not acknowledged, grieved, and repaired to the best of our human abilities.

The task for this chapter will be to provide a framework for thinking about how nations emerging from revolution might transition toward a just peace through a process of restorative justice that lends itself to social reconciliation.[2] The chapter proceeds in three parts. I begin with a clarification of the terms "forgiveness" and "reconciliation" so as to set a foundation for understanding these concepts throughout the chapter. In the second section, I describe restorative justice and why it may be most efficacious *jus post* revolution for nations in transition from the brutalities of oppression. Finally, I engage the critiques and strengths of South Africa's Truth and Reconciliation Commission (TRC) to illustrate how restorative justice as public truth-telling can create a shared historical memory of past abuses, validate the experiences of victims of oppression and violence, and hold perpetrators accountable, all in order to contribute to a process of social transformation.

The spirit of the hybrid inductive-deductive method remains in this chapter. I work deductively in advocating for the value of concepts like justice, forgiveness, repentance, and reconciliation, including how these are understood in the global Christian context as represented by Thomas Aquinas and the traditional Southern African philosophy of *ubuntu*. I work inductively by describing these concepts in dialogue with the experiences of those who have faced or committed oppression and violence and emerged with a desire to forgive and/or repent and be reconciled to one another. In accordance with the South African context, I pay special attention to those who have endured and perpetrated apartheid, and to what can be learned from South Africa's own attempts at restorative justice as enacted in the Truth and Reconciliation Commission.

FORGIVENESS AND RECONCILIATION

Because of their importance in enacting restorative justice after revolution, I begin with a clarification of how I am using the terms "forgiveness" and "reconciliation." In the context of the aftermath of a revolution that has overturned an oppressive regime, which has committed mass violations of human rights, I understand forgiveness to be something that victims extend to perpetrators regardless of the perpetrators' remorse or even desire for forgiveness. In this respect, I follow Robert J. Schreiter's insight that forgiveness is initiated by victims. In a theological analogy, Schreiter describes God as a victim of our sinfulness. Thus God is not for us "a source of indifferent mercy . . . [but rather] our sin causes God to be wrathful" and mercy "comes to us from a God who has felt the enmity deeply."[3] In the same way, victims may view perpetrators as objects of their wrath and causes of their grief.

Through forgiveness victims endeavor to release themselves from the burden of negative and destructive thoughts and feelings toward perpetrators. These feelings may hinder victims from living lives free of fear and desolation.

There are five important factors indicated by this description of forgiveness: First, the proper subject of forgiveness is primarily the well-being of victims, and only secondarily the well-being of perpetrators who may feel the positive effects of having been forgiven. As John W. de Gruchy explains, "Forgiveness enables those who forgive to overcome their bitterness and redeem their future, and those who sinned against them to recover their own humanity."[4] A perpetrator may benefit from being forgiven, but the initiator and primary subject of forgiveness is the victim. Second, according to this conception of forgiveness, victims can forgive perpetrators whom they have never met, or who are dead, as is sometimes the case following revolution or other massive social unrest. Thus, Daniel Philpott notes that "sometimes forgiveness will involve no reciprocal apology, acceptance, or even acknowledgment on the part of the perpetrator."[5] Third, since it does not depend on a perpetrator's apology this conception emphasizes that "victims cannot be expected to forgive on cue" as though forgiveness is simply a direct and presumed response to a perpetrator's expression of repentance.[6] In this way, again, forgiveness empowers victims and the activities or responses of perpetrators are secondary. Fourth, victims can engage in processes of forgiveness without the desire to be in an ongoing relationship with perpetrators.[7] Since forgiveness is victim-centered it does not require relationship. Indeed, some victims may find it easier to forgive and be free from an impulse toward revenge if they are not in active relationship with their perpetrators. This characteristic does require a caveat, however, when victims are actually victim-groups who, as a group, will continue to live in close proximity to perpetrator-groups following conflict. In such situations, which arise often after intra-national conflicts, it is unrealistic to think that members of victim-groups will have no contact or relationship whatsoever with members of perpetrator-groups. These cases warrant that, not just forgiveness, but also social reconciliation, be cultivated. Finally, forgiveness is a lifetime process to which victims may have to recommit themselves regularly. Those who have been severely traumatized are rarely able to offer forgiveness "once-and-for-all-time." Feelings of rage and possibly even desires for retaliation may continue to resurface. It is therefore best to speak of a continual openness toward forgiveness, rather than its final and absolute achievement.

Reconciliation is both related to and distinct from forgiveness. In the context of gross human rights violations victims and perpetrators often find themselves continuing to live in close proximity to one another. Whether or not this is a preferred state of being, it is often unavoidable. Thus reconciliation will normally involve both victims and perpetrators who in basic recognition of their common humanity, *minimally* commit themselves to a cessation of cycles of retaliation and revenge. *Maximally,* reconciliation may mean that the two individuals and/or groups choose to develop or redevelop a relationship that was damaged by the perpetrators' actions. This maximal form of reconciliation will likely include forgiveness in that it marks a shared commitment wherein victims extend forgiveness and perpetrators express remorse as necessary to the process of rebuilding damaged relationships. In this way, I concur with John de Gruchy that "the word of forgiveness is a key moment in the process of reconciliation"[8] but it does not constitute reconciliation itself. Maximal reconciliation following mass violations of human rights also requires some form of justice that is "understood as redemptive and reconciling, justice as the exercise of love and power in a way that heals relationships and builds community."[9] As I will argue, retributive justice is less efficacious than restorative justice for pursuing the goal of post-revolutionary reconciliation. *Jus post* revolution commitments to reparations and developing a just economy are also part of maximal efforts to promote social reconciliation. Finally, just as forgiveness is not a once-and-for-all event, reconciliation requires commitment across decades, and even generations. It involves sharing the truth of what has come before with those who never experienced it themselves; doing this in a way that emphasizes the evils of violence and oppression, but also the common humanity that opposes these evils and compels us to pursue justice and social transformation. In this way, reconciliation at its best is a lengthy, even multigenerational process of giving a community new life: it is conceived by those who struggle to be free from oppression and those who initiate and succeed in revolutionary struggle; it is nourished by those who negotiate to end the revolution with an eye toward a just peace; and it is brought to birth by those who enjoy the fruits of struggle and new life in a community committed to raising up the common good.

UNDERSTANDING RESTORATIVE JUSTICE

Restorative justice repairs relationships that have been damaged due to injustice. It prioritizes the human dignity that is a common possession of both victims and perpetrators of injustice. To gain a deeper understanding of restorative justice, I examine it in three parts. First, I explore Thomas Aquinas's understanding of the relationships among distributive, commutative, and general justice to illustrate the similarities between general justice that aims at the common good and post-conflict restorative justice. Second, I examine the traditional Southern African conception of *ubuntu* to show how restorative justice has been conceived of in the South African context. This is important as a conceptual girder for understanding how and why the TRC prioritized and enacted restorative justice. Finally, I suggest three goals or aims of transitional justice after oppression and conflict and argue that restorative justice best promotes these goals for positive social transformation and reconciliation.

Thomas Aquinas and General Justice

Thomas Aquinas distinguishes varying types of justice that correspond with a person's many diverse relationships, whether to oneself, to other individuals, or to the community as a whole. Since Aquinas claims that "the aspect of the common good differs from the aspect of the individual good," he identifies particular justice as distinct from general justice for pursuing these distinct goods.[10] Particular justice is directed toward and guides our behaviors in relation to ourselves and other individuals. Particular justice is further subdivided into distributive and commutative justice.[11] Distributive justice seeks equality of proportionality among people and goods, such that each individual person's particular needs are met.[12] Commutative justice can be directed either toward restitution, which seeks to return in equal measure something that has been taken from someone unjustly;[13] or reparation,[14] which demands that action be taken to compensate for wrongs that cannot be merely repaid.[15] Restitution thus involves either returning what has been taken, or at least the value of what has been taken. Reparation acknowledges that some injustices take things from people that cannot simply be returned. The German word "wiedergutmachung"—translated as "reparations," literally means "to make good again." In the German context this word captures the tensions of reparative justice well. It is used to describe efforts at compensation of the Jewish community following the Holocaust. Of course, no efforts can fully compensate for, or "make good" on such a horrific breach of our common humanity, and the term "reparation" evokes this tension. Nevertheless, for Aquinas reparation seeks to "make good again," or repair, situations of injustice that defy a more facile restitution.

General justice, with which we are especially concerned, is directed not toward individual goods, but toward the common good. Aquinas refers to this as "the virtue of a good citizen,"[16] which assists people in "direct[ing] the acts of all the virtues to the common good."[17] It is thus through the virtue of general justice that people act in ways that benefit not only the good of individuals, but also the good of the community. Conceptually, then, Aquinas's general justice resembles restorative justice. General justice seeks the common good as its overarching aim such that concerns for distributive (equality of proportionality) and commutative (reparation and restitution) justice are secondary. This is not to say that distributive or commutative justice are unimportant for building up the common good, but that, conceptually, the common good is the goal, and distribution and commutation should be viewed as means toward realizing that goal. Likewise, restorative justice after revolution should aim at the common good. These efforts may include aspects of distributive and commutative justice; for example promoting policies of land reform, or compensatory reparations for victims' families. But acts of distributive and commutative justice are at the service of the larger goal of promoting the common good, and do not take precedence over it. In this way general or restorative justice provides the telos—the common good—which then shapes the manner in which distributive and commutative justice are sought.

Building on Aquinas's notion of general justice, restorative justice can be understood as justice that aims at the common good, renewing and restoring the relationships that govern and create our societies. This conception of justice is especially important in divided communities emerging from violent oppression and revolutionary struggle, where there exists a special duty to foster intentionally a commitment to a common humanity. Aiming at the common good involves a rejection of the dehumanizing policies and practices of the former regime, and instead an obligation to recognize the dignity and rights of all people.

Ubuntu

The notion of ubuntu is perhaps the most fundamental concept for understanding restorative justice and its relationship to forgiveness and reconciliation in the aftermath of apartheid. The concept of ubuntu is not, however, unique to South Africa. Rather, it is a common anthropological philosophy among those Africans who share the heritage of the Bantu linguistic group. Among others these would include those in Southern Africa who speak Nguni and refer to ubuntu, as well as the Shona of Zimbabwe who refer to *unhu*, the Swahili speaking peoples of East Africa who refer to *utu*, and the Kikuyu of Kenya who speak of *umundu*.[18] The philosophy of ubuntu has been thoroughly adopted into African Christian theologies, most notably through the theological commitments of South African Archbishop Desmond Tutu. Ubuntu posits that human beings are deeply interconnected, and indeed are fully human only in communion.[19]

Ubuntu can be understood as a form of African humanism that is deeply communitarian in nature. It declares that all human beings share a sacred quality that can be damaged, but never entirely lost.[20] In this way, ubuntu correlates with Catholic social thought. It is similar to the notion of human dignity, which arises from the doctrine that human beings are created *imago Dei*. For example, in its section on "The Dignity of the Human Person," *Gaudium et Spes* confirms that human beings are "created 'to the image of God,'" and are thus "capable of knowing and loving [their] Creator."[21] In *Pacem in Terris* it is this dignity, flowing from the *imago Dei*, which calls us to recognize the rights of individuals.[22] Nevertheless, in contradistinction to individualist anthropologies which sometimes color our understanding of the doctrine of *imago Dei* in the West, ubuntu embraces an "African sense of community."[23] Rather than the Cartesian formulation, "I think therefore I am," ubuntu contends that "I am because we are," that is to say one person's humanity is conjoined to his/her community. The IsiNguni word has been translated into English as "a person is a person through other persons."[24] Thus ubuntu stresses that it is only through belonging to a community that persons discover, express, and maintain their full humanity. "Everyone belongs and there is no one who does not belong . . . A person is socialized to think of himself/herself as inextricably bound to others."[25] To understand how ubuntu relates and contributes to restorative justice and social reconciliation, we must clarify how ubuntu comprises an integrated personal-social ethic, and how ubuntu is damaged and restored.

Since ubuntu expresses what it means to be fully human, it propounds a particular kind of ethic. This moral code put forth by ubuntu is a personal-social amalgam. As a personal ethic, ubuntu demands that human beings are the "basis for all ethical actions."[26] In their personal ethics, every individual human being ought to strive to be "moral, social, relational, and compassionate . . . and it is these qualities that make him or her attain his or her personhood."[27] One can only fulfill his/her humanity through other people,[28] and ubuntu illustrates what the ideal person ought to be.[29] According to Desmond Tutu, ubuntu encourages "humanness, gentleness, and hospitality, putting yourself on behalf of others, being vulnerable. It embraces compassion and toughness. It recognizes that my humanity is bound up in yours, for we can only be human together."[30]

Ubuntu likewise encourages social virtues in that it disposes a person toward "values that contribute to the well-being of others and of community."[31] Through the quality of ubuntu, people ask themselves how their behavior affects the common good. The needs of the community are generally put before those of the individual. Self-improvement is encouraged, but it is presumed that such improvements will be placed at the service of the community. "Ubuntu does not mean that people should not enrich themselves. The question therefore is: are you going to do so in order to enable the community around you to improve."[32] In this way, Thomas Aquinas's notion of general justice, as directed toward the common good, and ubuntu as valuing the well-being of community mirror one another. Moreover, both view right relationships amongst members of a community as among the highest social goods. Thus both lend to a greater understanding of restorative justice as that which repairs relationships to facilitate the common good.

It is possible to damage one's ubuntu, or fundamental humanity, but not to lose it entirely. Behaving in ways that dehumanize, objectify, and degrade one's self and others, or (in the light of its concern for right relationships) that alienate human beings from one another harms ubuntu.[33] Theologically, such actions are generally understood as forms of sin. To suggest that someone has violated ubuntu is thus to condemn sinful behavior and to protect the community, and ultimately the wrong-doer as part of the community, from such destructive behavior. This means that it is the community who defines the person and who judges "whether one has attained full humanity (in the moral sense) or not. Yes, a person has dignity, which is inherent; but part of being a person is to have feelings and moral values that contribute to the well-being of others."[34] Ubuntu is thus bestowed and sustained by a community who seeks to be in right relationship with one another. That is a community that seeks "social harmony," or a peace that is marked by justice.[35] In this moral framework, justice is understood as that which restores the fullness of ubuntu: the personhood of all people, in relation to one another, and for the sake of the community and all its members.

When a person fails to fulfill ubuntu by treating themselves or others inhumanely, the community can restore the wayward person through forgiveness and reconciliation. In this way, ubuntu includes a hope that people will repent their inhumanity and that they will return to right relationship with the community.[36] "No matter what wrong an individual has done to the community, that individual remains a human being worthy of humane and equal treatment."[37] To continue to treat as human one who has, through his/her own inhumanity, violated ubuntu is itself an extremely powerful act of humanness. Thus, ubuntu "embraces forgiveness"[38] —if a person persists in actions that harm the community he/she can be "ostracized or rejected" for a time, but "not to have the capacity for forgiveness would be to lack ubuntu."[39] Individual capacity for forgiveness and reconciliation is not only a personal virtue, it is also a social and even political good in that it enables right relationships—peace and social harmony—for the common good.

The need for ubuntu, like the need for general justice, becomes most obvious in communities where it has been seriously violated. Thus, a robust understanding of ubuntu is essential to comprehending black South Africans' remarkable willingness to engage in restorative justice, to struggle for forgiveness and reconciliation *post* revolution against apartheid. Ubuntu includes a sense that one's humanity "is diminished when others are humiliated or diminished, when others are tortured and oppressed."[40] Apartheid, since it dealt in the currency of racism and segregation—the anti-right-relationship—arguably functioned as a full onslaught against the ubuntu of all South Africans regardless of color. By contrast, ubuntu "counters the narrative of apartheid"[41] and thus provides hope for forgiveness and reconciliation.

Following apartheid, for those invested with a deep respect for the notion of *ubuntu,* forgiveness and reconciliation may have been understood as primary ways, not only of treating perpetrators as human beings, but also of reclaiming their own humanity before those who had attempted to wrest it away. Because Southern Africans who uphold ubuntu view their humanity as deeply dependent on others, there is a sense that *not* to forgive, *not* to seek reconciliation does harm to the *victim* of violence, not just the perpetrator. "To forgive," remarks Desmond Tutu, "is not just to be altruistic. It is the best form of self-interest. What dehumanizes you inexorably dehumanizes me. [Forgiveness] gives people resilience, enabling them to survive and emerge still human despite all efforts to dehumanize them."[42] To intentionally hold a grudge or seek revenge is to harm one's own ubuntu, or to damage one's own humanity. Instead, through forgiveness victims reclaim their ubuntu. Ubuntu thus suggests that to encourage a victim to forgive is an act of solidarity with the victim. Ubuntu affirms that the perpetrator is not the true subject of forgiveness. Victims who struggle to forgo vengeance and instead forgive those who have harmed them are subjects of the very forgiveness they extend; forgiveness restores victims' full ubuntu and frees them from lives of isolation and desperation.

Moreover, interpersonal expressions of forgiveness in the context of ubuntu may even be considered a means of protecting the wider community through reconciliation. To reconcile with perpetrators is to take away their power to commit violations of ubuntu. A victim may choose to forgive and seek reconciliation with a perpetrator in order to reintegrate him/her into the community because *not* to do so is considered threatening for the community as a whole. "One who does not belong or has not been made part of the community is considered to be a danger."[43] As we have seen, through forgiveness and reconciliation victims assert their ubuntu before the one who violated it. This assertion of humanity is meant in part to defuse the possibility of further violence. Like social reconciliation, it intends to stop cycles of retaliation and revenge. The victim says, in effect, "By forgiving you, I demonstrate that I am human, invested with ubuntu and you must not violate my humanity through violence." Thus in forgiving, victims acknowledge the humanity both of themselves and of the perpetrators. By humanizing perpetrators, victims make them less frightening and thus take away the power the perpetrators wield over them—perhaps even in the victims' memories. Through forgiveness and reconciliation victims reintegrate perpetrators into the wider community, thus diminishing the chances for new waves of violence and helping the community commit to social reconciliation. Reasserting *ubuntu* through a processes of forgiveness and reconciliation humanizes both victim and perpetrator, whose actions had damaged the dignity of the entire community.[44] Furthermore, to reintegrate the perpetrator into the community through forgiveness and reconciliation is viewed as crucial to the restoration of right relationships and thus the future safety of the whole community.

WHY RESTORATIVE JUSTICE?

The South African context has affirmed that justice is a necessary precondition for post-revolutionary social reconciliation. Following the 1994 elections, the new, democratically elected South African government established the TRC to pursue restorative justice through the promotion of truth-telling, reparations, and social reconciliation. While the TRC was not without substantial problems, which I discuss below, it is nevertheless considered among the most effective processes of post-conflict transitional justice to date. In part this efficacy emerges from the struggle against apartheid itself: revolutionaries understood reconciliation as a goal that was operative in conditioning *jus ante, jus ad,* and *jus in* armed revolution responses and tactics. Thus despite decades of enmity South Africa was well prepared to engage a process of social reconciliation following the negotiations to hand over power. Also, South African theologians and revolutionary leaders were adamant in their rejection of "cheap" reconciliation that glosses over injustice "to avoid the fact of conflict or to shield those who were perpetrators of violence."[45] Instead they understood justice as the price of reconciliation, and many would eventually see restorative justice as the most efficacious form of justice for promoting the common good in the aftermath of revolution.

Understanding justice as necessary for social reconciliation means rejecting "cheap" reconciliation. In its intense critique of what it calls "Church theology," *The Kairos Document*, which I discussed in chapter 4, cautioned against "cheap" reconciliation saying that reconciliation had been made into "an absolute principle that must be applied in all cases of conflict or dissention."[46] The Kairos theologians argue that it is not possible to divorce reconciliation from justice. Cheap reconciliation posits a false dichotomy, setting up justice and peace as alternatives, rather than acknowledging that they are indicative of each other.[47] "To advocate cheap reconciliation," explains Miroslav Volf, "clearly means to betray those who suffer injustice, deception, and violence . . . such a concept of reconciliation really amounts to a betrayal of the Christian faith . . . an adequate notion of reconciliation must include justice as a constitutive element."[48] Not only *can* post-conflict reconciliation include some form of justice, it *must* do so to be true reconciliation. Recall that a commitment to the cessation of violence and victimization is a *minimum* criterion for the pursuit of reconciliation.

Determining that justice is a constituent element of reconciliation next demands that we consider what form of justice best promotes it. If we are seeking to establish a just peace post revolution we must address two questions: (1) What are the aims of transitional justice after revolution; what contributes to building a just peace in the aftermath of oppression and violence? (2) What type of justice most enables these desired outcomes? In accord with these questions, the rest of this section describes several aims that seem to stave off cycles of retaliation and revenge after oppression and violence, and argues that restorative justice is often the best option for pursuing these aims.

Building peace and stemming cycles of violence after revolution involves establishing a sense of justice for those people and groups who have been subject to the degrading, structural, and direct violence I described in chapter 4. Here, I suggest a nonexhaustive list of three goals for promoting this sense of justice in post-revolutionary societies. These goals build upon and reinforce one another. Promoting justice after oppression and violence must include clear efforts to: (1) Establish a historical record of past atrocities and human rights violations; (2) Validate victims' experiences of violence, and (3) Render some form of judgment upon perpetrators.

Working toward a just peace after oppression and violence involves engaging in concerted efforts to establish a historical record of atrocities and human rights violations. This ought to include both discrete incidences of politically motivated violence, such as the torture or murder of individuals; and an account of structural or institutionalized violence, such as forced migrations, unjust military conscriptions, and policies or actions that humiliated and demeaned particular racial or ethnic groups. Having a truthful account of the past is fundamental to a sense that justice has been achieved. Indeed, Audrey R. Chapman argues that it is a prerequisite for building a common future after severe conflict.[49] Likewise, Donald Shriver argues that an established record of the truth is key to stopping cycles of violence.[50] A relatively uncontested record of human rights abuses is important and meaningful because it provides a shared narrative of national history which enables the community both to honor the fractured past through memory, and to move forward together into a common future.

Second, efforts at transitional justice ought to validate victims' experiences by supporting process that deconstruct the "narrative of the lie" formerly promoted by oppressors. Here, I am drawing on the work of Robert Schreiter who contends that in order to heal from the past, victims of violence need validation in the form of hearing and speaking truths that correspond to their experiences. Schreiter argues that, far from being "senseless," violence is quite rational. It relentlessly pursues the goal of destroying a victim's identity by unraveling "the fragile webs of meaning we weave about ourselves" thus undermining our sense of self and security.[51] Having used violence to destroy victims' narratives of identity and security, perpetrators seek to impose on their victims their own narrative of meaning, "the narrative of the lie."[52] The purpose of violence then, is not simply to put an end to a victim's narrative; "that is done most efficiently by simple execution—but to provide another narrative so that people will learn to live with and acquiesce to the will of the oppressor."[53] Despotic regimes seek to impose the narrative of the lie through degrading, structural, and direct violence. They replace victims' senses of self, the sense that they are loved, and invested with worth and dignity, with a narrative which suggests that they are vulnerable, isolated, powerless against pain and aggression, and sometimes even subhuman. Alternatively, speaking and hearing the truth after traumatic violence enables victims to articulate a new narrative by which they can reestablish their identities. By integrating the experience of violence into this newly formed identity, the victim reestablishes a sense of safety. Truth-telling uncovers the narrative of the lie. It affirms the perpetrators' guilt, whether or not they repent, and the victims' innocence thereby validating their experiences and emotions.

Third, establishing a sense of justice means that perpetrators must be held accountable for their actions. Minimally this requires that some form of judgment be rendered upon them. It may also involve requiring perpetrators to perform reparative actions. Holding perpetrators accountable necessitates a firm stance against negotiated settlements that involve blanket amnesty. These are not always avoidable, but they should be eschewed as much as possible. Blanket amnesty is largely indiscernible from impunity. In post-oppressive contexts, blanket amnesty constitutes freedom from prosecution without conditions for all people who have committed politically motivated crimes regardless of the circumstances surrounding the atrocity. It is problematic for several reasons. It attempts to bypass justice on the way to peace and reconciliation. It thus warps social realities by denying that reconciliation is intimately linked to justice and indeed, impossible without it. Moreover, blanket amnesty compromises the first two goals for establishing a sense of justice after reconciliation. By providing no incentive for perpetrators to participate in truth excavation it jeopardizes the creation of a historical record of atrocities. By not holding perpetrators accountable, blanket amnesty invalidates victims' experiences of abuse and injustice. Instead, transitional justice processes must find ways of holding perpetrators accountable and declaring the abuses of human rights committed by the regime to be wrong.

Following revolution, restorative justice may be the most efficacious form of justice for pursuing these important goals. In advocating restorative justice, I do not intend to argue that retributive justice, in which perpetrators are charged with crimes, acquitted or convicted, and sentenced accordingly, is morally suspect. Nor do I want to suggest that it ought not be a viable alternative for handling perpetrators who refuse to engage or cooperate with a process of restorative justice.[54] Instead, I argue that retributive justice is often neither possible nor most desirable in situations emerging from histories of serious human rights violations as it does not necessarily forward the important goals that lend to a sense of justice and positive social transformation.

First, retributive justice is often not possible in societies emerging from histories of violence and conflict. The sheer magnitude of atrocities and the time passed—often decades—between the violations and the investigation of crimes make gathering evidence prohibitively difficult.[55] Moreover, many regimes include some form of amnesty for perpetrators as a condition of the surrender of power.[56] What is needed in these cases is a form of justice that allows for conditional amnesty that does not give perpetrators absolute immunity. Again, South Africa's TRC provides a helpful model in which amnesty is exchanged for truth-telling, and thus forwards the important goals of validating victims' experiences, establishing a truthful record of human rights violations, and rendering a moral judgment on perpetrators.

Second, retributive justice is often not desirable in regions emerging from situations of conflict characterized by gross human rights violations for at least two reasons. First, because the likelihood of successful prosecutions is somewhat low, again due to the difficulties of gathering evidence for atrocities; and second, because of the concomitant likelihood that perpetrators will not cooperate with attempts to uncover the truth of human rights abuses for which they are responsible and for which they may be prosecuted. Retributive justice in legal courts operates via an adversarial method. One assumption in the practice of retributive justice is that adversarial questioning of witnesses and the accused will bring the fullest truth to light, while also protecting the rights of the accused. But this adversarial method also generally discourages perpetrators from participating in the excavation of the truth since they typically wish to avoid the punitive consequences of retributive justice. Indeed, with retributive models it is in the interest of those who have committed violations of human rights to hide the truth as much as possible. Combined with lack of physical evidence that is often a problem following decades of oppressive rule this leaves little hope that the truth will emerge if retributive justice is held up as absolute justice, or the only meaningful form of justice. Instead, it is often only through the perpetrator's recollection of his/her crimes that a reasonably full historical account of human rights abuses can be established. In light of this reasoning, the model of restorative justice enacted by the TRC chose to tie grants of amnesty to disclosure of the truth, and this was judged as preferable to potentially unsuccessful prosecutions since it forwarded important goals for establishing a sense of justice.

Highlighting the benefits of restorative justice is not to say that retributive justice via a legal system ought never to be pursued following mass violations of human rights, or that efforts at prosecution through such bodies as the International Criminal Court should never be supported. However, if the goals following conflict are to establish a record of violence, validate victims' experiences, and render judgments on perpetrators as part of establishing a sense of justice that can be a foundation for social transformation and reconciliation, then retributive justice will frequently fail to capture these aims, and restorative justice will more fully capture them. Especially in areas where former enemies will continue to live in close quarters after conflict, establishing a just peace is crucial to the cessation of cycles of retaliation and revenge. In such situations, efforts at restorative justice may be both more possible and more preferable. What remains most clear is that some form of justice is a precondition to social reconciliation.

Restorative justice is an efficacious form of justice that contributes to a process of "costly" reconciliation post-revolution. Key to the notion of restorative justice is the conviction that justice and reconciliation are not opposed to one another, but are instead mutually cooperative. Moreover, restorative justice is rooted in a clear understanding that "relationship is the basis of both the conflict and its long-term solution."[57] When oppression or violent conflict occurs, a relationship is damaged; in reconciliation based on a foundation of restorative justice it moves toward healing. Restorative justice aims at reconciliation by striving to transform broken communities via the establishment of a shared historical memory of past atrocities, validation of victims experiences, and rendering a moral judgment against the actions of perpetrators. Restorative justice, like ubuntu, views reintegration of perpetrators into the community as a positive way of protecting the community from new outbreaks of violence. Thus emphasis is placed on healing relationships and restoring a sense of common humanity among both perpetrators and victims.

Restorative justice's stress on healing relationships can be contentious. For example, in the case of South Africa, some argue that no genuine relationship ever existed between the oppressors and the oppressed. Thus to speak of restoring a relationship, or indeed reconciling two groups to one another, does not make sense. "There is nothing to go back to, no previous state or relationship one would wish to restore."[58] Despite the lack of a historical relationship between oppressed and oppressor, however, I would contend that both general justice and ubuntu help us recognize that there is a moral relationship that requires reconciliation after gross violations of human rights; that is, a common humanity shared by both oppressed and oppressor that requires restoration and can thus benefit from a process of restorative justice and social reconciliation.

ENACTING RESTORATIVE JUSTICE: THE TRC

Despite the intensely ugly nature of the apartheid regime and its behavior toward political prisoners, Nelson Mandela, who had been a major architect of both nonviolent and armed struggle, emerged in 1990 after twenty-seven years in prison not to cry for revenge or retaliation, but rather to encourage South Africans to work together for a just peace that would include the reconciliation of the national community via a process of restorative justice. Given that apartheid constituted the absolute antithesis of reconciliation—recall that the word "apartheid" means "apartness" and "by its very nature is both unjust and divisive"[59]—this call for reconciliation from those arguably most traumatized by apartheid is rather astonishing. Perhaps it is even more remarkable that many oppressed South Africans aimed for eventual reconciliation among South Africa's racial groups even throughout the years of brutal repression and armed revolution, referring to this goal as "the struggle within the struggle."[60] The humanism of ubuntu that encourages a commitment to restorative justice for the common good cannot be underestimated when thinking about why many black South Africans waged their struggle against apartheid with an intention to reconcile, and emerged from it with a willingness to forgive. As we saw in chapter 4, this intention to reconcile pervaded the struggle, inspiring a tandem approach to revolution in which *Umkhonto we Sizwe* waged controlled and limited armed resistance, while the masses of ordinary South Africans continued practices of nonviolent resistance.

The TRC was established in 1995 by an act of its newly elected democratic parliament. Archbishop Desmond Tutu was chosen as the commission's chairperson. Tutu had attained almost iconic status during the years of apartheid for his role as a proponent of what we now consider just peacemaking strategies, and he was known for a fervent commitment to reconciliation as part of a just peace post revolution. Hearings and investigations began in 1996.[61] It is clear that Mandela's administration took seriously the potential role that the TRC could play in working toward a just peace in the wounded South Africa:

> The commission's empowering act provided the most complex and sophisticated mandate for any truth commission to date, with carefully balanced powers and an extensive investigatory reach. Written in precise legal language and running to over twenty single-spaced pages, the act gave the commission the power to grant individualized amnesty, search premises and seize evidence, subpoena witnesses, and run a sophisticated witness-protection program. With a staff of three hundred, a budget of some $18 million each year for two-and-a-half years, and four large offices around the country, the commission dwarfed previous truth commissions in its size and reach.[62]

The full resources of the new South African government were committed to establishing a sense of justice and staving off cycles of retaliation and revenge. Indeed, John W. de Gruchy argues that Mandela was "committed to pursuing the path of reconciliation as an integral part of the process of achieving the goal of liberation."[63] The TRC was charged with a threefold task of investigating human rights violations, processing applications for amnesty, and making recommendations regarding reparations for victims and their families.

As one of the most successful truth commissions to date, the TRC provides an excellent example of how to begin to enact restorative justice in post-revolutionary communities. Both the weaknesses of the TRC and its strengths offer important lessons for pursing restorative transitional justice after oppression and violence. In the remainder of this chapter, I first explore three critiques leveled against the TRC and draw out their implications, and second discuss implications of one of the major strengths of the TRC expressed in its design of amnesty in exchange for truth-telling.

Critiques of the TRC

A foundational concern that critics have with the TRC involves a sense of confusion about what type of reconciliation was being sought. "The TRC did not have consensus on . . . the nature of the reconciliation it was mandated to pursue."[64] On this point, Audrey R. Chapman relays a conversation she had with Charles Villa-Vicencio, who sat on the commission. She reports that Villa-Vicencio suggested that three separate ideas regarding reconciliation were operative.[65] First, there were those for whom reconciliation was the same as interpersonal forgiveness, that is, forgiveness between individuals regarding individual acts of violence. A second group sought reconciliation as the ability to peacefully coexist as members of a national community. This group envisioned the TRC as establishing the conditions under which groups within South Africa would forgo vengeance. The final group advocated an exclusive focus on uncovering the truth of human rights violations as a means to reconciliation in the future, and thus saw little concrete hope for reconciliation to be enacted via the commission itself. Since Archbishop Tutu, along with other prominent clergy members, is viewed as having been a proponent of the first position, the TRC has been critiqued for focusing too heavily on individual violations of human rights, and reconciliation between individuals.[66]

I have argued elsewhere that criticism of the TRC based on a strong dichotomy between "individual" and "social" reconciliation may represent a failure to understand the operative anthropology of communitarian cultures, and I will not rehash these arguments now.[67] Nevertheless, the charge that the TRC focused too heavily on forgiveness between individuals unquestionably points to an important concern for how institutional violence—founded in the case of South Africa on acute racism—is taken into account by truth and reconciliation commissions seeking to establish a foundation for social reconciliation after severe oppression. The sustained degrading and structural violence of apartheid as a system, Chapman argues, was dealt with "primarily as background."[68] This suggests that to be more successful at promoting the fullness of truth, and thus restorative justice and social reconciliation, the TRC might have viewed itself as investigating and exposing the system of apartheid itself, uncovering the truth of its moral bankruptcy, and reconciling the community so as to move forward with a new system dedicated to a just peace. Likewise, other post-revolutionary societies ought to heed the admonition that social transformation will require careful attention to structures of violence that fomented revolution in the first place and that engender feelings of anger and powerlessness that could compound into new cycles of violence. Moreover, as remains clear in the new South Africa, structures of violence and their effects linger after oppression unless they are intentionally dismantled. Low wages, unemployment, poverty, profound economic inequality, inadequate housing, preventable disease and death remain severe social ills in South Africa twenty years after the transition to democracy.

Besides this major conceptual concern were several administrative or procedural ones. First, Priscilla Hayner suggests that despite having been empowered to seek aggressively for the truth through subpoena, and search and seizure, the TRC did not use these powers effectively. Because of this Hayner critiques the TRC for prioritizing reconciliation over and above a thorough search for the truth.[69] If this critique is accurate its importance must not be dismissed. We have already noted that justice is a precondition for social reconciliation. In the South African case truth-telling was held up as a primary vehicle for justice. Establishing the truth renders a moral judgment on the perpetrators and validates the harrowing experiences of the victims while also establishing a record of human rights abuses. In this way, truth-telling facilitates all three of the aims of restorative justice that I outlined above. Truth commissions should use all means at their disposal to forward these aims in order to facilitate social reconciliation and a just peace.

A second procedural critique suggests what is perhaps an unavoidable flaw in the TRC's rubric of amnesty in exchange for truth-telling. Because amnesty was conditioned upon truth-telling it is possible that it encouraged applications only from those who "reasonably feared prosecution."[70] Perpetrators who expected that enough evidence of their crimes existed to warrant arrest, prosecution, and conviction chose to engage in a process of restorative justice in order to avoid these default forms of retributive justice that would be triggered by their refusal to acknowledge their crimes. In other words, this critique suggests that those perpetrators who had good reasons to fear the consequences of a process of retributive justice confessed the truth, while those who felt relatively secure from those consequences did not. These latter may have felt that they had little incentive to submit themselves to restorative justice, and thus avoided justice all together. There may be little that can be done here save to remind perpetrators that telling the truth, repenting, and accepting moral censure for their crimes restores their own humanity and admits them again to the human community. So long as these things remain of little value to perpetrators then their human dignity remains damaged.

A third procedural critique speaks to the nature of reconciliation itself. To gain amnesty, perpetrators were required to fully disclose the truth, but they were not required to show remorse. This has led some to charge that the TRC pressured victims to forgive without placing concomitant pressure on perpetrators to apologize.[71] Moreover, some officials wanted amnesty to be conditioned on displays of remorse.[72] While acknowledging that this critique helpfully intends to prioritize the experience of victims and protect them from further harm, it should be pointed out that there are multiple problems with placing the condition of repentance on applications for amnesty. First, it would depend on the erroneous notion that remorse can be objectively known. De Gruchy recognizes the tension here noting there are moral problems in offering "pardon to those who show no regret."[73] Nevertheless, he also acknowledges that we cannot effectively "evaluate remorse" or know when expressions of remorse are sincere.[74] Second, requiring remorse could invite false demonstrations of repentance and thus jeopardize the integrity of an amnesty process that is dependent upon remorse. Third, mandating repentance may foment more resentment than reconciliation as perpetrators weigh the costs and benefits of making insincere apologies in exchange for their freedom. Finally, while it is designed to protect victims, mandatory repentance may have the opposite effect: it could suggest to victims that *because* perpetrators are apologizing, they are somehow *obligated or expected* to express forgiveness. Thus, concerns about the relationships between forgiveness, repentance, and reconciliation strike at the heart of social transformation following oppression and revolution. As I noted in my definitions of these terms above, a victims' capacity to forgive does not hinge on a perpetrators' capacity to repent. Furthermore, the philosophy of ubuntu suggests that to encourage a victim to forgive is an act of solidarity with the victim, who is the main subject of the healing and restorative power of forgiveness. At the same time, reconciliation, since it involves the rebuilding of relationships and the recognition of a common humanity, will likely involve genuine expressions of remorse; but true repentance cannot practically be demanded from perpetrators under threat of prosecution. In short, requiring the full disclosure of the truth is a far more objective mandate for amnesty than repentance. At least in theory, with a commission empowered to investigate, subpoena, search, and seize, truth testimony can be examined against evidence to check its veracity. Mandatory truth-telling is thus more likely to facilitate justice and less likely to violate the core meanings of other key components of social transformation: forgiveness, repentance, and reconciliation.

No effort at post-conflict reconciliation is ever perfectly successful. Having noted weaknesses in how the TRC functioned, it is helpful to remember the theological insights of Augustine discussed in chapter 2: no justice, no peace will be perfected in this "earthly city" tainted as it is by personal and structural sin. In light of this theological reality, it is important to see truth commissions and other vehicles of restorative justice as points of departure for longer processes of reconciliation that will not come to fruition rapidly, but instead are fulfilled across generations.

Amnesty, Truth, and Confrontation

As already alluded to above, the question of amnesty for perpetrators of oppression and violence is highly contentious, and with good reason. Many argue that amnesty amounts to impunity: that it negates justice and allows those responsible for unimaginably horrible crimes to avoid the consequences of their actions. Indeed this has been a serious problem in post-conflict situations where blanket amnesty meant immunity from any form of accountability or judgment. Amnesty that merely asks victims to "forgive and forget" invalidates their experiences and revictimizes them.[75] Thus, amnesty as amnesia does not promote justice for victims. Donald Shriver notes that "It seems psychologically unquestionable that perpetrators of injustice like to forget, but that their victims cannot forget."[76] Rather than encouraging victims to "forgive and forget" then, Shriver suggests that perpetrators "remember and repent" and victims "remember and forgive" as the best prescription for "the restoration of political health."[77]

Despite these very genuine concerns about how justice is related to amnesty, amnesty is often a condition of negotiations for a transition of power in communities emerging from oppression and violence.[78] The question is thus frequently not whether or not to offer amnesty, but how to condition amnesty so as to forward the goals of restorative justice. The South African government did this by tying amnesty to full disclosure of the truth, so as to develop a historical record of atrocities, validate victims' experiences, and render a moral judgment upon perpetrators. This is amnesty not as amnesia, but as *anamnesis*: proper, or intentional remembering.

The South African context suggests that for amnesty to function as anamnesis, and as a tool to forward the goals of restorative justice and reconciliation, it ought to include two related conditions: full disclosure of the truth, and willingness of perpetrators to endure confrontations with victims. Disclosure must be public, must be judged to be complete, and must correspond to the best available evidence. By their nature full disclosures are admissions of guilt, though not necessarily of regret or repentance. In making public declarations of the truth, perpetrators must, if victims desire (and certainly some will not), endure confrontations in which victims or their representatives can question perpetrators. These conditions can thus often, though not always, occur simultaneously as perpetrators disclose the truth and victims listen and potentially question perpetrators.[79]

Full disclosure is important for forwarding restorative justice and reconciliation for at least two reasons. First, it constitutes in and of itself a form of justice for victims, and as we have seen justice is a constitutive element of social reconciliation. In reflecting on El Salvador's process of transitional justice Stephen Pope refers to full disclosure of the truth as an example of Thomas Aquinas's classic definition of justice: to give each person his/her due. "Truth-telling is an important expression of justice. The perpetrator owes the truth both to his victim and the wider community, which has also been harmed . . . the perpetrator pays to the victim a debt of commutative justice."[80] In full disclosure, the perpetrator remits the truth that is owed. Likewise, by requiring truth in exchange for amnesty, the community makes a claim for commutative justice. The overarching goal of the common good shapes the form taken by commutative justice: truth-telling.

Second, full disclosure helps a community meet the goals of establishing a historical record of atrocities, validating victims' experiences, and holding perpetrators accountable, which contribute to a sense of justice. In the case of the TRC, the sheer volume of stories and the number of perpetrators who confessed their guilt forced the population formerly in power to move from a space of denial to "corporate shame," with the realization that the privileges they enjoyed came at the price of deep injustice.[81] The "TRC helped reclaim a history that was denied and shredded."[82] Thus, it provides a clear example of how a truth and reconciliation commission can engage in a social process of deconstructing the narrative of the lie such that the experiences of victims are validated. Moreover, insofar as victims and victim-groups recognize the proceedings of a commission as the conduit of justice, they can begin to trust and take ownership of a legal system that formerly victimized them. Rather than feeling themselves and their experiences discounted, the process of full disclosure and confrontation becomes both the means to and the end of justice. It is the means to justice, because it validates a long invalidated experience; it outs the narrative of the lie, and establishes a record of the truth. It is the end of justice because when perpetrators are compelled to publicly admit their guilt and own their role in violations of human rights, a moral judgment is rendered against them. As Peter Storey puts it, the TRC helped victims to see "that even with amnesty, their tormentors are judged."[83] The community as a whole declares that the actions of the perpetrators were wrong and unjustifiable. Full disclosure of the truth forwards the goals of restorative justice and can thus contribute to a pursuit of the common good.

Confrontations between victims and perpetrators can have restorative effects for both, and for the common good as a whole.[84] Speaking of the importance of encounters between members of conflicting groups, John Paul Lederach argues that "acknowledgment through hearing one another's stories validates experience and feelings and represents the first step toward restoration of the person and the relationship."[85] Lederach concludes that confrontation is a critical moment in social transformation from "unpeaceful" to "more peaceful" relationships.[86] Here I offer two thematic reasons for its importance: confrontation symbolizes a shift in power, and it offers the opportunity to begin a longer process of reconciliation.

First, public confrontation in which perpetrators reveal the truth and victims or their representatives may question or engage the perpetrator signifies a shift in former power imbalances that can be healing and restorative for victims. Previous encounters between those who have been victimized and their perpetrators empowered the perpetrators and left the victims violated and vulnerable. A truth commission constitutes a new, more controlled confrontation, in which the victims have the opportunity to see that those who formerly unjustly wielded power over them are indeed human beings who, like themselves, are ultimately responsible to other human beings and vulnerable to the powerful machinations of the state. This shift in power is represented by the process of a commission itself. Public truth-telling and confrontation represents a ritualistic movement from the shrouded practices of the repressive regime to the potential justice and transparency of the new government. Even the physical spaces, such as courtrooms where politically motivated sham trials mocked genuine justice, are transformed into spaces for confrontations in which the truth is told and heard. In such confrontations, truth-telling takes on a highly symbolic nature: the lies the previous regime used to justify human rights abuses are publicly repudiated and a moral judgment is rendered against the perpetrators; justice is embodied in the very physical spaces formerly used to systematize injustice. Moreover, the TRC model demanded that perpetrators apply for amnesty; amnesty was conveyed by apartheid's victims, as represented by the TRC's amnesty committee; and many of those who failed to meet the requirements of amnesty were prosecuted. These procedures were far from perfect, and many of them remain subjects of rigorous debate, but there is little question that they represented a major shift in structures of power and justice in South Africa. Those groups who were formerly dehumanized and disenfranchised now claimed ownership over the very social and political spaces and judicial processes that had formerly victimized them.

Second, confrontation provides an opportunity to begin a longer process of reconciliation. It is important to remember that reconciliation is not a managed process, nevertheless confrontations can be graced moments. A moment of confrontation, studded with the perpetrators full disclosure of the truth and admission of guilt, marks an opportunity for both victim and perpetrator to acknowledge openly that "there is something from the past to be forgiven."[87] Some victims experience truth-telling as a form of moral accountability and justice, and an opportunity to offer forgiveness (though this is by no means a uniform response and many victims simply find themselves unready to convey forgiveness). For victims who want and are able to express forgiveness, it can further their sense of justice since forgiveness itself entails blame. The perpetrators were wrong, and their actions defiled the basic humanity of themselves and their victims. A victim who is able to forgive a perpetrator condemns the perpetrator's actions—that is, by pointing out that the perpetrator committed a grave wrong, requiring forgiveness. Confrontations may also enable perpetrators to admit their need for forgiveness and accept it when it is offered,[88] and to repent and apologize for their actions. Forgiveness and repentance in moments of confrontation can initiate the long process of reconciliation.

Narratives that evidence the beginnings of social reconciliation abound. Desmond Tutu describes the testimony at the TRC surrounding the Bisho Massacre in which thirty peaceful protesters were gunned down by South African defense forces.[89] The first officer to testify raised the ire of the entire courtroom because he came across as "hard, unsympathetic."[90] When the second witness, Colonel Horst Schobesberger, took the stand the atmosphere was extremely tense. He admitted that he had given the order to open fire. Then he turned directly to the victims and said: "I say we are sorry. I say the burden of the Bisho massacre will be on our shoulders for the rest of our lives. We cannot wish it away. It happened. But please, I ask specifically the victims not to forget, I cannot ask for this, but to forgive us, to get the soldiers back into the community, to accept them fully . . . This is all I can do. I'm sorry, this I can say, I'm sorry."[91] Tutu describes the tension in the room dissipating: "It was as if someone had waved a special magic wand which transformed anger and tension into this display of communal forgiveness."[92] Schobesberger saw the confrontation, which he was required to endure with victims as a condition of his amnesty, as an opportunity to acknowledge his guilt, and his victims' suffering. This confrontation enabled Schobesberger and his victims to deconstruct the narrative of the lie; to restore the memory of the Bisho massacre, making it a matter of public record. Schobesberger accepted both the moral censure of the truth commission and the gratuitous forgiveness of his community. Together victims and perpetrators in a moment of tense confrontation, contributed to a process of restorative justice and social reconciliation.

CONCLUSION

The notion of reconciliation spans and shapes both *jus ante* armed revolution and *jus ad* and *jus in* armed revolution. It likewise imbues the tandem approach to just revolution that I described in the previous chapter. An intent to reconcile means exhausting nonviolent just peacemaking strategies to overcome oppression. Should these fail, the intent to reconcile, must shape how armed resistance is introduced and employed. Moreover, articulating reconciliation as a goal of revolutionary struggle, and holding out hope for eventual reconciliation can inspire the masses to continue peaceful resistance in the midst of armed struggle so that nonviolent just peacemaking practices continue to form the bedrock of revolutionary resistance while armed strategies are used as minimally as possible to force effectively negotiations. Keeping reconciliation "in readiness of mind" throughout the revolutionary struggle considerably strengthens the chances of promoting and achieving it when freedom is won.

The telos of any armed conflict that is just—whether war or revolution—is to establish a just peace. To profess a genuine commitment to a just peace in the aftermath of oppression means promoting the common good and a social reconciliation that staves off cycles of violence. This requires justice that seeks to restore relationships and rebuild communities. Rather than encouraging additional violence in the name of retaliatory justice, or revenge, restorative justice compels us to set the foundation for peace in a shared understanding of the past that validates victims and holds perpetrators morally accountable. It aims at the common good, striving to heal broken relationships, and endeavoring to turn whole communities from violent impulses, to a sense of justice that promotes forgiveness, repentance, and reconciliation. Reconciliation can emerge from processes of restorative justice that demand full disclosure of the truth in moments of confrontation between perpetrator and victim. In this way restorative justice promotes reconciliation and seeks, after the revolution, to rebuild a community that will share a sense of common humanity, and a renewed commitment to the common good.

NOTES

1. Transitional justice is "the study and practice of trying to establish principled justice after atrocity by employing a range of approaches, including both judicial and nonjudicial measures, to help address a legacy of mass human rights abuses." Kirsten J. Fisher and Robert Stewart, "After the Arab Spring: A New Wave of Transitional Justice?" in *Transitional Justice and the Arab Spring*, Kirsten J. Fisher and Robert Stewart, eds., (New York: Routledge, 2014), 1.

2. Due to time and thematic constraints I focus in this chapter on restorative justice and social reconciliation in the aftermath of oppression and violence. It should be noted, however, that there are many other aspects of the emerging notion of *jus post bellum* that include long-term efforts of nations to, for example, build a more just economy, meet citizens' basic needs, and rebuild damaged infrastructure. I would direct the reader to the work of political philosopher Brian Orend including "*Jus Post Bellum:* The Perspective of a Just War Theorist," *Leiden Journal of International Law*, 20 (2007): 571–591; and *The Morality of War*, 2nd edition, (Petersborough, Ontario: Broadview Press, 2013). See also the contributions of Mark Allman and Tobias Winright in *After the Smoke Clears: The Just War Tradition and Post-War Justice* (Maryknoll, NY: Orbis Books, 2010); and "Growing Edges of the Just War Theory: *Jus ante bellum, Jus post bellum,* and Imperfect Justice," *Journal of the Society of Christian Ethics*, 32.2, (Fall/Winter 2012): 173–191. In addition, for more on the relationship between restorative justice and reconciliation see Daniel Philpott, *Just and Unjust Peace: An Ethic of Political Reconciliation*, (New York: Oxford University Press, 2012).

3. Robert J. Schreiter, *Reconciliation: Mission and Ministry in a Changing Social Order* (Maryknoll, NY: Orbis Press, 1992), 44.

4. John W. de Gruchy, *Reconciliation: Restoring Justice,* (Minneapolis, MN: Fortress Press, 2002), 177.

5. Philpott, 261.

6. Schreiter, 60.

7. This is especially important in situations where to be in active relationship with perpetrators may mean further victimization, as might be the case for abused spouses, for example.
8. de Gruchy, 170.
9. de Gruchy, 201.
10. Thomas Aquinas, *Summa Theologiae,* trans., English Dominican Fathers, II.II.58.7, ad 2. Available at http://www.newadvent.org/summa/.
11. Aquinas, II.II.61.1.
12. Aquinas, II.II.61.1.
13. Aquinas, II.II.61.4 and II.II.62.1.
14. In the original Latin, Aquinas uses the word *contrapassum.*
15. Aquinas, II.II.61.4.
16. Aquinas, II.II.58.6.
17. Aquinas, II.II.58.5.
18. Julius Gathogo, "African Philosophy as Expressed in the Concepts of Hospitality and Ubuntu" in *Journal of Theology for Southern Africa,* 130 March, (2008), 45.
19. For a theological treatment of ubuntu, see Michael Battle, *Reconciliation: The Ubuntu Theology of Desmond Tutu* (Cleveland, OH: The Pilgrim Press, 1997).
20. Mluleki Mnyaka and Mokgethi Motlhabi, "The African Concept of Ubuntu/Botha and its Socio-Moral Significance," *Black Theology* 3.2 (2005): 220.
21. Second Vatican Council, *Gaudium et Spes: Pastoral Constitution on The Church in the Modern World,* §12 available at http://www.vatican.va/archive/hist_councils/ii_vatican_council/documents/vat-ii_cons_19651207_gaudium-et-spes_en.html.
22. John XXIII, *Pacem in Terris,* §9–27 available at http://www.vatican.va/holy_father/john_xxiii/encyclicals/documents/hf_j-xxiii_enc_11041963_pacem_en.html.
23. Gathogo, 46.
24. Mnyaka and Motlhabi, 218.
25. Mnyaka and Motlhabi, 221–222.
26. Mnyaka and Motlhabi, 221.
27. Mnyaka and Motlhabi, 221.
28. Mnyaka and Motlhabi, 223.
29. Gathogo, 40.
30. Desmond Tutu quoted in *The Words of Desmond Tutu,* Naomi Tutu, ed., (London: Hodder and Stoughton, 1989), 69.
31. Mnyaka and Motlhabi, 217.
32. Nelson Mandela quoted in Gathogo, 45.
33. Albert Nolan, *God in South Africa: The Challenge of the Gospel* (Claremont, South Africa: David Philip Publishers, 1988), 80.
34. Mnyaka and Motlhabi, 224.
35. Desmond Tutu describes this "social harmony" as the "*summum bonum*—the greatest good." See Desmond Mpilo Tutu, *No Future Without Forgiveness* (New York: Doubleday, 1999), 31.
36. Mnyaka and Motlhabi, 226.
37. S. Netshiomboni, *Ubuntu: Fundamental Constitutional Value and Imperative Aid,* (Pretoria: University of South Africa Press, 1998), 6.
38. Mnyaka and Motlhabi, 225.
39. Mnyaka and Motlhabi, 225.
40. Desmond Tutu quoted in Gathogo, 45.
41. Battle, 47.
42. Tutu, *No Future without Forgiveness,* 31.
43. Mnyaka and Motlhabi, 222.
44. Mnyaka and Motlhabi, 223.
45. Schreiter, 18.
46. "The Kairos Document," 3.1. Available at http://www.sahistory.org.za/archive/challenge-church-theological-comment-political-crisis-south-africa-kairos-document-1985.

47. Miroslav Volf, "Forgiveness, Reconciliation, and Justice: A Christian Contribution to a More Peaceful Social Environment," in *Forgiveness and Reconciliation: Religion, Public Policy, and Conflict Transformation,* Raymond G. Helmick and Rodney L. Peterson, eds., (Radnor, PA: Templeton Foundation Press, 2001), 35. Allman and Winright make a similar claim in "After the Smoke Clears," that "justice and peace are not competing values. They are complimentary" (105).

48. Volf, 36.

49. Audrey R. Chapman, "Coming to Terms with the Past: Truth, Justice, and/or Reconciliation," *Annual of the Society of Christian Ethics,* 19, (1999): 238.

50. Donald W. Shriver, Jr., "Forgiveness: A Bridge Across an Abyss of Revenge" in *Forgiveness and Reconciliation: Religion, Public Policy, and Conflict Transformation,* 156.

51. Schreiter, 30.

52. Schreiter, 34.

53. Schreiter, 34.

54. Again, Allman and Winright make a similar point in "After the Smoke Clears": "Robust post-war justice includes elements of restorative justice alongside retributive, social, procedural, and criminal justice" (105).

55. Audrey R. Chapman, "Truth Commissions as Instruments of Forgiveness and Reconciliation," in *Forgiveness and Reconciliation: Religion, Public Policy, and Conflict Transformation,* 258.

56. This was the case in Argentina, Chile, Guatemala, and Sierra Leone. See Priscilla B. Hayner, *Unspeakable Truths: Facing the Challenge of Truth Commissions* (New York: Routledge, 2002), chapters 4 and 5.

57. John Paul Lederach, *Building Peace: Sustainable Reconciliation in Divided Societies* (Washington, DC: United States Institute of Peace, 1997), 26.

58. Antjie Krog, *Country of My Skull: Guilt, Sorrow, and the Limits of Forgiveness in the New South Africa* (New York: Three Rivers Press, 1999), 143.

59. John W. de Gruchy, "The Struggle for Justice and the Ministry of Reconciliation" in *Journal of Theology for Southern Africa ,* 62 (1988), 45.

60. de Gruchy, "The Struggle for Justice and the Ministry of Reconciliation," 47.

61. Hayner, 41.

62. Hayner, 41.

63. de Gruchy, *Reconciliation: Restoring Justice,* 37.

64. Chapman, "Truth Commissions as Instruments of Forgiveness and Reconciliation," 262.

65. Chapman, "Truth Commissions as Instruments of Forgiveness and Reconciliation," 262.

66. Chapman, "Truth Commissions as Instruments of Forgiveness and Reconciliation," 273.

67. See Anna Floerke Scheid, "Interpersonal and Social Reconciliation: Finding Congruence in African Theological Anthropology," *Horizons,* 39.1 (Spring 2012): 27–49.

68. Chapman, "Truth Commissions as Instruments of Forgiveness and Reconciliation," 273.

69. Hayner, 42.

70. Hayner, 43.

71. Chapman, "Truth Commissions as Instruments of Forgiveness and Reconciliation," 269.

72. Chapman, "Truth Commissions as Instruments of Forgiveness and Reconciliation," 271.

73. de Gruchy, *Reconciliation: Restoring Justice,* 177.

74. de Gruchy, *Reconciliation: Restoring Justice,* 177.

75. Robert Schreiter, "Mediating Repentance, Forgiveness, and Reconciliation: What is the Church's Role?" in *The Spirit in the Church and the World, The Annual Publication of the College Theology Society,* Bradford E. Hinze, ed., (New York: Orbis Press, 2003), 61.

76. Shriver, 152.

77. Shriver, 156.

78. Kent Greenawalt, "Amnesty's Justice" in *Truth v. Justice: The Morality of Truth Commissions,* Robert I. Rotberg and Dennis Thompson, eds., (Princeton, NJ: Princeton University Press, 2000), 92.

79. Peter Storey, "A different kind of justice: Truth and reconciliation in South Africa," in *The Christian Century* (September 10–17, 1997): 790.

80. Pope, 830.

81. Storey, 791.
82. de Gruchy, *Reconciliation: Restoring Justice*, 160.
83. Storey, 793.
84. For more on the cathartic results of disclosure and confrontation see Judith Herman, M.D., *Trauma and Recovery: The Aftermath of Violence—from Domestic Abuse to Political Terror* (New York: Basic Books, 1992).
85. Lederach, 26.
86. Lederach, 64–65.
87. Donald W. Shriver, Jr., *An Ethic for Enemies: Forgiveness in Politics* (New York: Oxford University Press, 1995), 7.
88. Volf, 45.
89. Tutu, *No Future without Forgiveness*, 150–151.
90. Tutu, *No Future without Forgiveness*, 150.
91. The testimony of Colonel Horst Schobesberger at the TRC. Quoted in Tutu, *No Future without Forgiveness*, 151.
92. Tutu, *No Future without Forgiveness*, 151.

Chapter Six

Just Revolution and the "Arab Spring"

In this final chapter, I begin by binding the elements of the previous chapters together, briefly summarizing the conclusions I have drawn regarding *jus ante*, *jus ad,* and *jus in* armed revolution, as well as *jus post* revolution. This summation serves to present the theory of just revolution and the criteria as I have presented them in outline. Next, I cautiously begin what inevitably needs to be a longer and more in depth discussion about how these conclusions interact with the recent string of uprisings across North Africa and the Middle East, often referred to as the "Arab Spring." Given the ongoing nature of these revolutionary movements and transitions, I make my remarks hesitantly and cautiously. They serve merely as brief observations for beginning what must necessarily be an ongoing analysis as events across North Africa and the Middle East continue to unfold.

SUMMARY: AN ETHIC FOR JUST REVOLUTION

All revolutions which seek to be just must begin with nonviolent resistance only. It is possible that nonviolence alone will enable revolutionaries to achieve their political goals. If a revolution can be won using only nonviolence, then it should not progress to a state of armed revolution. Just peacemaking theory expands our notion of what constitutes nonviolent strategies for building up peace and justice and avoiding resort to the use of force. A just revolution employs nonviolent direct action to surface tensions in the unjust system, and to make known the will of the people through mass participation in the revolutionary movement. It seeks to establish and advance participatory mechanisms and respect for human rights in the revolutionary movement itself. These mechanisms prevision the justice and peace that the just revolution aims to establish at the national level, and prepares the citizenry for meaningful participation in a new government. Revolutionaries should anticipate the regime's attempts to suppress the popular struggle, and seek to empower ordinary people through grassroots organizing as a bulwark against this suppression. Finally, revolutionaries should seek to engage the international community and the United Nations in their struggle for justice.

While armed revolution, like warfare, ought to be avoided and understood as a grave and serious undertaking it nevertheless may be morally justified in certain extreme cases. The just war criteria adapted and revised for revolutionary contexts are helpful in guiding a just armed revolution. A *just cause* for armed revolution manifests as grave wrongs and injustices requiring self-defense. These grave wrongs include degrading, structural, and/or direct repressive violence. In addition, a population should seek to define who, for them, constitutes a *legitimate authority* to lead the people in armed revolution. The legitimate authority encourages the already emerging political participation of all for the sake of the common good, is supported by the broad population, and endeavors to control and limit violence and the use of force. The legitimate authority is also the caretaker of the just revolution's *right intention* to effect eventual reconciliation amongst enemies for the sake of establishing a just peace. Moreover, armed revolution may only be undertaken as a *last resort*. Last resort is indicated by the criminalization and violent suppression of participatory, nonviolent resistance, and by the escalation of repressive practices such that the regime demonstrates that it views dissenting citizens as opponents to be defeated or eliminated. Finally, just revolution includes a *reasonable hope of success* of liberation from sinful injustice. The "reasonableness" of this hope is to be determined by the oppressed themselves, who may view revolutionary self-defense as a necessary component of protecting themselves and the common good.

Following the just war tradition's criteria for *jus in bello*, just armed revolution maintains *proportionality* of means. It thus demands that armed resistance be coupled with regular attempts at negotiation. Furthermore armed resistance should be graduated, beginning with those means, such as sabotage, that intend to incur no loss of life, and escalating to forms of resistance that include loss of life only as is necessary to promote negotiation, and decrease overall violence. In addition, just revolution must observe the criterion of *noncombatant immunity* by declaring armed revolution, refraining from direct, intentional attacks on civilians or civilian infrastructure as revolutionary means, and investigating and policing revolutionaries who commit abuses of human rights.

Whether a revolution has been entirely nonviolent or has included armed resistance, its aftermath ought to involve an intentional plan of transitional justice. Restorative justice, even if it is combined with punitive or retributive measures, is often the most effective form of justice for staving off cycles of retaliation and revenge and for helping former enemies living in close quarters to work together to build a just peace. Restorative justice aims at the common good, and can be designed to enable the post-conflict community to work toward social reconciliation by establishing a historical record of past atrocities and human rights violations, validating victims' experiences of violence, and rendering a judgment upon perpetrators. In practice this may include conditional amnesty that includes truth-telling and possible confrontation between victims and perpetrators, the prosecution of those who fail to cooperate with the conditions of amnesty, and support for both perpetrators who wish to express repentance, and victims who wish to struggle toward forgiveness.

THE "ARAB SPRING"

The Arab Spring, which erupted in early 2011, has been called the "culmination of a century of Arab popular struggle for freedom and sovereignty."[1] Most recognize the immediate precipitating act of the uprisings in street vendor Mohamed Bouazizi's desperate act of self-immolation when his unlicensed vegetable stand was shut down by Tunisian authorities. Bouazizi's radical protest sparked a series of demonstrations across the country that eventually led Zine al-Abidine Ben Ali, Tunisia's dictatorial leader for more than two decades, to flee the country. "Within days, a temporary president and national unity government were in place in Tunisia."[2] The Tunisian revolution ignited similar uprisings across North Africa and the Middle East as people who had endured decades of injustices in the form of degrading, structural, and direct repressive violence at the hands of corrupt and authoritarian regimes sought to overthrow the people and systems that oppressed them.[3] Authoritarian regimes in Yemen and Egypt crumbled under the weight of nonviolent resistance, and the Libyan regime of Muammar Gaddafi succumbed to a combination of nonviolent and armed resistance coupled with international intervention. Citizens of several other nations from Oman, to Algeria, from Bahrain to Morocco, engaged in protests that yielded a variety of responses from the promise of reforms, to violent repression. In Syria Bashar al-Assad resists change so vehemently that he met nonviolent resistance with severe violent repression. Pockets of rebels, some made up of defectors from Assad's own military, now conduct armed resistance against the regime. What may have begun as revolution in Syria, has devolved into a horrifically violent civil war.

As I discuss the revolutionary ethics of the Arab Spring here two caveats are necessary. First, the moniker "Arab Spring" can be both helpful and obfuscating. It is helpful because it acknowledges the connectedness among the uprisings that have occurred in several nations across North Africa and the Middle East. It is obfuscating insofar as it suggests that these events are more related than they in fact are. A full understanding of the Arab Spring would involve an in depth examination of each nation, its history, its culture/s, and the organizations mounting nonviolent and armed resistance in each uprising, as well as those social and political forces mitigating for and/or against change. While the events across the Middle East are undoubtedly related, we must heed the warning of University of Cairo professor Hasan Hanafi that "there is a danger arising from generalized judgments, especially generalizing a very complex phenomenon" such as the revolutionary uprisings across the Middle East.[4] It would be a mistake to view the Arab Spring as a single event rather than a series of distinct, complex, but related events.[5] I will continue to refer to the "Arab Spring," but with this caveat in mind.

Moreover, this first caveat points to a second, related one. Given both the complexity and ongoing nature of the Arab Spring, I cannot here engage in the kind of thorough analysis that these events ultimately demand. Circumstances on the ground shift daily both in those countries that have already forced reforms and regime transitions and in those that continue to struggle toward change. I hope to proceed with deeper analysis in future work, and as the events of the Arab Spring continue to unfold, but meanwhile this chapter will necessarily make only preliminary remarks that scratch the surface of what is necessary to evaluate the ethics of the Arab uprisings. I remain open, flexible and tentative in the observations I make here.

With these caveats in mind I turn now to several observations regarding the ethic of just revolution that I have posited and the Arab Spring. I will touch on aspects from each of the phases of just revolution, beginning with *jus ante* armed revolution, and continuing through *jus ad* and *jus in* armed revolution, and *jus post* revolution.

Jus ante armed revolution and the Arab Spring

A decidedly positive development of the Arab Spring is the continued affirmation of the effectiveness and moral authority of nonviolent struggle against oppression. Every nation engaged in the Arab Spring began by employing nonviolent resistance. Indeed, citizens of Tunisia, Yemen, and Egypt forced regime change using nonviolent means only. It is arguable that Tunisia and Yemen are now in the transitional, if at times precarious, *jus post* revolution phase. This is more complex in Egypt where many consider the revolution to be ongoing in light of a military coup that forced the democratically elected Mohammed Morsi from office.[6] Now, four years after protesters ousted Hosni Mubarak, Egypt remains in a state of intense volatility with governing authorities targeting activists across the political spectrum. Nevertheless, the revolutionary experiences of these countries give credence to just peacemaking theorists' insistence that the use of nonviolent practices prior to any consideration of the use of force has become morally normative.[7] Here I make four observations about nonviolent strategies and the Arab Spring.

First, nonviolent direct action in the form of protests and demonstrations played perhaps the most important role in instigating and spreading these revolutionary uprisings. Tunisians demonstrated in streets and squares across the country surfacing and confronting the social conditions that led Bouazizi to set himself aflame, and illustrating that "sustained and broad-based popular mobilization can lead to political change, even in a police state."[8] Egypt's Tahrir Square became the center of nonviolent direct action with eighteen days of protests demanding an end to the regime of Hosni Mubarak.[9] When his attempts to make concessions failed to quell protesters, and his military forces refused to fire on unarmed peaceful demonstrators, Mubarak stepped down. Yemeni citizens demonstrated against the three-decade rule of Ali Abdullah Saleh, eventually forcing him from power. Masses of people engaged in nonviolent direct action across the Middle East powerfully illustrating the will of the people and in some cases helping to engender political transformation.

Second, the Arab uprisings have been dependent upon grassroots networks for organizing mass resistance to dictatorial regimes and empowering ordinary people to become political actors. Grassroots organizations are attributed with laying the groundwork for the Arab Spring: "The revolt's intensity and broad scope . . . reflect that it did not emerge from a vacuum. It is rather, the culmination of decades of activism by scores of groups small and large that have struggled unsuccessfully for civil and political rights."[10] In Egypt, for example, the organizing efforts of groups like the April 25 Movement, Kefaya! ("Enough!"), and the We Are All Khaled Said Facebook page[11] belie any description of the uprisings as purely spontaneous. The Arab Spring confirms the importance of networks of grassroots organizations, of the kind envisioned by just peacemaking theorists. These groups have been active and ready to organize and empower ordinary people to participate in mass demonstrations when the opportunity for confrontational nonviolent direct action presented itself.

The third observation draws on the just peacemaking practice of "advancing democracy and human rights." Many scholars have noted that the uprisings challenge the notion of "Arab Exceptionalism," or the idea that "countries in the region [of the Middle East] come pre-installed with resistance to processes of democratization and globalization."[12] Mass participation in demonstrations, and popular demands for free and fair elections challenge the notion that Arabs automatically reject participatory or democratic practices in favor of autocratic rule. Indeed, Al Jazeera English's senior political analyst, Marwan Bishara, describes democratic activism and participation as major features of the revolutionary movements across North Africa and the

Middle East. "For centuries" argues Bishara, "these Arab citizens and their social and political movements have been either unfairly demonized or totally ignored in the West—by both its leaders and the media . . . But today's Arabs . . . characterized as unreceptive to democracy and freedom . . . are now giving the world a lesson in both."[13] While democratic participation in government will undoubtedly be culturally different from how it is manifested in the United States, Western Europe, Southern Africa, etc. what is clear is that Arabs desire participation in the structures that govern their lives, and accountability of those structures to the people most effected by them. As Rami G. Khouri notes, however, "it will take at least a decade to show if the change now under way is irreversible" so as to create "legitimate and participatory governance systems" and "institutionalize citizen rights and limits to state power in enforceable constitutional systems with the rule of law protected by an independent judiciary."[14] The Arab Spring has been a force for advancing human rights and participatory democracy in the Middle East, but the outcome of this wave of participation remains uncertain.

Finally, nonviolent international assistance likely contributed to troops decisions regarding whether or not to carry out orders to suppress protest pointing to the indispensable nature of international support for revolutionary movements in a political context of globalization. Sharon Erikson Nepstad cogently argues that military defections have been a key component of successful nonviolent revolutions since dictators typically depend on the military to repress dissent.[15] When the military defects, dictatorial regimes have less power to repress and the revolution is more likely to succeed. Thus nonviolent movements ought to encourage military defections. Nepstad argues for a number of factors—political, economic, and moral incentives—that sway the decision to defect or remain loyal. A major factor that influences defection is whether or not the military perceives the regime to be strong enough to withstand civil resistance. Here international assistance in the revolution becomes especially important. Nepstad encourages revolutionaries to court international assistance by ensuring that peaceful demonstrations are "televised globally" so that any repression is met with "international condemnation."[16] This condemnation may result in sanctions, which weakens the regime in the eyes of its military and may thus encourage defections; conversely, however, lack of sanctions may make a regime appear strong and discourage defections.[17] The military's decision to defect, in the case of Egypt, and to remain loyal to the regime, in the case of Bahrain helped determine the short-term outcomes of those revolutionary movements. After initially supporting Egypt's Hosni Mubarak, once repression became severe the Obama Administration shifted its support to protesters. President Obama's condemnation of Mubarak suggested to members of the military that the "regime was fragile."[18] At stake was $1.3 billion in U.S. aid received annually by the Egyptian military.[19] The "Egyptian military *as a whole* shifted its support from the regime to the movement."[20] By contrast, international response to revolution in Bahrain confirmed the military's perception that the Khalifa family regime was strong and would withstand protest. The United States did not apply sanctions, and two nations—Saudi Arabia and the United Arab Emirates—sent troops to help suppress dissent.[21] Protests are ongoing, but "they have failed to win over the armed forces and they have not been able to oust the Khalifa family."[22] Lack of international assistance for Bahrain's protesters is one factor in military decisions to remain loyal to the regime, and thus far, the nonviolent revolution has not been successful.

Nonviolent resistance has been a key component in forcing regime change and reforms in the Arab Spring. The success of just peacemaking practices in Tunisia, Egypt, and Yemen testifies to the value of nonviolent resistance for promoting just revolution, and affirms the validity of demanding that nonviolence ought to be the initial response to oppression.

Jus ad and *jus in* armed revolution and the Arab Spring

It is arguable that all of those nations that have engaged in uprisings during the Arab Spring have had just causes for their revolutionary activity: grave wrongs and injustices have been committed against the citizenry of the countries involved, including varying degrees of degrading, structural, and direct repressive violence. Thus political scientist Katerina Dalacoura remarks, "More than anything else, the rebellions were a call for dignity and a reaction to being humiliated by arbitrary, unaccountable, and increasingly predatory tyrannies."[23] As we have seen, citizens of several nations were able to wage revolution against these injustices with relative success using only nonviolent means. Revolutionaries in Libya and Syria, however, turned to armed strategies. Here I discuss interconnected observations regarding the criteria of legitimate authority, last resort, proportionality, and right intention in the Arab Spring.

The Arab Spring illustrates that legitimate authority for conducting armed revolution remains among the most difficult criteria to fulfill, on the part of the revolutionaries, or to determine, on the part of outside observers. Whether because autocrats purposefully foment discord among the people which prevents them from rallying together around a particular revolutionary authority;[24] or because the subjects of dictatorships have become suspicious of any person or group claiming authority, some Arab Spring revolutionaries have seemed reluctant to name, for themselves, a legitimate authority to lead the rebellion. Indeed, Wael Ghonim, the facilitator of the influential We are All Khaled Said Facebook page, which called thousands to demonstrate in Tahrir Square, boasted that Egypt's was a "leaderless revolution" in which no one had "primacy over others."[25] While I can applaud Ghonim's egalitarian sentiment, I am nevertheless convinced that the Arab Spring also demonstrates why it is important for revolutionaries to name for themselves a legitimate authority. In Ghonim's Egypt, the Supreme Council of the Armed Forces (SCAF) filled the vacuum of leadership and has arguably taken more power than is justifiably theirs. SCAF called for elections soon after the removal of Mubarak rather than waiting until protest groups could form genuine and competitive political parties.[26] Eventually the SCAF took it upon themselves to overturn the outcome of these elections, initiating a coup against Egypt's President. Dalacoura foresaw the potential problem posed by Egypt's lack of revolutionary authority, noting that "the dominant position of the army following the overthrow of Mubarak is an advantage in terms of continuity and stability but could pose a serious threat to the prospects of democratic reform."[27] The problems of Egypt's transition may have been either avoided or at least mollified had a clearer authority arisen from the ranks of the revolutionary groups themselves. The lack of effective leadership among revolutionaries in some Arab Spring nations led political scientist Ali A. Mazrui to remark, "It's definitely a fragile situation. And leadership in any of these instances could be captured by others . . . each revolution could still be captured by other groups. And we're having our fingers crossed that whoever captures it is concerned about the welfare of the people."[28] To promote new or transitional governments with genuine concern for the common good, revolutionaries would do well to declare for themselves a legitimate authority who enjoys broad support among the population and is accountable to them, and whose duty it will be to limit violence and promote political participation.

Defining a legitimate authority can also be crucial for garnering international support and assistance. In the early days of armed resistance in Libya, the *Los Angeles Times* ran the headline: "U.S. wants to know who's in charge of Libyan revolution."[29] The Obama administration spent days trying to determine to whom in Libya they could speak regarding humanitarian and potential military assistance. Shortly thereafter, the body known as the National Transitional Council (NTC) of Libya—"the main and most supported opposition group" had declared itself Libya's legitimate authority and underwent a "series of recognitions" throughout the international community, including eventual recognition by the United Nations.[30] While the United Nations and NATO forces cannot, in accordance with international law take sides in a civil war, the UN Security Council did choose, in accordance with the "responsibility to protect" norm discussed in chapter 3 to assist in protecting civilians from violence, and later to aid Libya's transitional government.[31] The international community's confusion and queries about who rebels considered their legitimate authority in Libya makes it clear that revolutionaries who value international assistance and support must declare a clear authority or authorities. Given the importance of international support for helping revolutions to succeed, a legitimate authority remains indispensable for meeting revolutionary goals.

Concerns about the criteria of last resort and proportionate means are tied together in the context of Syria, where revolution has morphed into civil war. On the one hand, "In Syria, regime violence almost certainly has been the primary reason behind the protest movement's growth and radicalization."[32] The Assad regime responded to nonviolent resistance with severe violent repression, including ordering the army to attack unarmed civilians, killing four on the first day of demonstrations.[33] In the aftermath of these killings, the number of protesters increased until thousands marched in the streets of the city of Deraa. The next wave of repression involved "several tanks and helicopters" sent "to seal off the city;"[34] over one hundred people were killed. The violent repression served to expand the spirit of revolution, so that protests spread from Deraa and erupted across the country.[35] The repressive actions of the regime caused the armed forces in Syria to split with thousands of Syrian soldiers defecting, siding with revolutionaries, and re-grouping to form the Free Syrian Army, which conducts armed resistance against the regime. Moreover, in light of the August 2014 chemical attack on a Damascus suburb there is ample evidence of Assad's intentions to escalate action against citizens, who he seems to view as opponents to be defeated or eliminated. Indeed, in a recent February, 2015 interview Assad declared that when rebels take over an area, the civilians living there naturally choose to flee to Syrian state controlled territory. He seems to reason that any Syrians who continue to live in rebel controlled territory, including those who have never taken up arms, have somehow either forfeited their protected status as civilian noncombatants, or at least can expect to become civilian casualties.[36]

Connected to last resort is the notion that armed resistance was insufficiently graduated in the Syrian armed movement. This raises questions about the fulfillment of the criterion of proportionality on the part of those engaged in armed resistance. While repression was severe enough to cause military defections, it is possible that the division of the military in Syria led to a hasty resort to armed force. It is also possible that ethnicity played a role in the escalation of conflict there: the division of the armed forces broke down along ethnic lines with the largely Alawite officer corps supporting the regime and the largely Sunni conscripts supporting rebels.[37] These ethnic divisions likely exacerbated the situation leading to greater violence and less willingness to negotiate. The disproportionate use of force has deeply complicated the prospects for post-conflict reconciliation in Syria. At present the criterion of proportionate means, coupled with and moderated by a right intention toward future reconciliation, or a respect for noncombatant immunity is absent. The Syrian regime accuses rebels of carrying out attacks on civilians, but rebels deny these reports.[38] Thus, in the situation of Syria, while it is clear that the Assad regime is morally bankrupt, thus far it is not clear that revolutionaries are conducting armed resistance in a way that leaves open the future possibility of reconciliation among disparate ethnic groups and disputing factions.

Similar points could be made about Libya, which likely met the criterion of last resort, but also moved quickly instead of gradually to take up arms against the unjust regime. Muammar Gaddafi's rhetoric and actions, including the killing of hundreds of protesters, testified to his view of Libyan citizens as opponents worthy of elimination. Gaddafi alternately referred to protesters as "hirelings [of foreign enemies]," "rats," and "germs."[39] In language disturbingly resonate with that of the perpetrators of the Holocaust and the Rwandan genocide, he dispersed the armed forces to "secure and cleanse [the streets] from these rats"[40] and declared: "we will issue a call to the millions, from the desert to the desert. And I and the millions will march in order to cleanse Libya, inch by inch, house by house, home by home, alley by alley, individual by individual, so that the country is purified from the unclean."[41] Thus, Libyan revolutionaries were arguably legitimately at a moment of "last resort." That said, armed resistance was not graduated. "In the case of Libya, the Libyan opponents of Gaddafi moved very rapidly towards becoming an armed insurrection rather than a protest movement."[42] Just one month after initial protests, the United Nations authorized a no-fly zone over Libya as well as military action deemed necessary to protect civilians. Under the cover of this protection, the armed movement was able to seize Libya's capital and kill Gaddafi in the process. The degree to which the lack of graduated armed resistance will continue to affect Libya's transition remains to be seen.

Jus post revolution and the Arab Spring

Transitional justice will be of urgent significance across the nations engaged in the Arab Spring. Whether the revolutions maintained nonviolent tactics only, or turned to armed resistance, all will need seriously and systematically to address the violent human rights violations of their former regimes both prior to and during the 2011 uprisings. Undoubtedly post-revolutionary nations will need to utilize a number of strategies in transitioning from a social context of autocracy and human rights violations, to one of participatory governance and respect for human dignity.

As we saw in chapter 5, following apartheid, the TRC employed a sometimes controversial approach to restorative justice that coupled Christian understandings of forgiveness and reconciliation with the Southern African humanist philosophy of ubuntu. This marriage of Christian theology and African philosophy arguably succeeded in beginning an important process of truth-telling and social reconciliation following apartheid. Moreover, this remarkable transition led to a major contribution of the African continent to the burgeoning field of transitional justice: the idea that a uniform approach to post-conflict justice and reconciliation may be a new form of imperialism that ought to be resisted in favor of local resolutions to conflict and inculturated notions reconciliation. In light of this concern, this section on *jus post* revolution for the Arab Spring explores how reconciliation might be inculturated in the context of the Middle East and North Africa. Given how important theologies of forgiveness have been in post-conflict contexts shaped by the Christian faith, I begin by exploring Islamic understandings of forgiveness that may be similarly salient for promoting reconciliation in contexts shaped by Islam. Thus I ask whether Islamic ways of understanding forgiveness could be helpful in socio-political arenas where the majority of citizens are Muslims. I compare and contrast forgiveness in Islam to forgiveness in Christianity, highlighting ways in which Islamic understandings could possibly both help and hinder reconciliation following the Arab Spring. Second, I examine the Islamic virtue of *sabr,* patience, arguing that it may be even more effective than forgiveness in functioning positively to stave off cycles of retaliation and revenge in Muslim contexts. Third, I describe the rituals of *sulh* and *musalaha* (settlement and reconciliation) as explained by George E. Irani. Irani has been instrumental in bringing this pre-Islamic ritual operative in the Middle East to the attention of scholars and practitioners in the fields of transitional justice and peace studies. Irani points to a promising possibility for the inculturation of reconciliation after the Arab Spring.

Islam understands mercy and forgiveness as key attributes of God. God is "oft forgiving"[43] and is the ultimate source of forgiveness for human transgressions. The merciful nature of God is also a model for relationships amongst human beings. The Prophet inculcated the merciful nature of God in his relationships to human beings and their communities, providing an example of forgiveness for all Muslims. During what is referred to as the Prophet's Meccan period (610–622 AD), when he endured persecution for his beliefs, he refused to harbor ill will against his enemies, declaring instead "May God, who is the greatest among forgivers, forgive you."[44] Likewise, the Prophet prayed for those who persecuted him, using words familiar to Christians, "Forgive them Lord, for they know not what they do."[45] Moreover, when his followers pled with him to inflict punishment on those who were persecuting Muslims, the Prophet responded: "I have not been sent to curse anyone but to be a source of *ramah* (compassion and mercy) to all."[46] Thus, the example set by the Prophet is one of forgiveness and compassion, even for enemies.

In personal relationships, forgiveness is viewed in Islam as a central virtue.[47] While Islam allows that vengeance is sometimes justifiable, it "is seen (by some interpreters) as less virtuous than forgiving."[48] Thus, "Islam . . . encourages believers to select forgiveness over revenge."[49] Nevertheless, Islamic theology holds that genuine forgiveness from one who is injured demands and only comes following repentance and reparation on the part of those who have done the injury. "Forgiveness is valid and concrete only when repentance and atonement are sincerely manifested by the perpetrator, or by the offender."[50] This deep concern for apology and compensation as acts that are necessary prior to genuine forgiveness is echoed in the Muslim response to the call for reconciliation in South Africa. South African Muslims who organized against apartheid argued that "reconciliation demands repentance on the part of oppressors and a fundamental redistribution of wealth and power."[51] Thus, Islam affirms Martha Minow's insight that vengeance and the desire to see wrong-doers punished "embodies important ingredients of moral response" to unjust injury that indicate a victim's own sense of self-worth and dignity.[52] Nevertheless, when perpetrators repent and compensate, or make reparation, for the violations they have committed, Islam views forgiveness as the best choice.[53]

The notion that genuine forgiveness is conditional on repentance and reparation differs in significant ways from the Christian theology of forgiveness espoused by Desmond Tutu and others who participated in the TRC; as well as operative in the minds of Christian theologians and those who theorize about the TRC. Recall that this strand of Christian theology considers the victim, or one who is injured, to be the subject of forgiveness; that is to say, the one who is injured is both the bestower of forgiveness and its primary beneficiary. In forgiving, the one who is injured is released from the burden of harboring impulses toward hatred and vengeance. Victims can offer pardon even in the absence of repentance and reparation. Moreover, a Christian who struggles to practice forgiveness does not do so in one single act, but as a spirituality, or way of life. From a Christian perspective, this understanding of forgiveness empowers victims to forgive in their own time and according to their own progression and healing, or indeed, to withhold forgiveness. It avers that victims do not forgive as a rote response to apologies or compensatory actions. The Islamic theology of forgiveness that demands repentance and reparation prior to forgiveness contests this Christian formulation. In considering this challenging theology of forgiveness, I suggest that it could either hinder or help post-revolutionary reconciliation in the context of the Arab Spring.

On the one hand, conditioning forgiveness after revolution on the repentance and compensatory actions of those who have done injury is problematic insofar as it might exclude forgiveness of the dead. The dead cannot apologize or make reparations. Victims of dead perpetrators may thus be locked into a need for apologies and reparations that cannot be adequately fulfilled. On a personal level, these victims may be denied the potentially positive effects of forgiveness. On a social level, denying the possibility of forgiveness may well prompt cycles of retaliation as victim-groups unleash vengeance against living persons who either symbolize, or seem to sympathize or align themselves with, the views and ideologies of dead perpetrators. To take Libya as an example, most would agree that Muammar Gaddafi is a perpetrator of crimes against humanity; he is ultimately responsible for untold suffering and the deaths of thousands of people. He is also dead, having been killed in the midst of Libya's revolution. While his death alone may constitute a kind of conciliatory vengeance for some, he cannot apologize for his actions or make reparations. Are victims of Gaddafi and his regime simply left out of the human capacity for forgiveness? What recourse is there in such a situation for victims of the dead?

On the other hand, conditioning forgiveness after revolution on remorse and reparation may point to a helpful combination of retributive and restorative justice that could promote social reconciliation in some contexts. Retributively, this theology of forgiveness demands that perpetrators accept censure, show remorse, and indeed sacrifice or diminish themselves so as to compensate the one they have injured. This inclination addresses the criticism leveled against Christian conceptions of forgiveness in the political sphere, which suggests that a Christian theology of forgiveness ignores the genuine human need for retributive punishment as part of a reassertion of the dignity of those who are injured (whether or not this criticism is fair or accurate). Moreover, the Islamic conception of forgiveness, by demanding reparation for victims, acknowledges a key aspect of restorative justice—making amends for the wrong done. In this process of "retribution" and "reparation" the *ummah* (community) can be restored. In this way, Islamic notions of forgiveness perhaps place a firmer emphasis on apologies and reparations as a components of justice than do Christian ones.

For nations emerging from revolutionary struggle across the Middle East, the Islamic conception of forgiveness suggests that retributive measures alone may be a starting point, but not the whole of transitional justice that seeks social reconciliation. In following revolutionary uprisings, "So far . . . " remark Fisher and Steward, "the primary focus has been on prosecutions."[54] Egypt, for example, has already begun a process of retributive justice: the trials of former president Hosni Mubarak on charges of killing protestors and corruption have already begun. But retributive measures like these must lead to, or be accompanied by reparative ones in a cultural context where most citizens are Muslim if there is to be hope that a desire for vengeance will give way to the preferred path of forgiveness and social reconciliation.

Sabr, or patience, is a concept that is perhaps even more promising than forgiveness for promoting reconciliation in post-revolutionary Islamic contexts. In his work developing a framework for peacebuilding in Islamic communities, Mohammed Abu-Nimer identifies *sabr* as a key Islamic virtue. *Sabr* "implies a multiplicity of meanings which cannot be translated into one English word."[55] It conveys the virtues of thoroughness, perseverance, and a "firmness of purpose" that direct the person toward systematic and intentional action in the face of difficult situations. Thus *sabr* wards off hasty or spontaneous reactions to injury and encourages instead thoughtfulness and care. Abu-Nimer explains that *sabr* inculcates "a cheerful attitude of resignation and understanding in sorrow, defeat, or suffering, as opposed to murmuring or rebellion, but saved from mere passivity or listlessness, by the element of constancy or steadfastness."[56] Thus, there is no true English equivalent for the Arabic word *sabr,* though the closest preferred translation seems to be "patience."

Like forgiveness, the importance of patience is illustrated both in the Qur'an and in the life of the Prophet. Akbar Ahmed names patience as among the "central Qur'anic concepts."[57] The Qur'an exhorts Muslims to practice patience in over fifteen places.[58] Moreover, particularly during his Meccan period the Prophet "showed no inclination toward the use of force in any form, even for self-defense" and instead "focused on the values of patience and steadfastness in facing oppression."[59] The Prophet's Meccan period is thus characterized by the cultivation of both forgiveness—as described above in his response to those who persecuted him—and patience, suggesting a link between the two ideas in the practice of Islamic virtue. Indeed, there seem to be two important parallels between the Christian concept of forgiveness that I have suggested has been useful in promoting post-conflict reconciliation in Christian socio-political contexts, and the Islamic concept of patience. These similarities suggest that patience may be a key component of post-conflict reconciliation in Islamic socio-political contexts.

First, like forgiveness in the Christian tradition, the subject and primary beneficiary of patience in Islam is the one who practices it. In his commentary on the Qur'an's verses on patience, Abdullah Yusuf Ali remarks: "Lest you should think that such patience only gives an advantage to the adversary, you are told that the contrary is the case: the advantage [lies] with the patient, self-possessed, those who do not lose their temper or forget their own principles of conduct."[60] Thus, Yusuf Ali holds that the primary subjects and beneficiaries of patience are those who inculcate it, even toward their enemies. Indeed, perhaps even more so than forgiveness, patience is presented as the remedy for impulsive retaliation and vengeance since it inclines the virtuous to reject spontaneous reactions to injury. Quoting the Prophet, Abu-Nimer argues that: "Power resides not in being able to strike another, but in being able to keep the self under control when anger arises."[61] For Muslims, cultivating patience may be even more important, then, than cultivating forgiveness for those who wish to stave off destructive cycles of retaliation and revenge. This suggests the need for further research as to how patience might apply in social and political life in the same way that scholars have endeavored to understand how forgiveness applies in social and political contexts around the world.

Second, as we have seen, in Christian contexts following mass violations of human rights, forgiveness and reconciliation amongst human beings are not once-and-for-all events, but more of a "spirituality"[62] to which victims recommit themselves regularly. The practice of patience in Islam strikes a similar chord. In her ethnographical work documenting the lives of Islamic women in Cairo, cultural anthropologist Saba Mahmood retrieves the notion of patience for empowering Muslim women. Mahmood narrates the spiritual journey of Nadia. Nadia describes herself as having found strength through the story of Ayyub, who Mahmood describes as the "equivalent of Job in the Judeo-Christian tradition."[63] The example of Ayyub's patient perseverance (*sabr*) in the face of suffering is an example to Nadia who understands patience not only in the traditional sense of suffering without complaint, but more as trust in the goodness and wisdom of God, whose purposes outstrip our human capacity to understand them.[64] Mahmood explains that for Nadia, patience is decidedly not a passive acquiescence to injustice or abuse. "*Sabr* in the sense described by Nadia and others does not mark a reluctance to act. Rather it is integral to a constructive project: it is a site of considerable investment, struggle, and achievement."[65] This sense of "struggle," "construction," and "achievement" resonates with Christians' attempts to forgive those who have most deeply hurt them. Cultivation of patience in Islam, like forgiveness in Christianity, involves a "deep commitment to God" that "empowers people."[66] Patience and forgiveness are not once-and-for-all events but instead constitute spiritual practices that one commits to cultivating throughout one's life. The power available through patience to Muslims who have been victims of human rights violations, is thus similar to the grace available to Christians through forgiveness: it is a power to forgo vengeance and find one's dignity instead restored through the practice of patience.

For post-revolutionary Islamic contexts, encouraging victims of human rights violations, especially Muslim victims, to cultivate patience—*sabr*—will be at least as important for staving off cycles of retaliation and promoting social reconciliation as encouraging them to forgive perpetrators. Patience is steadfast faith in God's love even in the face of overwhelming injustice and suffering. It encourages careful, thoughtful response to injury and discourages hasty, spontaneous reactions of vengeance.

Just as South Africans combined Christian notions of forgiveness with the indigenous philosophy of *ubuntu,* Middle Eastern nations emerging from revolution may consider combining efforts at forgiveness with adaptations of local, indigenous rituals to assist in social transitions and build peace and reconciliation in their communities. Of particular promise are the traditional practices that have been studied and described by George E. Irani and others: *sulh* (settlement) and *musalaha* (reconciliation).[67] "In a sense, sulh and musalaha can be considered as forms of arbitration supported by rituals."[68] These traditional practices emerged in pre-Islamic Arab contexts, and thus

Irani and Funk describe them as active amongst both Muslims and Christians across the Middle East.[69] The culturally indigenous nature of sulh and musalaha is auspicious for aiding in social reconciliation after the Arab Spring revolutions. Since it is pre-Islamic[70] and practiced by adherents of various religions, it has the power to reach across an even broader community than the Islamic notions of forgiveness or patience alone. This may mitigate to some degree Fisher and Stewart's justifiable concern that "transitional justice measures . . . based on Islamic law . . . would not be supported by significant parts of the population" involved in the Arab Spring revolutions.[71]

The ritualized process of sulh and musalaha as described by Irani and Funk involves roughly five components and "follows a similar format in most of its usages."[72] First, one of the parties in conflict calls a truce *(hudna)*, which, like a cease fire, puts an end to bloodshed, retaliation, and revenge.

Second, conflicting parties identify elders and respected people in the community to act as *musilahs* or *jaha*, (mediators), of the conflict. Unlike in typical Western conflict resolution, third party mediators for sulh and musalaha ought not be disinterested parties with nothing at stake in the outcome of the resolution. Indeed, scholars identify the need for mediators who are trustworthy members of the communities involved in conflict. This tradition portrays conflict mediators not as "mere facilitators."[73] Instead, they are invested with power and responsibility to offer clear proposals for resolving problems, and are expected to do so.

Third, those who have been selected as jaha carry out their duty to investigate the situation of conflict and propose solutions. "The task of the jaha is not to judge, condemn, or punish the offending party."[74] Instead, they are to find remedies to the dispute that preserve the honor and dignity of all families and parties to conflict, including both victims and perpetrators. In concert with notions of restorative justice, they are charged with helping to protect the community as a whole in order to "reaffirm the necessity of ongoing relationships in the community."[75] The solutions proposed should prioritize the well-being of the disputants, as well as the peace and security of the full community. In managing this delicate task, the jaha rely not simply on technical rationality for problem solving. Instead, they draw on religious wisdom, cultural narratives, and a people's history.[76] The goal is to "consult" "preserve" and "cultivate" a "community's wisdom."[77] In this way, the community as a whole, represented by the jaha, deliberate and come to consensus for the resolution of the conflict so as to restore the full humanity of everyone involved.

Fourth, victims or their families are compensated for their losses. Irani suggests that historically this involved a process in which conflicting parties made a public account of all of their losses. The side which was judged to have lost less paid reparations to the side which was judged to have lost more.[78] In the case of a murder, the perpetrator's family pays *diya* (blood money) to the family of the victim. Irani and Funk explain that the diya is "set by the mediators. This 'blood money' (or exchange of goods) may prove quite costly to the family of the perpetrator, but the symbolic significance of the compensation is at least as important as the substance of the payment. The exchange of money or goods substitutes for the exchange of death."[79] In this way, reparation takes the place of revenge. The capacity to accept reparation instead of revenge, even in a situation where revenge might seem justified, is considered virtuous and raises the esteem of the victim's family.

Fifth, the sulh is closed and sealed with a ritual of musalaha (reconciliation). Musalaha is a public ceremony that incorporates several ritualistic components. The conflicting parties begin by forming parallel lines on a road, they "exchange greetings" and make and accept apologies.[80] Next, members of the groups shake hands. Formerly conflicting parties pay ritualized visits to one another's homes. Finally, the reconciled parties share a meal together. In situations where the conflict has a clear perpetrator, the meal is hosted by the perpetrator's family.[81] There are resonances between the Islamic conception of forgiveness described above, and the rituals of sulh and musalaha. Forgiveness in Islam requires repentance and reparation; sulh and musalaha ritualize these experiences of repentance and reparation, making them expectations that are supported and encouraged by the full community. This communal support and ritualization may make apologies and reparations easier to make, and thus facilitate social reconciliation.

Arab Spring nations emerging from revolution may find it helpful to adapt the rituals of sulh and musalaha for supporting a process of repentance, reparation, and reconciliation in local communities. In particular, communities might consider including in their adaptations of sulh and musalaha the important component of restorative justice and social reconciliation that has thus far been missing from transitional strategies in the region: truth-telling. Truth-telling has been identified as a key component of social reconciliation after mass violations of human rights. As we saw in the previous chapter, it functions in several ways to validate victims' experiences of violation, hold accountable those responsible for violations, and establish a historical record of violations which can contribute to a common social memory of the past and a foundation upon which to build a shared future. Since advocates for restorative justice have argued that the truth is owed to victims as a form of justice,[82] truth-telling could be viewed in the process of sulh and musalaha as one form of reparation or compensation for past injuries that could be enabled by the jaha. Commentators have already suggested that Truth and Reconciliation commissions could be helpful in the post-revolutionary context of the Arab Spring. For example, Vandewalle notes, "Since the settling of scores seems inevitable in Libya after decades of Gaddafi's deliberate divide-and-rule policies, the international community would need to help establish a Libyan version of the Truth and Reconciliation Commission."[83] Likewise

Hafez Ghanem of the Brookings Institute has also suggested that a TRC is in order in Egypt. "The objective of this commission would be to discover and reveal crimes perpetrated by all sides over the last two years and, by doing so, help achieve national reconciliation."[84]

The socio-political revolutions across the Middle East and North Africa present new challenges and opportunities for *jus post* revolution. The lessons of the TRC in South Africa illustrated that religious and cultural insights can be combined effectively to forward and support efforts toward restorative justice and social reconciliation. Islamic notions of forgiveness and patience, and the indigenous practices of sulh and musalaha may be key components of post-revolutionary reconciliation after the Arab Spring.

CONCLUSION

This book is an attempt to devise a Christian ethic of political resistance and social transformation rooted in the just peacemaking theory, and the just war tradition. It depends upon the insistence in the Christian tradition that justice and peace are inextricably interwoven. Indeed, "justice is always the foundation of peace."[85] Many Christian theologians are rightly hesitant to affirm that the use of force has the moral power to contribute to peace, justice, and reconciliation. The general unlikelihood that force of arms can establish a just peace marked by social reconciliation is part of the reason why just war thinking must always begin with a presumption against the use of force. Thus, a Christian ethic of political resistance must affirm that nonviolent resistance is the foundation of a just revolution. However, I have argued here that in cases of brutal oppression and repression the violence of the state can ethically and effectively be countered through restricted armed resistance enacted as a supplement in tandem with nonviolent just peacemaking practices and in accordance with revised just war criteria. In response to the U.S. Bishops' concern that that theological ethicists have left underexplored the moral issues related to revolutionary activity, I have endeavored here to begin a discussion toward developing a practical theory of just revolution. This theory intends to empower people to struggle for liberation from injustice and to build a more peaceful world which values the dignity of all human beings.

NOTES

1. Rami G. Khouri, "The Long Revolt," *The Wilson Quarterly,* 35.3 (2011): 43.
2. Katerina Dalacoura, "The 2011 Uprisings in the Arab Middle East: Political Change and Geopolitical Implications," *International Affairs,* 88.1, (2012): 64.

3. For more on the conditions that led to revolution in various states see Khouri, 44; Fouad Ajami, "The Sorrows of Egypt" in *The New Arab Revolt: What Happened, What it Means, and What Comes Next* (New York: Council on Foreign Relations, Inc., 2011), 2–21; Michelle Penner Angrist, "Morning in Tunisia: The Frustrations of the Arab World Boil Over" in *The New Arab Revolt*, 75–80; and Richard N. Haass, "Reflections on the Revolution in Egypt" in *The New Arab Revolt*, 115–118. In addition, for a brief reference guide to the basics of the Arab Spring uprisings and their outcomes see http://www.bbc.com/news/world-19401680.

4. Hasan Hanafi, "The Future of Political Islam and the West: The Islamic Movement in the Arab World with a Focus on Egypt," *Religious Studies and Theology*, 32.1 (2013): 84.

5. See Lisa Anderson, "Demystifying the Arab Spring," *Foreign Affairs*, 90.3 (2011): 2.

6. See for example Judy Barsalou, "Post-Mubarak Egypt: History, Collective Memory, and Memorialization," *Middle East Policy*, XIX.2 (2012): 134–147.

7. Cartwright and Thislethwaite, "Support Nonviolent Direct Action," in *Just Peacemaking: The New Paradigm for the Ethics of Peace and War*, Glen H. Stassen, ed., (Cleveland, OH: The Pilgrim Press, 2008), 56. See also Erica Chenoweth and Maria J. Stephan, *Why Civil Resistance Works: The Strategic Logic of Nonviolent Conflict* (New York: Columbia University Press, 2011).

8. Dina Shehata, "The Fall of Pharaoh: How Hosni Mubarak's Reign Came to an End," *The New Arab Revolt*, 138.

9. See Shehata, 137.

10. Khouri, 45.

11. The Facebook page was named for an Egyptian citizen tortured and killed by the security police. For an account of the formation of the page and its role in fomenting nonviolent revolution see Wael Ghonim, *Revolution 2.0* (New York: Houghton, Mifflin, Harcourt Publishing Co., 2012).

12. Federico Caprotti and Eleanor Xin Gao, "Static imaginations and the possibilities of radical change: reflection on the Arab Spring," *Area*, 44.4 (2012): 510.

13. Marwan Bishara, *The Invisible Arab: The Promise and Peril of the Arab Revolution* (New York: Nation Books, 2012), xi.

14. Khouri, 46.

15. Sharon Erikson Nepstad, "Mutiny and Nonviolence in the Arab Spring: Exploring Military Defections and Loyalty in Egypt, Bahrain, and Syria," *Journal of Peace Research*, 50.3 (2013): 337–349.

16. Nepstad, 339.

17. Nepstad, 340.

18. Nepstad, 343.

19. Nepstad, 343.

20. Nepstad, 343. Italics in original.

21. Nepstad, 343.

22. Nepstad, 343.

23. Dalacoura, 67.

24. See for example, Dirk Vandewalle's remark that Libya's Muammar Gaddafi engaged in "decades" of "deliberate divide-and-rule policies." "To the Shores of Tripoli: Why Operation Odyssey Dawn Should Not Stop at Benghazi," in *The New Arab Revolt*, 273.

25. Ghonim, 294.

26. For more on the role of the SCAF and its activities in Egypt's transition see Khaled Elgindy, "Egypt's Troubled Transition: Elections without Democracy," *The Washington Quarterly* (Spring 2012): 89–104.

27. Dalacoura, 73.

28. Nirvana Tanoukhi, "Arab Spring and the Future of Leadership in North Africa: An Interview with Ali A. Mazrui," *Transitions*, 106 (2011): 148.

29. Paul Richter, "U.S. wants to know who's in charge of Libyan revolution," *Los Angeles Times* (March 2, 2011), available at http://articles.latimes.com/2011/mar/02/world/la-fg-libya-opposition-20110303.

30. Vasiliki Saranti, "Pro-Democratic Intervention, Invitation, or 'Responsibility to Protect'? Challenges to International Law from the 'Arab Spring,'" in *The Arab Spring: New Patterns for Democracy and International Law*, Carlo Panara and Gary Wilson, eds., (Leiden: The Netherlands, Koninklijke Brill NV, 2013), 188.

31. For details on the international community's role in Libya's transition see the report of New York University's Center on International Cooperation, drafted by Emily O'Brien and Richard Gowan, "The International Role in Libya's Transition: August 2011–March 2012," available at http://cic.es.its.nyu.edu/sites/default/files/libya_diplomatic_transition.pdf.

32. Dalacoura, 69.

33. Tony Badran, "Syria's Assad No Longer in Vogue: What Everyone Got Wrong about Bashar al-Assad" in *The New Arab Revolt*, 210.

34. Badran, 211.

35. Badran describes protests in Aleppo, Damascus, Homs, Latakia, and Qaumishli. Badran, 214.

36. For the full interview see http://www.bbc.com/news/world-middle-east-31311895.

37. Nepstad, 344.

38. Also of concern are the activities of the self-proclaimed "Islamic State in Iraq and Syria" (ISIS) fighters who control parts of Syria and who have committed serious violations of human rights. See "U.N. Panel Says War Crimes Spreading in Syria," *Wall Street Journal*, August 27, 2014.

39. Muammar Gaddafi, "Excerpts from Libyan Leader Muammar al-Qaddafi's Televised Address," in *The New Arab Revolt*, 416.

40. Gaddafi, 419.

41. Gaddafi, 420.

42. Al Mazrui in Tanouki's interview, 152. Al Mazrui contends this rapid movement to arms is one reason why the Libyan revolution did not "work out as smoothly" (152).

43. Qur'an 71: 10–12.

44. Quoted by Mohammed Abu-Nimer, "A Framework for Nonviolence and Peacemaking in Islam," *Journal of Law and Religion*, 15.1/2 (2000–2001): 248. See note 64.

45. Quoted in Abu-Nimer, 248.

46. Quoted in Abu-Nimer, 248.

47. Abu-Nimer, 248.

48. Mohammed Abu-Nimer and Ilham Nasser, "Forgiveness in the Arab and Islamic Contexts: Between Theology and Practice," *Journal of Religious Ethics*, 41.3 (2013): 480.

49. Abu-Nimer and Nasser, 480

50. Karim Douglas Crow, "Forgiveness in Muslim Thought and Practice: A Response to Augsburger's 'The Practices of Forgiveness and Reconciliation in Conflict Transformation,'" in *Peacebuilding By, Between, and Beyond Muslims and Evangelical Christians*, Mohammed Abu-Nimer and David Augsburger, eds., (Lanham, MD: Lexington Books, 2009), 13.

51. John W. de Gruchy, *Reconciliation: Restoring Justice* (Minneapolis, MN: Fortress Press, 2002), 124.

52. See Martha Minow, *Between Vengeance and Forgiveness: Facing History after Genocide and Mass Violence* (Boston: Beacon Press, 1999), 10.

53. Abu-Nimer and Nasser, 480. Indeed, Daniel Philpott notes that in "cases of murder and bodily assault"—dismayingly common in the midst of socio-political unrest—the Qur'an seems to recommend forgiveness particularly strongly. Daniel Philpott, *Just and Unjust Peace: An Ethic of Political Reconciliation* (New York: Oxford University Press, 2012), 160.

54. Kirsten J. Fisher and Robert Stewart, "After the Arab Spring: A New Wave of Transitional Justice?" in *Transitional Justice and the Arab Spring*, Kirsten J. Fisher and Robert Stewart, eds. (New York: Routledge, 2014).

55. Abu-Nimer, 251.

56. Abu-Nimer, 251.

57. Akbar Ahmed, *Postmodernism and Islam: Predicament and Promise* (London: Routledge Press, 1992), 48.

58. Abu-Nimar, 251.

59. Abu-Nimer, 230.

60. Quoted in Abu-Nimer, 253.
61. Abu-Nimer, 252.
62. Schreiter, 23.
63. Saba Mahmood, *Politics of Piety: The Islamic Revival and the Feminist Subject* (Princeton, NJ: Princeton University Press, 2005), 173.
64. Mahmood, 173–174.
65. Mahmood, 173–174.
66. Abu-Nimer, 252.
67. See George E. Irani and Nathan C. Funk, "Rituals of Reconciliation: Arab-Islamic Perspectives," *Arab Studies Quarterly,* 20.4 (1998): 53–73; and George E. Irani, "Islamic Mediation Techniques for Middle East Conflicts," *Middle East Review of International Affairs,* 3.2. (1999): 1–17.
68. George E. Irani, "Apologies and Reconciliation: Middle Eastern Rituals," in *Taking Wrongs Seriously: Apologies and Reconciliation,* Elazar Barkin and Alexander Karn, eds., (Stanford, CA: Stanford University Press, 2006), 138.
69. Irani and Funk, 66. Irani and Funk specifically name Jordan, Palestine, and Lebanon as countries where sulh and musalaha have been practiced by both Christians and Muslims. Daniel Philpot also includes Egypt as a nation where the rituals take place (160).
70. For more on the origins of sulh and musalaha see Sadik Kirazli, "Conflict and Conflict Resolution in pre-Islamic Arab Society," *Islamic Studies,* 50.1 (2011): 25–53.
71. Fisher and Stewart, 5.
72. Irani and Funk, 65.
73. Irani and Funk, 58.
74. Irani and Funk, 65.
75. Irani and Funk, 65.
76. Irani and Funk, 63.
77. Irani and Funk, 63.
78. Irani, "Islamic Mediation Techniques for Middle East Conflicts," 12.
79. Irani and Funk, 66.
80. Irani and Funk, 66.
81. Irani and Funk, 66.
82. See for example Steven Pope, "The Convergence of Forgiveness and Justice: Lessons from El Salvador" *Theological Studies,* 64 (2003): 830.
83. Vandewalle, 273.
84. Hafez Ghanem, "Egypt Needs Truth and Reconciliation," available at http://www.brookings.edu/research/opinions/2013/08/16-egypt-democracy-truth-reconciliation-ghanem.
85. The United States Conference of Catholic Bishops (USCCB), *The Challenge of Peace: God's Promise and Our Response,* 60. Available at http://www.usccb.org/upload/challenge-peace-gods-promise-our-response-1983.pdf.

Bibliography

Abu-Nimer, Mohammed, "A Framework for Nonviolence and Peacemaking in Islam" *Journal of Law and Religion,* 15.1/2 (2000–2001).
Abu-Nimer, Mohammed, and Ilham Nasser, "Forgiveness in the Arab and Islamic Contexts: Between Theology and Practice," *Journal of Religious Ethics,* 41.3 (2013).
Abu-Nimer, Mohammed, and David Augsburger, eds., *Peacebuilding By, Between, and Beyond Muslims and Evangelical Christians,* (Lanham, MD: Lexington Books, 2009).
African [Banjul] Charter of Human and Peoples' Rights. Available at http://www.achpr.org/instruments/achpr/.
Ahmed, Akbar, *Postmodernism and Islam: Predicament and Promise,* (London: Routledge Press, 1992).
Alden, Chris, *Apartheid's Last Stand: The Rise and Fall of the South African Security State,* (London: MacMillan Press Ltd, 1996).
Allman, Mark J., *Who Would Jesus Kill? War, Peace, and the Christian Tradition* (Winona, MN: St. Mary's Press, 2008).
Allman, Mark J. and Tobias L. Winright. *After the Smoke Clears: The Just War Tradition and Post War Justice,* (Maryknoll, NY: Orbis Books, 2010).
———. "Growing Edges of the Just War Theory: *Jus ante bellum, Jus post bellum,* and Imperfect Justice," *Journal of the Society of Christian Ethics,* 32.2 (2012): 173–191.
Anderson, Lisa, "Demystifying the Arab Spring," *Foreign Affairs,* 90.3 (2011): 2–7.
Aquinas, Thomas, *Summa Theologiae.* English Dominican Fathers, trans., Available at http://www.newadvent.org/summa/.
———. *De Regno,* in *Aquinas: Political Writings,* R.W. Dyson, ed. and trans., (Cambridge: Cambridge University Press, 2002).
Arendt, Hannah, *On Revolution,* New York: Penguin Books, 1990.
Aristotle, *The Nicomachean Ethics,* J.A.K. Thomson, trans., (London: Penguin Books, 2004).
Augustine, *City of God,* Marcus Dods, trans., (New York: The Modern Library, 2000).
———. *The Confessions,* R.S. Pine-Coffin, trans., (London: Penguin Books, 1961).
———. *Contra Faustum.* Available at http://www.newadvent.org/fathers/1406.htm.
———. *Letter 189: To Boniface.* Available at http://www.newadvent.org/fathers/1102189.htm.
———. *Letter 138: To Marcellinus.* Available at http://www.newadvent.org/fathers/1102138.htm.
Barkin, Elazar and Alexander Karn, eds., *Taking Wrongs Seriously: Apologies and Reconciliation,* (Standford, CA: Stanford University Press, 2006).
Barsalou, Judy, "Post-Mubarak Egypt: History, Collective Memory, and Memorialization," *Middle East Policy,* XIX.2 (2012).

Battle, Michael, *Reconciliation: The Ubuntu Theology of Desmond Tutu*, (Cleveland, OH: The Pilgrim Press, 1997).
Beinart, William, *Twentieth Century South Africa*, 2nd edition, (New York: Oxford University Press, 2001).
Biko, Steve, *I Write What I Like*, (New York: Harper & Row, 1978).
Bishara, Marwan, *The Invisible Arab: The Promise and Peril of the Arab Revolution*, (New York: Nation Books, 2012).
Bujo, Benezet, *Foundations of an African Ethic*, (New York: Crossroads Publishing Company, 2001).
Bylthe, James M., "The Mixed Constitution in Aquinas" in *Journal of the History of Ideas*, 47.4 (1986): 547–565.
Cahill, Lisa Sowle, "Just Peacemaking: Theory, Practice, and Prospects" in *Journal of the Society of Christian Ethics*, 23.1, (2003): 195–212.
———. *Love Your Enemies: Discipleship, Pacifism, and Just War Theory*, (Minneapolis: MN: Fortress Press, 1994).
Caprotti, Federico and Eleanor Xin Gao, "Static imaginations and the possibilities of radical change: reflection on the Arab Spring," *Area*, 44.4 (2012): 510–512.
Chapman, Audrey R. "Coming to Terms with the Past: Truth, Justice, and/or Reconciliation," *Annual of the Society of Christian Ethics*, 19 (1999): 235–258.
Chenoweth, Erica and Maria J. Stephan, *Why Civil Resistance Works: The Strategic Logic of Nonviolent Conflict* (New York: Columbia University Press, 2011).
Cherry, Janet, *Spear of the Nation: South Africa's Liberation Army* (Athens, OH: Ohio University Press, 2011).
Clark, Meghan J., "Integrating Human Rights: Participation in John Paul II, Catholic Social Thought and Amartya Sen," *Political Theology* 8.3 (2007).
Conquergood, Dwight, *Cultural Struggles: Performance, Ethnography, Praxis*, E. Patrick Johnson, ed., (Ann Arbor, MI: University of Michigan Press, 2013).
Cortright, David and George A. Lopez, eds., *Smart Sanctions: Targeting Economic Statecraft*, (New York: Rowman and Littlefield Publishers, 2002).
Council on Foreign Relations/Foreign Affairs *The New Arab Revolt: What Happened, What It Means, and What Comes Next*, (New York: Council on Foreign Relations, Inc., 2011).
Dalacoura, Katerina, "The 2011 Uprisings in the Arab Middle East: Political Change and Geopolitical Implications," *International Affairs*, 88.1 (2012).
de Gruchy, John W., *Reconciliation: Restoring Justice*, (Minneapolis, MN: Fortress Press, 2002).
———. "The Struggle for Justice and the Ministry of Reconciliation" in *Journal of Theology for Southern Africa* no. 62, (1988): 43–52.
de Macedo, Paulo Emílio Vauthier Borges, "The Law of War in Francisco Suárez: The Civilizing Project of Spanish Scholasticism" in *Revistada Faculdade de Direito da UERJ*, 2.22 (2012). Open access at http://www.epublicacoes.uerj.br/index.php/rfduerj/article/viewFile/4280/3165.
Denzin, Norman K., "The Call to Performance," *Symbolic Interaction*, 26.1 (2003): 187–207.
De Vitoria, Franciscus, *De Indis et de Iure Belli, Relectiones*, Ernest Nys, ed., (Washington, DC: Carnegie Institution, 1917).
Dooling, Wayne, *Slavery, Emancipation, and Colonial Rule in South Africa*, (Scottsville, South Africa: University of KwaZulu-Natal Press, 2007).
Elgindy, Khaled, "Egypt's Troubled Transition: Elections without Democracy," *The Washington Quarterly*, 5.2 (2012): 89–104.
Elshtain, Jean Bethke, *Augustine and the Limits of Politics*, (South Bend, IN: University of Notre Dame Press, 1998).
Epstein, Barbara, *Political Protest and Cultural Revolution: Nonviolent Direct Action in the 1970s and 1980s*, (Berkley and Los Angeles: University of California Press, 1991).
Farmer, Paul, Bruce Nizeye, Sara Stulac, and Salmaan Keshavjee, "Structural Violence and Clinical Medicine," PLoS Med 3.10: e449. DOI: 10.1371/journal.pmed.0030449 (2006). Open access available at http://www.plosmedicine.org/article/info%3Adoi%2F10.1371%2Fjournal.pmed.0030449#s2.

Fisher, Kirsten J. and Robert Stewart, eds., *Transitional Justice and the Arab Spring*, (New York: Routledge, 2014).
Gathogo, Julius, "African Philosophy as Expressed in the Concepts of Hospitality and Ubuntu" in *Journal of Theology for Southern Africa*, 130 (2008): 39–53.
Ghonim, Wael, *Revolution 2.0*, (New York: Houghton, Mifflin, Harcourt, 2012).
Gordon, Joy, *The Invisible War: The United States and the Iraq Sanctions*, (Cambridge, MA: Harvard University Press, 2010).
———. "Economic Sanctions, Just War Doctrine, and the 'Fearful Spectacle of the Civilian Dead,'" *Crosscurrents*, 49.3 (1999).
———. "Reply to George A. Lopez's 'More Ethical than Not,'" *Ethics and International Affairs*, 13.1 (1999): 149–150.
Hanafi, Hasan, "The Future of Political Islam and the West: The Islamic Movement in the Arab World with a Focus on Egypt," *Religious Studies and Theology*, 32.1 (2013).
Hauerwas, Stanley, *Performing the Faith: Bonhoeffer and the Practice of Nonviolence*, (Grand Rapids, MI: Brazos Press, 2004).
Hayner, Priscilla B., *Unspeakable Truths: Facing the Challenge of Truth Commissions*, (New York: Routledge, 2002).
Helmick, Raymond and Peterson, Rodney L., eds., *Forgiveness and Reconciliation: Religion, Public Policy, and Conflict Transformation*, (Philadelphia, PA: Templeton Foundation Press, 2001).
Henkin, Louis, "That 'S' Word: Sovereignty, and Globalization, and Human Rights, Et Cetera," *Fordham Law Review*, 68.1 (1999).
Herman, Judith, *Trauma and Recovery: The Aftermath of Violence—from Domestic Abuse to Political Terror*, (New York: Basic Books, 1992).
Himes, Kenneth R., "Intervention, Just War, and U.S. National Security," *Theological Studies*, 65 (2004): 141–157.
Hollenbach, David, *Claims in Conflict*, (New York: Paulist Press, 1979)
———. *Nuclear Ethics: A Christian Moral Argument*, (Mahwah, NJ: Paulist Press, 1983).
Hufbauer, Gary Clyde, Jeffery J. Schott, Kimberly Ann Elliot, and Barbara Oegg, *Economic Sanctions Reconsidered*, 3rd edition, (Washington, DC: Peterson Institute for International Economics, 2007).
International Commission on Intervention and State Sovereignty (ICISS), *The Responsibility to Protect* (Ottawa: International Development Research Center, 2001).
Irani, George E., "Islamic Mediation Techniques for Middle East Conflicts," *Middle East Review of International Affairs*, 3.2. (1999): 1–17.
Irani, George E., and Nathan C. Funk, "Rituals of Reconciliation: Arab-Islamic Perspectives," *Arab Studies Quarterly*, 20.4 (1998): 53–73.
Johnson, Allan G., *Privilege, Power, and Difference* (New York: McGraw-Hill, 2006).
Johnson, James Turner, *Morality and Contemporary Warfare*, (New Haven, CT: Yale University Press, 1999).
———. *Ideology, Reason, and the Limitation of War*, (Princeton, NJ: Princeton University Press, 1975).
Johnson, Sue and Richman, Joe, *Mandela: An Audio History*, Radio Diaries, (2004), "All Things Considered," NPR: Broadcast (April 26–30, 2004).
Joireman, Sandra, *Nationalism and Political Identity*, (London: Continuum, 2004).
Juckes, Tim J., *Opposition in South Africa: The Leadership of Z.K. Matthews, Nelson Mandela, and Stephen Biko*, (Santa Barbara, CA: Praeger Publishers, 1995).
"The Kairos Document." Available at http://www.sahistory.org.za/archive/challenge-church-theological-comment-political-crisis-south-africa-kairos-document-1985.
Karis, Thomas and Carter, Gwendolen M., eds., *From Protest to Challenge: A Documentary History of African Politics in South Africa 1882–1964, Volume I: Protest and Hope*, (Stanford, CA: Hoover Institution Press, 1977).
———. *From Protest to Challenge: A Documentary History of African Politics in South Africa 1882–1964, Volume III: Protest and Violence*, (Stanford, CA: Hoover Institution Press, 1977).

Keefer, Natalie "The Struggle for Human Rights in Myanmar," *Social Education,* 76.5 (2012): 258–260.
Khouri, Rami G., "The Long Revolt," *The Wilson Quarterly,* 35.3 (2011): 4.
King, Jr., Martin Luther, *Letter from a Birmingham Jail.* Available at http://www.africa.upenn.edu/Articles_Gen/Letter_Birmingham.html.
Kirazli, Sadik, "Conflict and Conflict Resolution in pre-Islamic Arab Society," *Islamic Studies,* 50.1 (2011): 25–53.
Klotz, Audie, "Norms Reconstituting Interests: Global Racial Equality and U.S. Sanctions against South Africa," *International Organization,* 49.3 (1995): 451–478.
Krog, Antjie, *Country of My Skull: Guilt, Sorrow, and the Limits of Forgiveness in the New South Africa,* (New York: Three Rivers Press, 1998).
Kurzman, Charles "The Arab Spring: Ideals of the Iranian Green Movement, Methods of the Iranian Revolution," *International Journal of Middle East Studies,* 44.1 (2012): 162–165.
Langan, John S.J., "Elements of St. Augustine's Just War Theory," *The Journal of Religious Ethics,* 12.1 (1984): 19–38.
Lederach, John Paul, *Building Peace: Sustainable Reconciliation in Divided Societies* (Washington, DC: United States Institute of Peace, 1997).
Lodge, Thomas, *Black Politics in South Africa Since 1945,* (Johannesburg, South Africa: Ravan Press, 1983).
———. *Sharpeville: An Apartheid Massacre and Its Consequences,* (New York: Oxford University Press, 2011).
Lopez, George A., "More Ethical than Not: Sanctions as Surgical Tools: Response to 'A Peaceful, Silent, Deadly Enemy,'" *Ethics and International Affairs,* 13.1 (1999): 149–150.
Mahmood, Saba, *Politics of Piety: The Islamic Revival and the Feminist Subject,* (Princeton, NJ: Princeton University Press, 2005).
Mandela, Nelson Rolihlahla, *The Struggle is My Life,* (New York: Pathfinder Press, 1986).
———. *Nelson Mandela Speaks, Forging a Democratic, Nonracial South Africa,* (New York: Pathfinder Press, 1993).
———. *Long Walk to Freedom,* (Boston: Back Bay Books, 1995).
———. "First letter from Nelson Mandela to Hendrik Verwoerd." Available at http://www.sahistory.org.za/archive/document-9-first-letter-nelson-mandela-hendrik-verwoerd.
Massingale, Bryan, *Racial Justice and the Catholic Church,* (Maryknoll, NY: Orbis Books, 2010).
May, Rollo, *Power and Innocence: A Search for the Sources of Violence,* (New York: W.W. Norton, 1972).
Miller, Richard, "War/Peace Materials: Resources for Fresh Ideas," *Annual of the Society of Christian Ethics,* (1987).
Minow, Martha, *Between Vengeance and Forgiveness: Facing History after Genocide and Mass Violence,* (Boston: Beacon Press, 1998).
Mitchell, W.J.T., "Image, Space, Revolution: The Arts of Occupation," *Critical Inquiry,* 39 (2012): 8–32.
Mnyaka, Mluleki and Mokgethi Motlhabi, "The African Concept of Ubuntu/Botha and its Socio-Moral Significance," *Black Theology* 3.2 (2005): 215–237.
Moses, Greg, *Revolution of Conscience: Martin Luther King and the Philosophy of Nonviolence,* (New York: The Guilford Press, 1998).
Nardin, Terry, ed., *The Ethics of War and Peace: Religious and Secular Perspectives,* (Princeton, NJ: Princeton University Press, 2002).
Nepstad, Sharon Erikson, *Nonviolent Revolutions: Civil Resistance in the Late Twentieth Century,* (New York: Oxford University Press, 2011).
———. "Mutiny and Nonviolence in the Arab Spring: Exploring Military Defections and Loyalty in Egypt, Bahrain, and Syria," *Journal of Peace Research,* 50.3 (2013): 337–349.
Netshiomboni, S., *Ubuntu: Fundamental Constitutional Value and Imperative Aid,* (Pretoria, South Africa: University of South Africa Press, 1998).
Nojeim, Michael J., *Gandhi and King: The Power of Nonviolent Resistance* (Westport, CT: Praeger Publishers, 2004).

Nolan, Albert, *God in South Africa: The Challenge of the Gospel,* (Claremont, South Africa: David Philip Publishers, 1988).
———. *Jesus Before Christianity,* (Maryknoll, NY: Orbis Books, 1976).
Orend, Brian "*Jus Post Bellum*: The Perspective of a Just War Theorist," *Leiden Journal of International Law*, 20 (2007): 571–591.
———. *The Morality of War,* 2nd edition (Petersborough, Ontario: Broadview Press, 2013).
Organization of African Unity, *African Charter on Human and People's Rights*, at http://www.achpr.org/instruments/achpr/.
Panara, Carlo and Gary Wilson, eds., *The Arab Spring: New Patterns for Democracy and International Law,* (Leiden, The Netherlands: Koninklijke Brill NV, 2013).
Philpott, Daniel, *Just and Unjust Peace: An Ethic of Political Reconciliation,* (New York: Oxford University Press, 2012).
Pontifical Council for Justice and Peace, ed., *Compendium of the Social Doctrine of the Church*, (Washington DC: United States Conference of Catholic Bishops, 2005).
Pope Francis I, *Evangelii Gaudium* (2013). Available at http://w2.vatican.va/content/francesco/en/apost_exhortations/documents/papa-francesco_esortazione-ap_20131124_evangelii-gaudium.html.
Pope John Paul II, *Evangelium Vitae* (1995). Available at http://www.vatican.va/holy_father/john_paul_ii/encyclicals/documents/hf_jp-ii_enc_25031995_evangelium-vitae_en.html.
Pope John XXIII, *Pacem in Terris,* (1963). Available at http://www.vatican.va/holy_father/john_xxiii/encyclicals/documents/hf_j-xxiii_enc_11041963_pacem_en.html.
Pope, Stephen, "The Convergence of Forgiveness and Justice: Lessons from El Salvador," in *Theological Studies*, 64, (2003): 812–824.
Populorum Progressio, in O'Brien, David J. and Shannon, Thomas A., eds., *Catholic Social Thought: The Documentary Heritage* (Maryknoll, NY: Orbis Press, 1992).
Posel, Deborah, "What's in a Name? Racial Categorisations Under Apartheid and their Afterlife" in *Transformations: Critical Perspectives on Southern Africa,* 47 (2001): 50–74.
Ramsey, Paul, *The Just War: Force and Political Responsibility,* (Lanham, MD: Rowman and Littlefield Publishers, Inc., 1983).
Regan, Richard, *The Moral Dimensions of Politics*, (New York: Oxford University Press, 1986).
Reuther, Rosemary Radford, *Sexism and God Talk* (Boston: Beacon Press, 1983).
Rodgers, Benedict, "The Saffron Revolution: The Role of Religion in Burma's Movement for Peace and Democracy," *Totalitarian Movements and Political Religions,* 9.1 (2008): 115–118.
Rotberg, Robert I. and Thompson, Dennis, eds., *Truth v. Justice: The Morality of Truth Commissions,* (Princeton, NJ: Princeton University Press, 2000).
Scheid, Anna Floerke, "Interpersonal and Social Reconciliation: Finding Congruence in African Theological Anthropology," *Horizons,* 39.1 (2012): 27–49.
Schreiter, Robert J., *Reconciliation: Mission and Ministry in a Changing Social Order*, (Maryknoll, NY: Orbis Books, 1992).
———. "Mediating Repentance, Forgiveness, and Reconciliation: What is the Church's Role?" in *The Spirit in the Church and the World*, The Annual Publication of the College Theology Society, Bradford E. Hinze, ed., (Maryknoll, NY: Orbis Books, 2003).
Schuld, J. Joyce, *Foucault and Augustine: Reconsidering Power and Love,* (Notre Dame, IN: University of Notre Dame Press, 2003).
Second Vatican Council, *Gaudium et Spes: Pastoral Constitution on The Church in the Modern World,* (1965). Available at http://www.vatican.va/archive/hist_councils/ii_vatican_council/documents/vat-ii_cons_19651207_gaudium-et-spes_en.html.
Shannon, T.A., ed., *War or Peace,* (Maryknoll, NY: Orbis, 1980).
Shriver, Donald W., *An Ethic for Enemies: Forgiveness in Politics,* (New York: Oxford University Press, 1995).
Simons, Harold Jack, *Struggles in Southern Africa,* (New York: St. Martin's Press, Inc., 1997).
South African Democracy Education Trust, *The Road to Democracy in South Africa, Volume 1 1960–1970,* (Cape Town, South Africa: Zebra Press, 2004).

Southern African Bishops Conference, *Pastoral Letter of Southern African Catholic Bishops' Conference On Christian Hope in the Current Crisis*, (1985). Available at http://www.sacbc.org.za/wp-content/uploads/2013/05/PASTORAL-LETTER-ON-THECHRISTIAN-HOPE-IN-THE-CURRENT-CRISIS.pdf.

Stassen, Glen, ed., *Just Peacemaking: The New Paradigm for the Ethics of Peace and War*, (Cleveland, OH: The Pilgrim Press, 2008).

———. "New Paradigm: Just Peacemaking Theory," in the *Bulletin of the Council of Societies for the Study of Religion*, 25 (1996).

———. "The Unity, Realism, and Obligatoriness of Just Peacemaking Theory" in *Journal of the Society of Christian Ethics*, 23.1 (2003): 171–194.

Storey, Peter, "A different kind of justice: Truth and reconciliation in South Africa" in *The Christian Century*, (September 10–17, 1997): 788–793.

Suárez, Franciso, *The Three Theological Virtues: On Charity*, Disputation XIII: On War, trans. Gladys L. Williams, Ammi Brown, and John Waldron, with revisions by Henry Davis, (London: Oxford University Press, 1944).

Sutherland, Bill and Matt Meyer, *Guns and Gandhi in Africa: Pan-African Insights on Nonviolence, Armed Struggle, and Liberation*, (Asmara, Eritrea: Africa World Press, Inc., 2000).

Suttner, Raymond, "The African National Congress (ANC) Underground: From the M-Plan to Rivonia," *South African Historical Journal*, 49 (2003): 123–146.

Tanoukhi, Nirvana, "Arab Spring and the Future of Leadership in North Africa: An Interview with Ali A. Mazrui," *Transitions*, 106 (2011): 148–162.

Templin, J. Alton, "The Ideology of a Chosen People: Afrikaner Nationalism and the Ossewa Trek, 1938," *Nations and Nationalism*, 5.3 (1999): 397–417.

Thomas, Scott, *The Diplomacy of Liberation: The Foreign Relations of the African National Congress Since 1960*, (London: Tauris Academic Studies, 1996).

Trocme, Andre, *Jesus and the Nonviolent Revolution*, Charles E. Moore, ed., (Farmington, PA: Plough Publishing House, 2007).

Truth and Reconciliation Commission Report, South Africa. Available at http://www.justice.gov.za/Trc/report/index.htm.

Tutu, Desmond, *No Future Without Forgiveness*, (New York: Doubleday, 1999).

———. *The Rainbow People of God: The Making of a Peaceful Revolution*, (New York: Image, Doubleday, 1994).

Tutu, Naomi, ed., *The Words of Desmond Tutu*, (London: Hodder and Stoughton, 1989).

"United States: Comprehensive Anti-Apartheid Act of 1986," 26 I.L.M. 77 (1987). Available at http://www.gpo.gov/fdsys/pkg/STATUTE-100/pdf/STATUTE-100-Pg1086.pdf.

U.S. Bishops, *The Challenge of Peace: God's Promise and Our Response* (1983). Available at http://old.usccb.org/sdwp/international/TheChallengeofPeace.pdf.

Villa-Vincencio, Charles, ed., *Theology and Violence: The South African Debate*, (Grand Rapids, MI: Wm. B. Eerdmans Publishing Co., 1988).

———. *Civil Disobedience and Beyond*, (Claremont, South Africa: David Philip Publishers Ltd, 1990).

Walzer, Michael, *Just and Unjust Wars: A Moral Argument with Historical Illustrations* (New York: Basic Books, 1977).

Williams, Rocky, "South African Guerrilla Armies: The Impact of Guerrilla Armies on the Creation of South Africa's Armed Forces," *ISS Monograph Series*, 127 (2006).

Index

Abu-Nimer, Mohammed, 147–149
accountability, 109, 120
African National Congress (ANC), xiii, 42, 65n11; ANCYL, 43, 44, 65n21, 65n27; Congress of the People from, 52–53; Defiance Campaign of, 45–46, 65n27; Programme of Action from, 44–46, 65n22, 65n27; sexism in, 43, 65n13; Women's League of, 43; *See also specific topics*
African nations, 61, 69n136
Afrikaner nationalism: Anglo Boer War and, 3–4; apartheid from, 4–5; National Party and, 5, 8–9
aggression, 105n61
Ahmed, Akbar, 148
Ali, Abdullah Yusuf, 148
All-In African Conference, 46, 60–61
Allman, Mark J., 25–26, 36n117, 75, 133n47, 133n54
amnesty, 120, 127; retributive justice and, 120–121, 133n56; TRC and, 125, 127
ANC. *See* African National Congress
ANC Women's League, 43
ANC Youth League (ANCYL), 43, 44, 65n21, 65n27
Anderson, Lisa, x
Anglican Church. *See* Tutu, Desmond
Anglo Boer War, 3–4, 5
anti-social war, 107n112

apartheid, 5, 10n18; origins of, xiii–xiv, 4–5, 8–9; racism related to, 2–3, 124–125
Aquinas, Thomas (saint), 85, 96, 103n28; common good, 34n79, 35n86; general justice of, 113–114; God in, 19–21; government forms in, 22, 103n28; just war in, 23–25, 33n40; legitimate authority in, 23–24, 75–76; natural law in, 21–22; peace in, 19, 22, 25, 34n62; power in, 24; right intention in, 25, 34n60, 79–80; self-defense and, 27; tyranny and, 22–23, 23–24, 26–27, 75; virtue in, 21
Arab Spring, 100–101, 103n23, 137; *jus ante* armed revolution in, 138–141; *jus in* armed revolution in, 141–144; *jus post* revolution in, 144–152; last resort in, 143–144; proportionate means in, 143; *See also specific countries*
Arab Spring transitional justice, 144; compensation in, 150–151; forgiveness in, 145–147; *jaha* in, 150; *musalaha* for, 149–151; reparation in, 145–147; repentance in, 145–147; *sabr* in, 147–149; *sulh* in, 149–150, 151; TRC compared to, 144–145; truth and, 151–152
Arendt, Hannah, x–xi, xii
Aristotle, 22
al-Assad, Bashar, 137, 143–144

Augustine (saint), 26, 33n21; Faustus and, 16–17; God and, 14, 16, 18–19, 75; just war of, 16–19, 33n40, 33n42, 79; Manichean dualism and, 13–14, 33n16; for order, 17–18; peace of, 14, 16, 18–19, 79, 104n40; pessimism of, 15–16; sin and, 24, 35n99; virtue of, 15

Bahrain, 141
banning, 45–46, 66n35; M-Plan and, 56; SACC and, 55
Bantu Authorities Act (1951), 6–7
Bantu Education Act (1953), 8
Bantu Women's League, 65n13
Beinart, William, 4, 7
Ben Ali, Zine al-Abidine, 137
Biko, Steve, 61
Bishara, Marwan, 103n23, 139–140
Bisho Massacre, 130
Black Consciousness Movement, 61
Boesak, Allan, 92, 93–94
Boniface, General, 13, 18–19
Botha, P.W., 10n18, 65n14
Bouazizi, Mohamed, 137
boycotts, 41–42
Brews, Alan, 92, 93–94
Buddhist monks, ix, xvin4
Burma (Myanmar), ix, xvin4

Cahill, Lisa Sowle, 19, 32n2, 32n6
Cajetan, Tommaso de Vio, 85
Catholic bishops: of South Africa, 87–88, 89; of U.S., ix, 26, 30–31, 34n62, 86, 104n42, 152
Chapman, Audrey R., 119, 124
Childress, James, xvin12, 72
Christian ethics, x, 12, 27, 34n62, 100; Islam compared to, 146, 147, 148–149, 149–150; for restorative justice, 80–81, 87–90, 113–114, 114–115, 144–145; Society of Christian Ethics, 28. *See also* Aquinas, Thomas; Augustine; just war tradition and Christian theology
Christology, 29–30
Cicero, 25
civil disobedience, 41
civil-political rights, 49, 66n52, 66n53
Civil Rights Movement (U.S.), 41
Clark, Meghan J., 67n59, 76

combatants: opponents compared to, 97, 101. *See also* noncombatant immunity
Commission of Enquiry into Certain Allegations of Cruelty and Human Rights Abuse against ANC Prisoners and Detainees by ANC Members, 99
Commission of Enquiry into Complaints by Former African National Congress Prisoners and Detainees, 98–99
communication, 56. *See also* languages
communism, 45, 65n27
community, 147, 149–151; in just peacemaking theory, 31, 37n151, 37n152; legitimate authority from, 78; *ubuntu* and, 115, 115–117
commutative justice, 113–114
compassion (*ramah*), 145
compensation, 150–151
Comprehensive Anti-Apartheid Act, 61
Congress Alliance, 65n27
Congress of the People, 52–53
Constantine (emperor), 12, 32n6
constitution (South Africa), 66n49
cultural entrenchment of racism, 3–5
cultural rights, 52, 67n59

Dalacoura, Katerina, 141, 142
Defiance Campaign, 45–46, 65n27
de Gruchy, John W., 111, 112, 123, 125
de Klerk, F.W., 106n95
democracy, 22, 65n21; advancement of, 46, 47–48, 139–140; in Freedom Charter, 48–49, 52–53; participation compared to, 76–77
direct repressive violence, 74, 103n10
distributive justice, 113–114
double effect, 27, 36n122, 91

economics, 49–50, 51, 67n59
education, 8, 67n79; languages for, 51–52; SASM, 100
Egypt, x, 139, 153n11; legitimate authority in, ix–x, 140–141, 141–142; mass participation in, 76–77; military defections in, 140–141; SCAF of, 142
El Salvador, 127
Elshtain, Jean Bethke, 16, 19, 24, 33n39
employment, 7–8, 50
enemies, 34n60, 79, 81, 104n41

escalation, 90–92, 98
ethics: of sanctions, 58–60. *See also* Christian ethics
ethnic groups, 52
evil, 13–14, 18, 33n21
extreme nationalism, 4–5

Facebook, 139, 141, 153n11
Farmer, Paul, 73–74
Faustus the Manichean, 16–17
Fisher, Kirsten J., 147, 150
forgiveness, 110–111, 132n7; in Arab Spring transitional justice, 145–147; reconciliation compared to, 111–112; *ubuntu* and, 116–117
Freedom Charter: civil-political rights in, 49, 66n52, 66n53; cultural rights in, 52, 67n59; democracy in, 48–49, 52–53; economics in, 49–50, 51, 67n59; education in, 51–52; housing in, 50–51; land distribution in, 50; mining industry in, 50; ratification of, 52–53; workers' rights in, 50
Friesen, Duane K., 53, 55
Funk, Nathan C., 149–150, 151, 155n69

Gaddafi, Muammar, ix, 137, 144, 147, 153n24
Gandhi, Mahatma, 53
general justice, 113–114
Ghanem, Hafez, 152
Ghonim, Wael, 76–77, 141–142
God, 13, 110; in Aquinas, 19–21; in Augustine, 14, 16, 18–19, 75
Gordon, Joy, 58–60, 68n127
government forms, 22, 103n28
grassroots organizing, 53–54, 55, 139; M-Plan, 56–57, 68n109; South African Council of Churches, 54–55, 57
Green Movement, ix
Grossman, David, 104n41
Group Areas Act (1950), 6–7
guerrilla warfare, 96–97, 107n112

Hanafi, Hasan, 138
Hani, Chris, 91
Hayner, Priscilla B., 98, 125
healing, 122

Hebrew scriptures, 30, 55; designation of, 33n41; God in, 13, 17, 20
Henkin, Louis, 58
Hollenbach, David, 66n52, 66n53, 67n59
hope, 93–94. *See also* reasonable hope of success
housing, 50–51, 65n13, 65n14
human rights, 47–48, 65n21, 99. *See also* Freedom Charter

Immorality Act (1950), 6
intentions: of legitimate authority, 77, 140–141; of MK, 78, 80, 82–83, 100, 108n124. *See also* right intention
international support, 63; military defections and, 140–141; Responsibility to Protect for, 58; sanctions as, 58–61, 68n127, 69n129, 69n136, 69n139; from UN, 57–58, 60, 61
Iran, ix
Irani, George E., 145, 149–150, 151, 155n69
Iraq, 59
ISIS. *See* Islamic State in Iraq and Syria
Islam: Christian ethics compared to, 146, 147, 148–149, 149–150; the Prophet of, 145, 148. *See also* Arab Spring transitional justice
Islamic State in Iraq and Syria (ISIS), 154n38

jaha (mediators), 150
Jesus Christ, 12, 13, 25, 30, 34n60, 55; just peacemaking theory from, 29–30, 31; unity and, 87, 88
John Paul II (pope), 104n37
Johnson, Allan G., 2
Johnson, James Turner, 27, 33n39
John XXIII (pope), 30
jus ad armed revolution, xiv, xv; in Arab Spring, 141–144. *See also* South African revolution
jus ad bellum, 25, 74–75; last resort in, 25–26; macro-proportionality and, 26–27; micro-proportionality and, 27; reasonable hope of success in, 26
jus ante armed revolution, xiv–xv; in Arab Spring, 138–141. *See also* just

166 Index

peacemaking practices
jus in armed revolution, xiv, xv, 71; in Arab Spring, 141–144; to decrease violence, 92–94; escalation in, 90–92, 98; noncombatant immunity in, 95–99; proportionate means in, 90–95, 143–144
jus post revolution, 40, 109–110, 131n2; in Arab Spring, 144–152; summary of, xv. *See also* transitional justice
just cause, 102n4, 103n10, 136; in South African revolution, xii, 72–75
justice, 112, 113–114; peace and, 19, 25, 30–31, 34n62, 109, 118, 119, 133n47. *See also* restorative justice; retributive justice; transitional justice
just peacemaking practices, 40, 64; democracy advancement as, 46, 47–53, 139–140; grassroots organizing as, 53–57, 68n109, 139; international support as, 57–61, 63, 140–141; from just peacemaking theory, 30, 31, 31–32, 32, 39–40. *See also* Freedom Charter; nonviolent direct action
just peacemaking theory, xiv, xv, 11, 36n128, 65n26; accountability in, 109; community in, 31, 37n151, 37n152; from Jesus Christ, 29–30, 31; just peacemaking practices from, 30, 31, 31–32, 32, 39–40; nonviolence in, 28–29; role of, 28–29
just war: in Aquinas, 23–25, 33n40; in Augustine, 16–19, 33n40, 33n42, 79
just war theory, xi, 75, 105n61; violence in, 79, 101–102
just war tradition, xi, 11; criteria in, xvin12, 136–137; principles from, xi–xii, xiv; stages of, xiv
just war tradition and Christian theology, 12, 104n37; Augustine in, 14–19, 26, 33n16, 33n21, 33n40, 33n42, 35n99; *jus ad bellum* in, 25–27; last resort in, 25–26; noncombatant immunity in, 27; proportionate means in, 26–27. *See also* Aquinas, Thomas

The Kairos Document, 77, 88–89, 118
Khouri, Rami G., 140

killing, 36n117; love and, 79; training for, 104n41. *See also* noncombatant immunity; proportionate means; *specific massacres*
King, Martin Luther, Jr., xvin8, 41

land distribution, 2, 50; Group Areas Act for, 6–7; Urban Areas Act for, 7–8
Langan, John, 24
languages, 8, 35n86, 67n79; for education, 51–52; *ubuntu* and, 114, 115
last resort, 136; in Arab Spring, 143–144; in *jus ad bellum*, 25–26; in South African revolution, 82–84; Villa-Vicencio on, 86–87
Lederach, John Paul, 37n152, 56, 128–129
legitimate authority, 136; in Aquinas, 23–24, 75–76; from community, 78; in Egypt, ix–x, 140–141, 141–142; intentions of, 77, 140–141; participation and, 76–77, 103n18, 103n22; violence and, 78–79, 90, 91, 92–94, 104n34, 105n54
Lelyveld, Joseph, 94
Libya, ix, 144, 147, 154n42; legitimate authority in, 142–143; sanctions from, 59
Lopez, George A., 59, 69n129
love: of enemies, 19, 34n60, 79, 81; killing and, 79; peace as, 19, 104n40

macro-proportionality, 26–27
Mahmood, Saba, 149
Mandela, Nelson, 66n35, 66n36, 107n97, 122; in Defiance Campaign, 45–46; on M-Plan, 56; on proportionate means, 90–91, 92, 93; right intention of, 80; for sanctions, 61; on *Umkhonto we Sizwe* (MK), 90–91, 93, 106n95; Verwoerd and, 46
Manichean dualism, 13; beliefs of, 13–14, 33n16; Faustus with, 16–17
Marikana Massacre, 9n4
Massingale, Bryan N., 3
mass participation, 42, 46, 135–136; in Arab Spring, 139–140; in Egypt, 76–77
Matthews, Joe, 56
Matthews, Z.K., 60
Maxeke, Charlotte, 65n13

Index 167

Mazrui, Ali A., 142, 154n42
mediators (*jaha*), 150
mercy (*ramah*), 145
micro-proportionality, 27, 91
migrant workers, 7–8
military defections (Egypt), 140–141
mining industry, 2, 9n4, 50
Minow, Martha, 105n46
miscegenation, 6
Mixed Marriage Act (1949), 6
MK. *See Umkhonto we Sizwe*
Montville, Joseph V., 4
Morsi, Mohammed, x
M-Plan, 56–57, 68n109
Mpumlwana, Malusi, 78, 107n96
Mubarak, Hosni, ix–x, 140
musalaha (reconciliation), 149–151
Myanmar. *See* Burma

National Party (South Africa), 5, 8–9
National Transitional Council (NTC), 142
Native's Land Act, 2
natural law, 21–22
negotiation, 46, 65n15, 66n36, 91, 106n95
Nepstad, Sharon Erickson, xi, 140
Nobel Peace Prize, 106n95
Nolan, Albert, 73, 88
noncombatant immunity, 27, 91, 136; in guerrilla warfare, 96–97; identification in, 97–98; in *jus in* armed revolution, 95–99; terrorism and, 96, 98; tyranny related to, 95–96; violations of, 95–96, 98–99
nonviolence, xiv–xv; in just peacemaking theory, 28–29; for revolution, xi, xviii8
nonviolent direct action, 42–45, 46–47, 141; mass participation in, 42, 46, 76–77, 135–136, 139–140; object of, 41–42, 64; with violence, 94, 99–101, 101–102
NTC. *See* National Transitional Council

Obama, Barack, 140
oppression, 1

PAC. *See* Pan-Africanist Congress
pacifism, 28–29
Pan-Africanist Congress (PAC), 62, 82, 92, 105n48

particular justice, 113
pass books, 2, 73
patience (*sabr*), 147–149
peace, xiii, 94–95; in Aquinas, 19, 22, 25, 34n62; in Augustine, 14, 16, 18–19, 79, 104n40; justice and, 19, 25, 30–31, 34n62, 109, 118, 119, 133n47; as love, 19, 104n40. *See also* just peacemaking practices
perpetrators, 110–111, 132n7
perseverance, 55
Philpott, Daniel, 111, 154n53
Pope, Stephen, 127
Population Registration Act (1950), 6
Poqo, 92, 93
power, 24, 75. *See also* legitimate authority
preventative war, 105n61
Prevention of Illegal Squatting Act (1951), 6
Programme of Action, 44–46, 65n22, 65n23, 65n27
the Prophet, 145, 148
proportionate means, 136; double effect related to, 27, 36n122, 91; in *jus in* armed revolution, 90–95, 143–144; in just war tradition and Christian theology, 26–27; Mandela on, 90–91, 92, 93; of MK, 90–91, 92, 93–95; reconciliation and, 91, 92, 92–93, 94–95
prosecution, 121
Public Safety Act (1953), 69n142
punishment, 107n111

Qur'an, 148, 154n53

R2P. *See* Responsibility to Protect
race: as social construct, 6, 10n27. *See also* apartheid
racial prejudice, 2–3
racism, 2–3, 124–125
racist legislation, 5; Bantu Education Act, 8; employment and, 7–8; Group Areas Act, 6–7; Population Registration Act, 6; Urban Areas Act, 7–8
ramah (compassion, mercy), 145
Reagan, Ronald, 61
reasonable hope of success, 26, 84–90, 136
reciprocity, 111, 132n7

reconciliation, 91, 109, 130–131; forgiveness compared to, 111–112; justice in, 112; *musaluha* as, 149–151; proportionate means and, 91, 92, 92–93, 94–95; as right intention, 80–81, 91, 104n42; *ubuntu* and, 117. *See also* Truth and Reconciliation Commission

remorse, 125, 130, 134n91

reparation, 113, 145–147

repentance, 109, 145–147

Responsibility to Protect (R2P), 58, 61, 69n139, 102n4

The Responsibility to Protect, 78

restitution. *See* reparation

restorative justice, 112, 133n54, 136–137; accountability in, 120; Christian ethics and, 80–81, 87–90, 113–114, 114–115, 144–145; healing and, 122; peace and justice in, 118, 119, 133n47; rationale for, 118–122; truth in, 119–120, 128–130; *ubuntu*, 114–117. *See also* Truth and Reconciliation Commission

retributive justice, 120, 147; amnesty and, 120–121, 133n56; prosecution through, 121; truth in, 121; vengeance related to, 81, 105n46, 146–147

Reuther, Rosemary Radford, 24

revolution: definition of, x–xi, 72; just war theory for, xi; nonviolence for, xi, xviii8; violence of, x–xi. *See also* South African revolution

Rhodesia, 91, 100, 108n124

right intention, 25, 34n60, 104n41, 136; reconciliation as, 80–81, 91, 104n42; in South African revolution, xii, 79–81

Russert, Bruce, 47–48, 66n48

sabotage, 90–91, 98, 107n111, 136

sabr (patience), 147–149

SACC. *See* South Africa Council of Churches

SADF. *See* South African Defense Force

Saffron Revolution, ix

Said, Khaled, 139, 141

Saleh, Ali Abdullah, 139

sanctions, 61, 69n139; African nations for, 61, 69n136; ethics of, 58–60; from Libya, 59; requests for, 60–61, 69n129; "smart", 59, 68n127; from UN, 60, 61

SANNC. *See* South African Native National Congress

SASM. *See* South African Students' Movement

SCAF. *See* Supreme Council of the Armed Forces

Schobesberger, Horst, 130, 134n91

Schreiter, Robert J., 110, 119

sedition, 96

self-defense, 27, 72–73

Sermon on the Mount, 29–30

settlement (*sulh*), 149–150, 151

sexism, 43, 65n13

Sharpeville Massacre, 62–63, 74

Shriver, Donald, 119, 127

sin, 14; Augustine and, 24, 35n99; *ubuntu* and, 115–116

Sisulu, Walter, 65n27

"smart" sanctions, 59, 68n127

Smith, Ian, 108n124

Smith, Michael Joseph, 57–58

social virtues, 115–117

Society of Christian Ethics, 28

Sophiatown, 7

South Africa: Anglo Boer War of, 3–4, 5; Catholic bishops of, 87–88, 89; constitution of, 66n49; ethnic groups in, 52; National Party of, 5, 8–9; oppression in, 1; *See also specific topics*

South Africa Council of Churches (SACC), 54, 57; active theology from, 54–55; banning and, 55; networks of churches and, 54

South African Defense Force (SADF), 62

South African Native National Congress (SANNC), 43, 65n11

South African revolution, xii–xiii, 40, 100; just cause in, xii, 72–75; last resort in, 82–84; peace from, xiii, 94–95; reasonable hope of success in, 84–90; right intention in, xii, 79–81; underground activity in, 56, 68n107, 68n109, 82. *See also* legitimate authority

South African Students' Movement (SASM), 100

Stassen, Glen, 28, 29

State of Emergency, 62, 74

Steward, Robert, 147, 150
Storey, Peter, 128
strikes, 41–42, 46
structural violence, 73–74
Suárez, Francisco, 26, 85–86, 105n61
subsidiarity, 103n22
sulh (settlement), 149–150, 151
Suppression of Communism Act, 45, 65n27
Supreme Council of the Armed Forces (SCAF) (Egypt), 142
Suttner, Raymond, 56, 68n107, 68n109
Swift, Louis J., 32n6
Syria, ix, 154n38; al-Assad of, 137, 143–144

tandem approach, 99–101
terrorism, 96, 98, 107n112
Tlhagale, Buti, 78, 104n34
transitional justice, xv, 109, 131n1. *See also* Arab Spring transitional justice
TRC. *See* Truth and Reconciliation Commission
truth, 125; Arab Spring transitional justice and, 151–152; full disclosure of, 127–128; in restorative justice, 119–120, 128–130; in retributive justice, 121
Truth and Reconciliation Commission (TRC), xii, 80, 99, 107n105; amnesty and, 125, 127; Arab Spring transitional justice compared to, 144–145; Botha and, 10n18; critiques of, 124–127; formation of, 123; remorse in, 125, 130, 134n91; truth in, 125, 127–130; Tutu and, 123, 124, 130
Tunisia, 137
Tutu, Desmond (archbishop), xiii, 54–55, 74; TRC and, 123, 124, 130; *ubuntu* and, 114, 115, 117, 132n35
tyranny: Aquinas and, 22–23, 23–24, 26–27, 75; noncombatant immunity related to, 95–96

ubuntu, 123; Catholicism and, 114–115; community and, 115, 115–117; damage of, 115–117; description of, 114; forgiveness and, 116–117; languages and, 114, 115; moral code of, 115; reconciliation and, 117; restorative justice related to, 116–117; sin and, 115–116; social virtues and, 115–117; Tutu and, 114, 115, 117, 132n35
Umkhonto we Sizwe (MK), 68n109, 98, 123; intentions of, 78, 80, 82–83, 100, 108n124; Mandela on, 90–91, 93, 106n95; *Poqo* compared to, 92, 93; proportionate means of, 90–91, 92, 93–95
UN. *See* United Nations
underground activity, 56, 68n107, 68n109, 82
United Nations (UN), 65n21, 142; international support from, 57–58, 60, 61; sanctions from, 60, 61
United States (U.S.), 61; Catholic bishops of, ix, 26, 30–31, 34n62, 86, 104n42, 152; Civil Rights Movement of, 41
Universal Declaration of Human Rights, 65n21
Unlawful Organizations Bill, 65n27
Urban Areas Act (1952), 7–8
U.S. *See* United States

Vandewalle, Dirk, 151, 153n24
vengeance, 81, 105n46, 146–147
Verwoerd, Hendrik, 5, 8, 66n36; Mandela and, 46; Sharpeville Massacre and, 62
Villa-Vicencio, Charles, 77, 83, 94; on last resort, 86–87; on legitimate authority, 78; on reconciliation, 124
violence, x–xi, 107n96; against Biko, 61; decrease in, 92–94; direct repressive, 74, 103n10; in just war theory, 79, 101–102; legitimate authority and, 78–79, 90, 91, 92–94, 104n34, 105n54; nonviolent direct action with, 94, 99–101, 101–102; reluctant use of, 93, 107n97; structural, 73–74; tandem approach related to, 99–101; types of, 72. *See also* nonviolence; proportionate means
violent repression, 62, 63; Sharpeville Massacre as, 62–63, 74
virtue, 15, 21; social virtues, 115–117
Vitoria, Francisco de, 25–26
Volf, Miroslav, 118, 133n47
Volk. See Afrikaner nationalism

Walzer, Michael, xii, 27, 97, 107n111; on guerrilla warfare, 96–97, 107n111, 107n112
We Are All Khaled Said Facebook page, 139, 141
Winright, Tobias L., 25–26, 133n47, 133n54
women, 43, 65n13

Xuma, Jacob, 73

Zimbabwe African People's Union (ZAPU), 108n124

About the Author

Anna Floerke Scheid, Ph.D. is assistant professor of theology at Duquesne University in Pittsburgh, Pennsylvania, USA. She completed her doctoral studies in Theological Ethics at Boston College in 2009, under the direction of David Hollenbach, S.J. She earned an MA in 2004 from Catholic Theological Union in Chicago, working closely with Robert Schreiter, C.PP.S. Presently, she teaches and researches in the area of social ethics with special attention to the ethics of conflict, peacebuilding, and post-conflict reconciliation. Her work appears in the U.S. journals *Horizons,* the *Journal of the Society of Christian Ethics,* and *Teaching Theology and Religion,* as well as the Nigerian journal, *The Bulletin of Ecumenical Theology.* Dr. Scheid and her husband reside in Pittsburgh with their three children.